TENERIFE
Gomera

Hints for using the Guide

Following the tradition established by Karl Baedeker in 1844, buildings, places of natural beauty and sights of particular interest are distinguished by one ★ or two ★★ stars.

To make it easier to locate the various places listed in the Sights from A to Z section of the guide, their coordinates on the large map included with the guide are shown in red at the head of each entry.

Coloured strips down the outside edge of the right-hand pages are an aid to finding the different sections of the guide. Blue indicates the introductory material, red the descriptions of sights, and yellow the practical information at the end of the book.

Only a selection of hotels and restaurants can be given: no reflection is implied, therefore, on establishments not included.

In a time of rapid change it is difficult to ensure that all the information given is entirely accurate and up to date, and the possibility of error can never be entirely eliminated. Although the publishers can accept no responsibility for inaccuracies and omissions, they are always grateful for corrections and suggestions for improvement.

Preface

This guide to Tenerife and Gomera is one of the new generation of Baedeker guides. These guides, illustrated throughout in colour, are designed to meet the needs of the modern traveller. They are quick and easy to consult, with the principal places of interest described in alphabetical order, and the information is presented in a format that is both attractive and easy to follow.

Playa Jardín, Puerto de la Cruz: one of the most beautiful beaches on Tenerife

The present guide is devoted to Tenerife, the largest of the Canary Islands, but also includes the smaller neighbouring island of Gomera, less developed for tourism but scenically no less interesting. The guide is in three parts. The first part presents a general survey of Tenerife, its topography, climate, flora and fauna, population, economy, history, original inhabitants, art and culture and famous people who have played a part in its history. A selection of quotations leads on to the second part, in which, after some suggested itineraries, the individual sights and features of interest are described. The third part contains a variety of practical information. Both the Sights and the Practical Information sections are in alphabetical order.

Baedeker guides are noted for their concentration on essentials and their convenience of use. They contain numerous colour illustrations and specially drawn plans, and at the end of the book is a fold-out map, making it easy to locate the various places described in the Sights from A to Z section with the help of the coordinates given at the head of each entry.

Contents

Baedeker Specials

Eternal

There is one cliché above all others that can truthfully be applied to the Canary Islands – "Eternal Spring". Admittedly even spring has its bad days, but without question this archipelago in the Atlantic is particularly favoured by climate. With temperatures ranging between 18° and 25°C (64° and 77°F) throughout the year, it is an ideal holiday destination for sun-starved visitors from more northerly lands.

Even in ancient times these paradisal islands seem to have had a mysterious drawing power. Homer must have been referring to the Canaries in his "Elysian Fields"; Plutarch referred to them as the "Blessed Islands"; and for Plato they were the remains of the lost continent of Atlantis. In our own jet age hundreds of thousands of visitors come to these sun-kissed islands every year.

Lido San Telmo

in Tenerife's tourist centre, Puerto de la Cruz

On Tenerife two completely different holiday regions await the visitor. The south of the island, where the sun always shines but as a result the vegetation is sparser and sometimes barren, boasts some lovely beaches sloping gently down to the sea and offers bathers and sunbathers everything they could wish for. In the north the steep cliffs are frequently lashed by fierce waves, but even here some beautiful beaches have been laid out in recent years, and there are also magnificent sea-water swimming pools. But in any case Tenerife is really too good for just a seaside holiday. In the centre of the island is a gigantic lunar landscape, the Caldera de las Cañadas, dominated by the great bulk of Mount Teide. The slopes of the Teno and Anaga hills are covered with luxuriant green and are still almost completely unspoiled.

Nature unspoiled

in the Barranco de Masca

Gomera

Luxuriant green forests in the Garajonay National Park

Spring

With its varied topography this, the largest island in the Canaries, is frequently described as a "mini-continent"; and it is indeed true that here, within a comparatively small compass, examples of all the world's different vegetation zones can be found, with a correspondingly varied flora.

Natural beauty and seclusion give Tenerife's smaller neighbour, the island of Gomera, its particular appeal. With its lush vegetation, reminiscent of primeval forests, its deep gorges and its idyllic valleys, Gomera offers endless scope for walks through wild and romantic scenery. Here, far from the stresses of everyday life, visitors can enjoy a completely relaxed holiday. On Gomera you can walk for hours, well away from the beaten tracks, without meeting any other human beings.

Bathing enthusiasts, however, should not pitch their hopes too high on Gomera, which has only small beaches of dark sand, sometimes sprinkled with stones.

A journey to the Canaries is never primarily a cultural trip. Although there are a number of pretty village churches, and in recent years a number of interesting museums have been opened, the islands' principal attractions are still their mild climate and the scope they offer for a variety of leisure pursuits.

Facilities for nearly every conceivable kind of sport are available, and the numerous leisure parks cater for old and young, while Tenerife offers an endless variety of entertainment for the evening.

These two "green pearls in the Atlantic" are only a few hours' flight from London and other European cities, so there is no excuse for not returning again and again.

Drago
The dragon tree of Icod, the symbol of Tenerife

Joie de vivre
The Canaries are full of it

Playa de las Américas
where many new sandy beaches have been created in recent years

Nature, Culture History

Facts and Figures

General

Tenerife is the largest island in the archipelago of the Canaries. Along with Gran Canaria, it lies almost in the centre of this group of islands. Altogether the Canary Islands (Islas Canarias) consist of seven major islands and six smaller ones in the Atlantic, lying some 100 km (62 mi.) off the north-west coast of Africa (Morocco and Western Sahara) and about 1100 km (685 mi.) from the Spanish mainland (Cádiz). The whole archipelago extends for 500 km (310 mi.) from east to west and 200 km (125 mi.) from north to south.

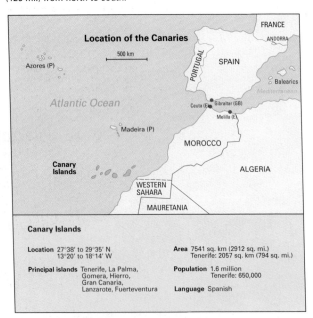

Location of the Canaries

500 km

Azores (P)

Atlantic Ocean

Madeira (P)

Canary Islands

FRANCE

ANDORRA

PORTUGAL

SPAIN

Balearics

Mediterranean

Ceuta (E) · Gibraltar (GB)

Melilla (E)

MOROCCO

ALGERIA

WESTERN SAHARA

MAURETANIA

Canary Islands

Location 27°38' to 29°35' N
13°20' to 18°14' W

Principal islands Tenerife, La Palma, Gomera, Hierro, Gran Canaria, Lanzarote, Fuerteventura

Area 7541 sq. km (2912 sq. mi.)
Tenerife: 2057 sq. km (794 sq. mi.)

Population 1.6 million
Tenerife: 650,000

Language Spanish

The Canaries offer an extraordinarily varied range of scenery, with each of the islands possessing its own specific characteristics. Tenerife is frequently claimed to be the most beautiful of the Canary Islands.

Atlantic archipelagos

Along with the Azores, Madeira and the Cape Verde Islands the Canaries belong to the Macaronesian Islands (the "Blessed Islands"), which all show common features in flora and fauna, are all of volcanic origin and have similar topographical patterns.

◀ *The picturesque little hill town of Taganana in the Anaga range. On terraced fields round the town fruit and vegetables are grown for home consumption*

It is not known for certain how the Canary Islands got their name. The designation "Isla Canaria" appears for the first time on a Spanish chart of 1339. In antiquity the group was known as the Blessed or Fortunate Islands; later the name Canaria was applied by Pliny the Elder (AD 23–79) to the island now known as Gran Canaria. Pliny related the name to the large dogs (Latin *canis*, dog) that lived on the island. There were certainly dogs in the Canaries in Pliny's time, but they were not unusually large.

The Romans associated the islands with the kingdom of the dead that lay in the west; and it is possible that this had something to do with the name, for in ancient mythological conceptions the dead were conducted into the underworld by dogs. It has also been suggested that the bird known to the Romans as *canora* (from Latin *canere*, to sing) may have lived on the islands. Still another possibility is that the name may have come the cape of Canauria (probably the present Cape Bojador) on the African coast. The origin of the name Tenerife is also not entirely certain. Early Spanish sources suggest that in the language of the Guanches (see Early Inhabitants) *tener* meant either "snow mountain" or "snow-covered mountain" , referring to the island's most striking geographical feature, Mount Teide.

Name

The Canary Islands are divided between two Spanish provinces. The westerly islands of Tenerife, La Palma, Gomera and Hierro form the province of Santa Cruz de Tenerife (chief town Santa Cruz), while the eastern islands of Gran Canaria, Fuerteventura and Lanzarote form the province of Las Palmas de Gran Canaria (chief town Las Palmas). The two provinces make up the Comunidad Autónoma de Canarias (the autonomous region of the Canary Islands). Like the other 16 Spanish autonomous regions, it has its own parliament of some 60 members. Las Palmas and Santa Cruz alternate as capital of the region.

Administration

Although it is situated in the latitude of the central Sahara Tenerife has astonishingly lush vegetation. A view of the north-west coast

Canary Islands / Islas Canarias

Each of the provinces is headed by a governor appointed by the Spanish government, with their seats in Santa Cruz and Las Palmas. Each island has a degree of self-government, with a Cabildo Insular (Island Council) that is responsible, among other things, for health services, road construction, water supply and culture. The lowest tier of local government is the *ayuntamiento* (municipality).

Autonomy

The Canaries were granted these powers of self-government in 1972 under the Spanish policy of decentralisation. Many people in the Canaries feel, however, that they do not go far enough, and the degree of independence to be aimed at is a recurrent theme of local political controversy. The Unión del Pueblo Canario (UPC, Union of the Canarian People) campaigns for complete independence, but it is a long way from commanding a majority, and radical separatist organisations find little popular support. A large proportion of the population would favour an extensive measure of self-government within a Spanish federal state.

Topography

Geology

In geological terms the Canaries are quite young. The age of the eastern islands of Lanzarote and Fuerteventura is estimated to be between 16 and 20 million years, and that of Gran Canaria between 13 and 14 million years, while the western islands are believed to have come into being even later – Tenerife and Gomera perhaps between 8 and 12 million years ago, La Palma and Hierro only 2–3 million years ago. The variations in the surface topography confirm this picture of a reduction in age from east to west. Erosion has evidently been longer at work on Lanzarote and Fuerteventura, with their low rounded hills, than in the western Canaries with their rugged and mountainous terrain.

The origins of the archipelago are still not completely understood. The theory that it is a remnant of the lost continent of Atlantis, as described by Plato in his "Critias", which was believed to extend from the west African coast to America, has long since been shown to be untenable. The earlier belief that the Canary Islands, or at least Lanzarote and Fuerteventura, were once part of the African continent has also been conclusively disproved. It is well established that all the islands are of volcanic origin. In the 1970s the model of "hot spots" was used to explain the origin of the Canaries, on the analogy of the Hawaiian Islands. The basis of this theory is that at certain points in the earth's mantle – always the same points – magma (rock melted by the earth's internal heat) collects in the course of millions of years and is then discharged in volcanic eruptions. A process of this kind was believed to have given rise in the first place to the islands of Lanzarote and Fuerteventura. As a result of continental drift (which is estimated to take place in this region at the rate of up to 3 cm (over 1 in.) a year) the Canaries then moved further east, and as magma continued to accumulate at the same spot and thrust its way upward it formed other volcanic islands, ending with La Palma and Hierro. This theory, however, has since been superseded. In contrast to the Hawaiian Islands, the Canaries are not disposed in a linear arrangement and the individual islands show no regular sequence of volcanic activity. On some of the eastern islands there were volcanic eruptions at much later dates than on the western islands: thus the most recent eruption on Tenerife was in 1909, while the last eruption on Gomera was around a million years ago.

It is now fairly generally agreed that the Canaries lie on raised sections of the Atlantic seabed, here some 2000 m (6500 ft) deep. These sections, rising to varying heights, were thrust upward when the ocean bed (in this area between 150 and 180 million years old), in the course of its eastward movement was compressed and broken up off the African coast by tectonic forces resulting from the collision between the African and European Plates. Then on these uplifted sections, from the Middle Tertiary (around 30–40 million years ago) onwards, volcanic forces gradually built up the individual islands, until, some 16–20 million years ago, Lanzarote and Fuerteventura emerged from the sea.

There have been repeated volcanic eruptions in the Canaries, most recently on La Palma in 1949 and 1971. On Tenerife there were eruptions of Mt Chinyero (north-west of the Pico de Teide) in 1909 and Mt Chahorra (south-west of the Pico Viejo) in 1798. Such activity has left its mark on the topography of Tenerife with the greatest variety of volcanic landscapes found in the Caldera de las Cañadas, a gigantic open-air museum of many different types of volcanic rocks. The best known is a blue–black basalt; trachyte is a light-coloured rock with a rough surface; phonolite is greyish-green; obsidian (after a Roman named Obsidius who discovered it) is a dark glassy volcanic rock; pumice, which has the astonishing property of floating in water, is a ligthweight rock produced by the formation of bubbles in lava.

Volcanoes

The expanses of infertile lava, often still looking quite fresh, are known as *malpais* (badlands). After a period of weathering, however, the lava forms a soil that can be successfully cultivated if climatic conditions are favourable. Volcanic ash in particular contains nutrients that are essential for plant life. The people of the Canaries have learned by experience how to make the best use of the properties of the volcanic rock: thus pumice and lapilli (fragments of volcanic rock ranging in size between a pea and a nut) are used to retain moisture in the soil (see Economy).

Tenerife, the largest of the Canaries (2057 sq. km (794 sq. mi.)), is a triangular shaped island pointing north-east. At its broadest point the distance between the north and south coasts is just over 50 km (31 mi.), at its narrowest only about 15 km (9 mi.). Its length between the Punta de Anaga in the north-east and the Punta de la Rasca in the south-west is some 83 km (52 mi.).

Landscape

In the centre of the island is the Pico de Teide (3718 m (12,198 ft)), the highest point of the Atlantic islands. Encircling the peak is the Caldera de las Cañadas, a gigantic collapsed crater. To the north-east extends the Cumbre Dorsal, which slopes gradually down from 2200 m (7200 ft) to 1700 m (5600 ft) and then falls sharply to the plateau of La Laguna (550 m (1800 ft)). The north-eastern tip of the island is occupied by the

The Montañas de Anaga, in north-east Tenerife, are frequently shrouded in cloud

rugged Montañas de Anaga, which, like the Teno Hills in the extreme west of the island, consist of older basaltic rocks. These two ranges of hills are believed at one time to have been separate islands that were linked with one another by a later volcanic eruption. They divide the island into two totally different landscape zones: while the hill slopes in the north are covered with a luxuriant growth of vegetation the country to the south is more barren.

The hills are broken up by *barrancos* (gorges), which with one exception (the Barranco del Infierno) are no longer traversed by watercourses. In spite of this the lower reaches frequently offer favourable conditions for agriculture. On the flanks of the hills extend a number of wide and fertile valleys like the Valle de la Orotava in the north and the Valle de Güimar in the south. The rugged cliff coastline of the island is relieved here and there by small coves with beaches of black or light-coloured sand. The only stretch of low-lying coast is in the south.

Environment

Tourism

Air pollution in the Canaries is pleasantly low as a result of the low consumption of energy for heating, thanks to the mild climate, and the almost constantly blowing wind. Environmental problems are attributable mainly to the effects of expanding tourism. There have been extensive housing and hotel developments in recent decades, the effects of which are only too evident on the south coast, in Playa de las Américas and Los Cristianos. In addition to this over-building the growth of tourism has given rise to problems of water supply and waste disposal.

Water supply

On Tenerife, as on all the Canary Islands, water is rare and precious. Tourism, of course, makes increasing demands for water, but as a result of rising living standards consumption by the local population has also increased. The island's extensive banana plantations also require artificial irrigation: each banana plant needs something like 300 to 400 litres a year.

The scanty rain that falls on Tenerife seeps away into the porous volcanic soil and accumulates underground on impermeable layers of rock. These reserves of water are now being tapped: horizontal shafts are driven into the mountains to reach the water, and with the help of a thousand or so channels of this kind, with a total length of around 1500 km (930 mi.), the water is conveyed to the consumers, who store it in large cisterns. This water-supply system is owned and managed by joint-stock companies, whose shares are sold mainly to farmers and hotels. As a result of the rising demands of tourism the price of water has risen sharply in recent years, making many smaller farms uneconomic.

As a result of the increasing demand for water Tenerife's water table is steadily sinking, and it has become necessary to resort to other means of obtaining water. The main alternative source on Tenerife is the desalination of seawater. But this in turn leads to environmental damage, for to produce 100 litres of fresh water 6 litres of oil are required for heating. The use of environmentally friendly wind turbines or solar energy installations makes only a small contribution to the energy required by the desalination plants.

In the south of the island, where there is practically no rain, dry farming methods are used. The soil is covered by or mixed with volcanic stones (lapilli, pumice), which are porous and are thus able to store water. This technique also increases the condensation of layers of air near the ground, since the stones are warmed up during the day and cool off quickly at night. As a result the stones keep the soil moist.

The disposal of rubbish is also a major problem on Tenerife, and arrangements for recycling waste have not made much progress. The first containers for used glass were installed only in 1994–5, and only 1.7 kg of glass per head of population per year is collected on the island, compared with the Spanish average of 6 kg. A new law on the disposal of packaging came into force in Spain at the beginning of 1998, but there is likely to be a time lag in its enforcement in the Canaries.

Waste disposal

The mass of the population of the Canaries began to take an interest in ecological matters only in the late 1980s, when the membership of the ecological protection group, Coordinadora Ecologista de Tenerife, started to rise. Local politicians also gradually realised that an unspoiled environment was a major factor in fostering the development of the most important element in the island's economy, tourism. In recent years numerous laws on the protection of the environment have been introduced, though in many cases they amount only to declarations of intent. In fact, however, there has been a reduction in the number of permits for development projects (though there are numerous projects that have been granted permits but have not yet been carried out), and there is some evidence of a return to traditional Canarian architecture (for example in Puerto de la Cruz). The environmental protection laws provide, for example, for compensation for environmental damage, the acquisition of nature conservation areas by the Canarian government and heavier fines for ecological offences. Evidence of increased ecological awareness, too, is the César Manrique Prize, introduced in 1997, which is awarded by the Canarian government to individuals and institutions who have shown particular concern for the environment.

Nature

In the Canaries as a whole there are just under 150 nature reserves under statutory protection. They are divided into seven categories, the highest of which is the Natural Parks. The fauna, flora and geology of the Canaries are unique elements in the natural world of the island that have suffered little change at the hands of man. The Parque Nacional del Teide is the most popular National Park in the whole of Spain, attracting some 3.25 million visitors annually.

Nature reserves

15

Climate

Climate

The Canaries have a warm temperate climate – milder and more agreeable than would normally be expected in these latitudes. It is mainly influenced by the trade winds, but also by the zone of high pressure over the Azores and the cool Canary Current.

Weather conditions on Tenerife, as in the rest of the Canaries, can change with surprising rapidity. Long periods of bad weather, however, are rare. If the sun should happen to be concealed by clouds it is usually necessary to drive only a few kilometres to see a brilliant blue sky again. There is quite a considerable difference between the northern and the southern half of the island (see below, Trade winds). Particularly in winter, the chances of seeing the sun are markedly greater in the south of Tenerife.

Temperature

Temperature variations over the year are remarkably slight. Thus the average temperature in the northern coastal regions of Tenerife in January, the coldest month, is 17.8°C (64.0°F), with an absolute minimum of 10.5°C (50.9°F), while in August, the hottest month, it is 24.2°C (75.6°F), with an absolute maximum of 40.4°C (104.7°F). In the hill regions there is, of course, a temperature gradation according to altitude. In July and August the weather pattern is sometimes affected by three- or four-day heat waves coming from the Sahara.

Water temperatures are around 19°C (66°F) in winter and may reach 22°C (72°F) in summer.

Rainfall

Rainfall is mainly confined to the winter months, when it is brought by cyclones from northern latitudes. In the southern parts of the island, however, there is little rain even in winter. In the northern coastal regions the average annual rainfall is around 500 mm (20 in.); in the central regions it rises to 600–800 mm (24–31 in.); and in the mountains it falls again to 300 mm (12 in.). The snowline is around 1200 m (3900 ft).

Trade winds

Over the western Canaries a bank of cloud regularly forms at medium altitudes in the early morning, dispersing towards evening. The clouds rarely bring rain, but they do bring moisture in the form of mist and dew. The clouds are caused, throughout most of the year, by the trade wind blowing from the north-east, usually a moderate breeze.

In contrast to other climatic influences, the trade winds are constant. Their circulation begins at the Equator, where the sun's warming influence on the earth is at its highest (in the "intertropical convergence zone"). The warm air masses rise, becoming gradually cooler, and move at a height of 12–15 km (8–10 mi.) towards the Pole. After cooling still further they sink down to the surface of the earth about latitude 30° and flow close to the ground towards the Equator. As a result of the rotation of the earth, however, the current of air is diverted from its original direction, flowing from the north-east in the northern hemisphere and from the south-east in the southern hemisphere. Above about 1500 m (4900 ft) the winds are warm and dry; below that altitude they are moist and rather cooler. So long as the separation between the upper and lower layers (the "inversion" of the winds) is preserved

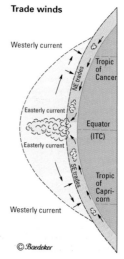

Trade winds

Westerly current

Tropic of Cancer

NE trades

Easterly current

Equator (ITC)

Easterly current

SE trades

Tropic of Capricorn

Westerly current

© Baedeker

there is little formation of cloud; but when the winds come up against a sufficiently high hill the inversion is disturbed. The cool, moist lower current is halted on the slopes exposed to the sun, becomes warmer and rises, whereupon it is cooled again and condenses; and clouds then form between 600 and 1700 m (2000 and 5500 ft). (It follows that there is no formation of cloud during the night). With the trade winds blowing from the north-east, the southern parts of the island are not affected in this way but are exposed only to warm dry winds blowing down from the hills.

The influence of the trade winds is less marked in winter. The sun's rays strike the northern hemisphere at a much more acute angle (whereas in the southern hemisphere the sun is vertically over the Tropic of Capricorn on December 22nd). The zone subject to the trade winds then moves further south, and the Canaries come under the influence of Atlantic troughs of low pressure.

Because of the Canaries' nearness to the Equator there is less variation in the length of the day between summer and winter than in more northerly latitudes. The longest day in summer lasts about 14 hours, the shortest in winter about 11 hours. There is a very short twilight period.

Daytime

Flora

The flora of the Canaries is unique in two respects. On the one hand there are found here, within a relatively small area, species of plants from almost every vegetation zone in the world; on the other hand there is a strikingly high proportion of endemic species (plants that are found only here). Altogether the flora of the Canaries comprises almost 2000 species, about a third of which are endemic.

Even the barren southern region of Tenerife produces a lush profusion of vegetation – as here in the Parque Ecológico at Los Cristianos – when there is a sufficient water supply

17

In the Mediterranean region, the Alps and southern Russia numerous fossils of fruits and leaves have been found that show that plants now occurring only in the Caucasus were once common in these other areas too. The climatic catastrophes of the late Tertiary era (the beginning of the Ice Age, the drying up of the Sahara) drove the subtropical flora of the period from its previous habitats, but the isolated location of the Canaries allowed it to survive there. Moreover the considerable differences of altitude on the islands made it possible for plants to adapt to changing conditions by migrating to different altitudes.

Major factors in the emergence of different vegetation zones on Tenerife have been differences in altitude and the influence of the trade winds. The lowest level is arid and barren, with a vegetation that includes the Canary date palm and succulents such as the *Pillar euphorbias*. This zone reaches up to altitudes of around 1000 m (3300 ft) in the south, but in the north it is confined to the coastal regions. Here the natural vegetation includes junipers and the dragon tree between 200 and 600 m (650 and 2000 ft), followed by laurels above 600 m. The zone of evergreen deciduous forest gives place at 1100 m (3600 ft) to the *fayal-brezal* formation *(fayal,* bog myrtle, *brezo,* tree heath). The tree heath can grow to a height of 15 m (50 ft), but may sometimes be no more than a shrub or a dwarf shrub. The fayal-brezal formation together with the zone of laurel woodland is also known as the Monte Verde zone.

In the northern half of Tenerife the pine forest zone begins at 1500 m (4900 ft), but in the south Canary pines grow from 1000 m (3300 ft) upwards. In both the north and the south of the island this zone ends at 2000 m (6500 ft). Between 2000 and 2700 m (8900 ft) the characteristic species are *retama* (Teide broom) and *codeso,* a low shrub with yellow flowers. Above this is the *violeta* (violet) formation, with few species. Here, with luck, you may find the Teide violet discovered by Alexander von Humboldt, which flowers in May or June.

Dragon tree

The most striking and most characteristic plant of the Canaries is the dragon tree (*Dracaena draco*). It belongs to the lily family and, with its tall stem and many branched crown, is closely related to the yucca. Dragon trees grow fast, reaching a height of 4–5 m (13–16 ft) in 50 years. Some old specimens are up to 20 m (65 ft) high. The dragon tree's branches end in a cluster of long dark green sword-shaped leaves. Since the tree sends out branches only after its first blossoming (after about 10 years' growth), there is little resemblance between the young tree and an older one like the mighty dragon tree of Icod. Dragon trees do not form annual rings, and the age of a tree can be determined only by the number of branches – an unreliable method, since the branches are put out at irregular intervals. The dragon tree of Icod is thought to be between 300 and 400 years old, and is certainly not older than 500–600 years. Dragon trees are now frequently planted as ornamental plants in parks and gardens; otherwise most of them are to be found in inaccessible places at altitudes between 200 and 600 m (650 and 2000 ft).

For the indigenous inhabitants of the Canaries the dragon tree had special significance: they used the resin from its stem, which turned red on exposure to the air ("dragon's blood"), as an ingredient in their healing salves.

The dragon tree: sacred to the Guanches

The Canary date palm (*Phoenix canariensis*) has spread from the Canaries all over the Mediterranean area. It is closely related to the date-palm of North Africa and the Arab countries, but it is shorter and sturdier and has a fuller and more decorative crown with larger and more luxuriant leaves. The small dates it produces are woody and have an unpleasant smell. On Tenerife it is found mainly in parks and bordering streets. There are large palm groves on Gomera.

Canary date palm

The Canary pine (*Pinus canariensis*) is a prominent feature of the landscape on Tenerife. Its long and flexible needles are always in clusters of three. Its hard, reddish heartwood *(tea)* has long been (and still is) used in the construction of wooden ceilings and balconies. At the pine's altitude of between 1000 and 2000 m (3300 and 6600 ft) the moisture in the clouds brought by the trade winds condenses on its branches and drips down its needles into the ground. The water thus obtained is not merely sufficient for the tree's own needs but makes a substantial contribution to the island's water supply.

Canary pine

Although the forests of the Canaries have been decimated over the centuries, there are still areas of laurel woodland on Tenerife, the finest being Bosque de las Mercedes near La Laguna. The Canary laurel (*Laurus canariensis*), like the Canary pine, makes a contribution to the island's water supply. It usually stands between 8 and 10 m (26 and 33 ft) high, but some trees reach 20 m (65 ft). The leaves, dark green in colour and elliptical and pointed in shape, can be used as herbs.

Canary laurel

The candelabra spurge (*Euphorbia candelabrum*), a plant endemic to the Canaries, where it is known as *cardón*, grows mainly on arid hillsides and rocks. At first glance it looks like a cactus, but is distinguished from

Candelabra spurge

a cactus by the poisonous milky sap in its stems, roots and fruit and by its inconspicuous flowers. The huge specimens to be seen in southern Tenerife are thought to be hundreds of years old.

A striking plant that is endemic to Tenerife is the Teide viper's bugloss: indeed the red variety, which grows to a height of up to 2 m (6½ ft), is a kind of emblem of Tenerife. The blue variety grows to a height of a metre.

Teide viper's bugloss

A typical representative of the succulents is the prickly pear (*Opuntia ficus indica*), which was brought to the Canaries in the 16th c. It is commonly found on hillsides up to medium altitudes. On this plant is reared the cochineal insect, which yields a red colouring substance; but

Prickly pear

The Teide viper's bugloss is at home in the Teide National Park, but is also grown in parks and gardens.

19

cochineal is now produced on any scale only on Lanzarote in the eastern Canaries.

Ornamental plants

In addition to the prickly pear and some species of agaves the Spanish conquerors also introduced to the Canaries a number of luxuriantly flowering ornamental plants. Oleanders, hibiscus and bougainvilleas are now to be seen in parks and gardens all over the islands, and the red poinsettias, which form dense bushes 3–4 m (10–13 ft) high, are ubiquitous features of the landscape in northern Tenerife during the winter months. A particularly exotic flower is the strelitzia with its striking inflorescences.

Food plants

The natural vegetation pattern of the islands was also altered by the introduction of various food plants, and plantations of bananas, fruit trees, vegetables and vines are now familiar features of the landscape.

The banana

The most important food crop on the islands, by a long way, is the banana. A small species of banana that is not sensitive to weather conditions has been grown on Tenerife since the end of the 19th c. (see Baedeker Special p. 26).

The stem of the banana plant, made up of long, stiff leaf sheaths, terminates in long fibrous leaves. When the plant is about a year old it produces a large club-like flower spike, with female flowers in the lower part and male flowers in the upper part. Depending on the amount of sunshine and the altitude (bananas flourish in the Canaries up to heights of 300–400 m (1000–1300 ft)), the fruit ripens in four to six months. A bunch of bananas weighs on average 25–35 kg, and occasionally as much as 60 kg. After producing the fruit the plant dies, but not before producing fresh shoots. The strongest of the shoots is preserved, and after another year this will in turn produce a bunch of bananas as long as a man's arm.

Environmental threats

The tourist boom and the extensive building developments associated with it have had serious consequences for the native flora. Some 75 per cent of endemic species are now threatened with extinction, and of these around 70 species are in acute danger of dying out.

Large-scale felling of the forests has also had devastating effects on ecological conditions. In the past great expanses of forest have been cleared to provide land for cultivation, and other forested areas have been destroyed by fire. In earlier centuries forest fires in the Canaries were started by volcanic activity and lightning: nowadays they are not infrequently started deliberately. In recent decades efforts have been made to replant the forests, which are not only essential to the islands' water supply but also help to prevent erosion on the hillsides. At first the new plantings were of eucalyptus, but in the last thirty years it has been mainly pines – though not the native *Pinus canariensis* but a fast-growing species from North America, *Pinus insignis*. In the event of a forest fire, however, this species is usually permanently damaged, whereas the native pine is highly resistant to fire. Only a few months after a forest fire fresh green shoots begin to appear on the trunk of a Canary pine, and in eight or ten years the fire damage has been wholly made good.

Fauna

The fauna of the Canaries shows a much narrower range of species than the flora – though here too endemic species are relatively numerous. Of the 328 species under statutory protection in Spain 63 are found in the Canaries.

Mammals

There are no large mammals in the Canaries apart from rabbits, hedgehogs and bats. In remote mountain regions mouflons may occasionally be seen. In the early 1970s some of these wild mountain sheep were released on Tenerife, and in the absence of any natural enemies they multiplied so rapidly that they are now a serious danger to the native flora. For this reason a certain number are permitted to be shot each year.

It is reassuring for visitors that there are no scorpions or poisonous snakes in the Canaries. Lizards, however, are everywhere to be seen, as well as an occasional slow-worm (a lizard with atrophied legs). In 1997 a giant lizard of the Gallotia genus was discovered in the Teno Hills, a species up to 50 cm (20 in.) in length that was thought to be extinct and was known only from the remains of its skeleton. It was believed to have been exterminated soon after the Spanish occupation of the Canaries, providing as it did a welcome source of meat for cats and goats as well as humans. A small population, now estimated at little more than 1500, managed, however, to survive in inaccessible regions in the Teno Hills.

Reptiles

Birds are well represented – blackbirds, blue tits, a species of robin, chaffinches, woodpeckers, various species of pigeon, buzzards, kestrels, seagulls, ibises. Occasionally the fluting tones of the *capirote,* the Canary nightingale, can be heard. But visitors who expect to see the familiar yellow canary living in the wild on the islands from which it takes its name will be disappointed: there is only one not very striking wild form, the Canary finch, with greyish-green plumage and no great talent as a songster. The familiar domestic canary was originally developed out of this species by Austrian and German breeders.

Birds

There are innumerable endemic species of insects. Butterfly-lovers are well catered for. Particularly striking are the Canary admiral and the brimstone butterfly, with orange-red forewings. The largest species found in the Canaries is the monarch butterfly, which has a wing-span of almost 10 cm (4 in.).

Insects

The waters round the Canaries contain an abundance of fish. Salmon, tuna, cuttlefish, moray, bass, ray and sprat are merely a few of the numerous species represented. The grey mullet is fished round the islands, and a local species known as the *vieja* frequently appears on the menu. Rocky areas round the coasts are the haunt of the conger eel. Coastal waters are free of sharks, but dolphins are common, swarms of them often accompanying the ferries.

Fish

The pilot whales that live in the waters between Tenerife and Gomera have developed into a tourist attraction, and excursions to see the whales regularly feature in tour programmes. In the early 1990s around 40,000 people took part in excursions of this kind, and the figure has now risen to some 650,000. Many boats sail much too close to the whales, and it has been established by marine biologists that the number of young whales has fallen markedly; the whales are less well nourished than a few years ago and have become shyer.

Whales

Population

The Autonomous Region of the Canary Islands has a population of around 1.6 million, including just under 50,000 foreign nationals. Tenerife has a population of 650,000, Gomera 20,000; population density on Tenerife is more than three times that of mainland Spain. The largest town on Tenerife is Santa Cruz de Tenerife (pop. 205,000), followed by La Laguna (127,000) and La Orotava (36,000).

It has been shown by anthropologists that the Canarians differ in some respects from other Spaniards, with many features that point to

Population

their descent from the indigenous inhabitants of the islands (see Early Inhabitants).

Language

As in the rest of Spain, Castellano (Castilian) is the language of government and business, and most Canarians also speak pure Castilian, although they tend, like South American Spanish speakers, to soften or elide the letter s.

Religion

The people of the Canaries are predominantly Roman Catholic, with only small minorities of Protestants. Catholicism is deeply ingrained in many families: in a survey carried out in 1995 41 per cent said they were practising Catholics.

Character

A statistical survey carried out in 1995 by the local newspaper "Gaceta de Canarias", indicated that 47 per cent of the islanders regard themselves primarily as "Canarios", with only 18 per cent feeling themselves essentially Spanish. It is notable that the people of the islands assess their personal circumstances in a very positive light: 81 per cent describe themselves as "content" with their life, and 59 per cent describe their position in life as "good". The Canarians place a high value on leisure: 37 per cent put "more free time" high on their list of priorities, well above owning their own home or having more money.

Family

In family life patriarchal structures reign supreme. The husband is still the head of the family, while the wife concerns herself mainly with bringing up the children and looking after the house. Nowadays, however, as a result of the high unemployment rate and low wage levels, combined with a fairly high cost of living, many women are obliged to contribute to the family budget. Although the individual family unit is the norm in the towns, the extended family is still common in rural areas – though here too the average number of children is falling.

The plaza is a popular meeting place, as here in Santa Cruz

After the end of the Franco dictatorship the social problems of the Canaries were very evident. It was estimated at that time that in some villages the illiteracy rate was as high as 50 per cent. It still ranges between 8 and 12 per cent – higher than in many other parts of Spain.

Unemployment is also higher than in mainland Spain. The number of registered unemployed in the Canaries is at present 177,000 (around a quarter of the population of working age), and the actual figure is probably still higher. Depending on the length of time in their previous employment, the unemployed can expect to receive an allowance for a period of between 12 and 18 months amounting to 48 per cent of their last pay.

In the past the usual way to escape from poverty was to emigrate, particularly to South America: there are said, for example, to be some 300,000 Canarians living in Caracas (Venezuela) alone. The South American states are now taking very few immigrants, and this has further aggravated the unemployment problem in the Canaries. There is still, however, a shortage of skilled workers, since many of them have left for the Spanish mainland, attracted by the better prospects there.

Like other regions heavily dependent on tourism, the Canaries are also facing the problems arising from conflicts between traditional values and the carefree and apparently upmarket lifestyles of the tourists. As a result the demands of the native population are increasing, and are leading in many instances to dissatisfaction with their lot, which in turn finds expression in a high level of alcoholism and a rise in the crime rate.

Social problems

Economy

In the last few years the Canaries have enjoyed a marked economic upswing. The average income, at 82 per cent of the average for the European Union, is now higher than in most other Spanish regions. A further indication of the recovery of the economy is the relatively low rate of inflation, which came down in the early 1990s at around 5 per cent and in 1997 was only 2.3 per cent (compared with just under 20 per cent in 1980). The economy is wholly dependent on a single source of income, tourism. The services sector contributes 79 per cent of the gross national product, and more than 70 per cent of workers are depend on tourism for their income, so that even a relatively small decline in the number of visitors would have a very negative effect on the general economic situation of the Canaries.

On January 1st 1986 Spain joined the European Community (now European Union). There was a separate agreement for the Canaries, which were fully integrated into the European Union only in 1993, when they became subject to the EU's agricultural and commercial policies. There still remain, however, a number of special conditions: under the POSEICAN programme (Specific Options Program for the Distance and Insularity of the Canaries) economic disadvantages (for example distance from other EU states) will be tackled.

European Union

The agricultural produce exported from the Canaries changed over the centuries. After the Spanish conquest of the islands the main crop was sugar; but by the end of the 16th c. competition from Central America, at lower prices, had brought about the decline of this branch of the economy. The main product then became wine, and in the 17th and 18th c. the heavy Malvasia (Malmsey) of the Canaries was much prized at European courts and particularly in Britain. But tastes changed, and disease attacked the vines (mould in 1852, mildew in 1878), leading to the complete demise of wine production. Interest then switched in the 19th c. to the rearing of the cochineal insect, a parasite on cactuses that

Agriculture

Economy

On the island of Gomera agriculture plays a much more important part in the economy than on Tenerife

yielded a red colouring substance and flourished on the newly planted fields of prickly pear. With the development of aniline dyes, however, the economic importance of the cochineal insect declined, and cochineal is now used only in the manufacture of lipsticks and for colouring aperitifs, aerated drinks and sweets. The cochineal insect is still reared on a modest scale on Tenerife and above all on Lanzarote in the eastern Canaries. The ailing economy of the islands was then given a boost by the cultivation of a small species the banana (*Musa cavendishii*) less vulnerable to weather conditions, which was brought in from Indochina and by about 1890 was being grown on a considerable scale on Tenerife. But this crop too has been in crisis in recent years (see Baedeker Special p. 26).

Cash crops

Tenerife's banana plantations are now mainly concentrated in the northern half of the island. The banana flourishes at heights of up to 400 m (1300 ft). In the south the main crops are tomatoes and potatoes, together with maize, wheat, barley, fruit, vegetables and fodder plants for domestic consumption. Of lesser importance is the growing of wine grapes.

Although bananas and tomatoes are still, by a long way, Tenerife's most important export products, in recent years increasing numbers of banana plantations have been abandoned, giving place to the cultivation of various exotic vegetables and cut flowers.

Over all the prospects for agriculture are not good. The contribution it makes to the gross national product has been steadily falling in recent decades and now stands at only 4 per cent.

Stock farming

Stock farming is of secondary importance, and locally reared cattle and pigs meet only part of the islands' requirements, while sheep farming is also of only minor importance. Goat farming, on the other hand, has increased substantially, thanks to support from the European Union. There are believed to be something like 100,000 goats in the province of Santa Cruz de Tenerife. Whereas formerly the herds ranged freely over the countryside they are now mainly kept in fenced fields. The goats are milked daily at noon by electrical milking machines. The average yield per goat is 3–4 litres in winter but only between half a litre and a litre in summer.

Both coastal and seagoing vessels are engaged in fishing in the waters round the islands, but their equipment is for the most part hopelessly antiquated. In addition, under an agreement with Morocco in 1995, the permitted fishing quotas have been considerably reduced. Much of the catch consists of tuna. As consumers' tastes are now very varied much of the fish consumed on the islands has to be imported.

Fishing

Industry

Industry contributes about 17 per cent of the gross national product. The scope for developing this branch of the economy is restricted by the high import prices of primary products and of energy. An installation of major importance is the large refinery at Santa Cruz de Tenerife, the second largest in Spain, which processes oil from Venezuela, partly for domestic consumption and partly for supplying seagoing vessels. There are also a number of wood-processing, papermaking, packaging and fish-canning factories. Craft products (e.g. embroidery) are produced in smaller (sometimes quite tiny) workshops.

Since 1852 the Canaries have been a free trade (duty-free) zone, and this has given an enormous boost to trade. Shortage of water, raw materials and electric power, however, puts a brake on economic development,

Commerce

Production of goat's cheese in the Arico cheese factory

Problems of the Banana Crop

It certainly is not big: indeed, on the small side. But it is well rounded, smooth and firm fleshed. And it is sweet – a tempting and toothsome fruit. This is the dwarf banana of the Canaries, whose growers are now facing problems.

The banana – by far the most important cash crop of the Canaries – is one of the world's most unusual plants. Related to the strelitzia flower, it grows to a height of 3–6 m (10–20 ft), with a false trunk composed of the tightly packed basal portions of its long, stiff leaf sheaths and topped by long fibrous leaves. After a year's growth a large flower spike carrying numerous yellow flowers enclosed in reddish-purple bracts emerges at the top of the false trunk, and thereafter it takes between four and six months, depending on amount of sunshine and altitude, until the fruit is ready for harvesting. The bananas grow in bunches, weighing between 25 and 50 kg, of between 150 and 300 individual fruits ("fingers"), grouped in clusters ("hands") of 10 to 20. Each plant produces only one bunch of fruit, after which it dies and is cut down; but it has already provided its replacement in the form of the shoots that grow out of its underground stem. Only the strongest of these is preserved, and in due time, after a year or so, this will in turn produce a bunch of bananas the length of a man's arm. Equally curious is the structure of the flower. The blossoms in the lower part of the flower spike are female, those in the upper part male. Perhaps no other plant has such a strongly sexual aspect. The form of the flower suggests power and potency: it is, indeed, phallic. And yet the banana plant is in fact totally asexual. The bananas – sweet-smelling, rich in vitamins – are produced only by the female flowers, without any process of fertilisation. As the bunch of bananas grows heavier it pulls the flower spike down, while the blossoms from which the fruit emerges themselves reach upward towards the sun, carrying with them the ripening bananas, which also turn upward and thus acquire their curved shape.

The original home of the banana was in southern Asia, in the valleys of the Himalayas. It was introduced to the West by Arab traders, and in the early 15th c. Portuguese seafarers sailing from Guinea carried it to the Canaries. There the banana (Spanish *plátano*, Spanish American *banana)*, was long regarded as a purely ornamental plant. Finally, however, Spanish settlers took it from the Canaries to the American colonies, where its value as a foodstuff was quickly recognised. In the Canary Islands themselves it began to be cultivated as a food plant only towards the end of the 19th c. The variety grown was *Musa cavendishii*, produced by crossing two wild species from south-east Asia, *Musa acuminata* and *Musa balbisiana*, which was small and thin skinned but unaffected by weather conditions. It was introduced on Tenerife in 1884 and soon afterwards on Gran Canaria, La Palma and Gomera. Thereafter it began to be exported, first to Britain and then to other European countries. For many years it was the islands' main export.

For some years now, however, banana growing in the Canaries has been in crisis. This is due mainly to the larger, handsomer and cheaper bananas from Central America that have been flooding European markets. Admittedly the small Canary bananas are not particularly handsome to look at; but thanks to the high level of sunshine in the islands they are particularly rich in sugar and accordingly are much sweeter and tastier than their competitors from the New World. But their skin is extremely thin and readily acquires brown

plants in the Canaries from being uprooted by the strong winds on the islands it is necessary to build walls or set up nets to provide shelter. Moreover the bananas need plenty of water to ripen, and water is a rare and precious commodity in the Canaries. And finally the wages of banana harvesters in the Canaries are higher than those of their counterparts in Central America.

The Canary banana could not have survived in recent years without state support. In 1972 the Spanish government banned the import of foreign bananas and undertook to subsidise the banana growers of the Canaries by guaranteeing the purchase of their crops. Since the establishment of the European common market, however, there is nothing to prevent American bananas from reaching Spain by way of other EU countries. The Canary banana growers, therefore, have had to reconsider their position. Many of them are

The banana harvest is continuous throughout the year, since each plant has its own growing rhythm

patches, which both spoils their appearance and makes transport more difficult and expensive. Hence the higher cost of Canary bananas. The production costs of *Musa cavendishii* are substantially higher than those of the related species grown in Central America, which also have the advantage of flowering in six months rather than twelve. To protect banana

switching to other kinds of fruit; some have given up and sold their land; while others again are happy to continue growing bananas and even look hopefully to the future, since Canary bananas can still find a market within the European Union thanks to restrictions that have been imposed on the import of *chiquitas* and *tucas* from Central America.

and as a result the balance of trade has long been in deficit. Imports, principally from mainland Spain, are increasing. Major imports include crude oil, consumption goods and foodstuffs as well as mechanical and electrical equipment and motor vehicles. Exports are largely restricted to agricultural products.

Energy

The continually increasing demand for energy (which almost doubled between 1985 and 1993) is almost wholly met by oil. Alternative forms of energy production are employed only in small private or experimental projects. Solar energy is used in a few sea-water desalination plants. The islands offer ideal conditions for the use of wind generators, with warm dry winds blowing at an average speed of 40 k.p.h. (25 m.p.h.); but so far there are only a few major projects for the use of wind energy on Tenerife.

Tourism

The beginnings of tourism on Tenerife date back to the 19th c., when the island was visited mainly by British and Scandinavian business travellers, scientists and naturalists. The first travel agencies began to operate in the early 20th c. Visitors now came to Tenerife not only for bathing and other holiday pursuits but also for the sake of their health. The two world wars naturally put an end to tourism in the Canaries, but recovery soon began. In 1950, for example, there were 15,000 foreign visitors to the Canaries. The British and the Scandinavians were now joined by German holidaymakers.

With the introduction of charter flights in 1957 the whole structure of tourism in the Canaries changed. Tenerife's main tourist centre, Puerto de la Cruz, was transformed, with the construction of numerous new hotels. From the late 1960s onwards the south coast of the island was increasingly developed for tourism. There were setbacks to this tourist boom in 1973–5 and in 1978, but in the eighties the tourist industry enjoyed growth rates of 10 per cent or more. The smaller islands of Gomera, Hierro and La Palma in the western Canaries now began to share in the boom. During the nineties there were occasional slight falls in the numbers of visitors, but over all the trend continued upwards.

Visitors

The number of visitors to the Canaries passed the 8 million mark in 1996. In 1997 the total was 8.4 million, 3.1 million of whom spent their holidays on Tenerife. The largest contribution was made to the total by British visitors, followed by Spaniards and Germans. Tenerife now has around 200,000 beds available for visitors, and the number is still increasing.

The greatly increased numbers of visitors in the last twenty years have had far-reaching effects on the economy and the landscape of the islands. Great stretches of the coasts are now built-up. Efforts are now being made to learn from the mistakes of the past and, by imposing rigid restrictions on tourist development, save what can still be saved. The measures taken include the cleaning up and improvement of beaches and tourist installations and provision for the protection of the environment. The concentration is now on qualitative rather than quantitative growth. The regional government is concerned to create alternatives to the "sun-and-sea" holiday. Other possibilities – sport, the experience of nature, *turismo rural* or *agro-turismo,* trade fairs and congresses – are being actively promoted. Cottages and farmhouses in the country are being rehabilitated for letting to visitors who want a quiet and relaxing holiday, thus helping the economy of the inland regions of the islands. This will preserve historic old buildings that would otherwise fall into ruin and will help to provide a market for local agricultural produce.

Transport

Tenerife has an excellent network of roads that is constantly being improved to cater for the increasing numbers of car-borne tourists. Motorways run north from Santa Cruz de Tenerife to Los Realejos and south to Fañabé, beyond Playa de las Américas, with an extension to Armeñime under construction (due for completion in 2000).

There are no railways on Tenerife, and public transport on the island is confined to buses.

Roads

There are regular ferry services between the various islands in the Canaries. The port of Santa Cruz plays a major part in the commercial life of the islands, and it is also an important hub of Spanish overseas trade. Almost all the islands' exports and imports pass through Santa Cruz.

Shipping

Tenerife has two international airports. Most charter flights use the Reina Sofía Airport in the south of the island, which was opened in 1978 and now handles some 7.5 million passengers a year. Within the next few years a new terminal and an additional runway will increase its capacity to 20 million passengers a year. The Los Rodeos airport in the north of the island handles 4 million passengers a year. The construction of an airport on Gomera began in 1991 and was completed in 1999.

Air travel

History

Earliest inhabitants	Until recently there were only speculative theories about the date of the earliest settlement of the Canaries. Scientists at the university of La Laguna now believe, however, that the first settlers arrived at some time after 500 BC and that there were several waves of immigrants (see Early Inhabitants, p. 34).
From 1100 BC	The existence of the Canaries was already known in antiquity. In the course of their exploratory voyages along the West African coast the Phoenicians and later the Carthaginians visit the islands, but no regular trading contacts develop.
25 BC to AD 23	King Juba II of Mauretania sends ships to the Canaries, which, on the evidence of Pliny the Elder, they seem to have reached.
1st c. AD	Pliny the Elder (AD 23–79) mentions the Canaries in his "Natural History" and gives (inaccurate) information about the size and distance of the islands.
2nd c.	The Greek geographer Ptolemy (c. 100–160) shows the islands on his map of the world – the first map to give degrees of longitude. He makes the prime meridian – the end of the then known world – pass through the western tip of Hierro, the Punta de Orchilla.
3rd c.	Roman ships land on the Canary Islands.
Late 13th c.	The Canaries, having fallen into oblivion for many centuries, are rediscovered by European seafarers questing for slaves.
1312	Lancelotto Mallocello, a Genoese navigator, cruises in Canarian waters and lands on the island later to be named after him, Lanzarote. He retains possession of the island until 1330.
1340–2	Portuguese and Spanish ships sail frequently to the Canaries, many of them coming from Majorca. Since they are usually heavily armed and carry horses, their objective is probably not merely trade.
1344	Pope Clement VI, claiming authority over "all lands to be discovered", appoints Luis de la Cerda, a scion of the Spanish royal family, king of the Canary Islands – though this title does not imply possession of the territory.
Late 14th c.	Roberto de Bracamonte succeeds Luis de la Cerda as king but, like him, is content with the purely theoretical royal title and makes no attempt to conquer the islands. He leaves this task to his cousin Jean de Béthencourt (see Famous People).
1402	Together with the Spanish nobleman Gadifer de la Salle (c. 1340–1422) Jean de Béthencourt, a Norman, makes the first attempt to win the Canaries for the Spanish crown. After occupying Lanzarote Béthencourt is granted the title of king of the Canary Islands. Gadifer de la Salle takes no part in further conquests after his claim to the title is rejected.
1405	Béthencourt conquers the islands of Fuerteventura and Hierro but fails in his attempts to take Gran Canaria and La Palma. He returns to Europe in 1406.

Béthencourt appoints his nephew Maciot de Béthencourt viceroy of the islands. In 1416, however, Maciot is compelled to retire on grounds of incompetence, but sells his office successively to the royal envoy Diego de Herrera, Prince Henry of Portugal and a Spanish count, Hernán Peraza the Elder.
  The situation about possession of the islands thus becomes thoroughly confused, and in subsequent years both Spanish and Portuguese ships are sent to conquer them.

1406–15

Hernán Peraza the Elder, who hitherto has alternated between Fuerteventura, Hierro and Gomera, finally establishes his authority on Gomera and builds the famous Torre del Conde. He and his successors rule the island with ruthless disregard for the interests of the inhabitants.

1445

The Spanish crown acquires by purchase the right of sovereignty over the islands of Fuerteventura, Lanzarote, Gomera and Hierro.

1478

After several unsuccessful attempts at conquest the whole of Gran Canaria comes under Spanish control in April 1483.

1478–83

The treaty of Alcáçovas settles the territorial disputes between Spain and Portugal. The Canaries are assigned to Spain, and Portugal is compensated by the whole of West Africa and other offshore islands.

1479

On his first voyage of discovery Columbus (in Spanish Cristóbal de Colón; see Famous People) puts in at Gran Canaria and then at Gomera. On his later voyages (1493, 1498, 1502) he calls in several times at these islands and once at Hierro.

1492

Alonso Fernández de Lugo, an Andalusian noble (see Famous People), lands on La Palma and establishes his authority over the whole island.

1492–3

Fernández de Lugo gradually conquers the whole of Tenerife, which has preserved its independence longer than any other of the Canary Islands. The island then, like Gran Canaria and La Palma, becomes directly subject to the Spanish crown. Supreme authority is exercised by *capitanes generales* (captains-general), who allocate the right to work land (but not to own it) and sell water rights.
  Gomera, Hierro, Fuerteventura and Lanzarote have the status of *señoríos*. The Spanish crown has sovereignty over these islands but grants rights of possession – in effect fiefs – to nobles and ecclesiastics, subject to duties payable to the governors of the islands and to the Spanish crown.

1494–6

Fernández de Lugo founds the town of La Laguna as his capital and the administrative centre of Tenerife.

1496

The indigenous population of the Canaries – apart from those who have been sold as slaves – become gradually assimilated to the Spanish conquerors.
  The islands rapidly acquire economic importance through the growing of sugar cane and later the production of wine.

16th–17th c.

After the Spanish conquest the slave trade is forbidden, but the ban is frequently evaded, as is shown by a further decree issued by Pope Paul III making trading in slaves a punishable offence.

1537

Britain makes several unsuccessful attempts to take the Canary Islands. An attack by Admiral Blake is beaten off.

1657

During the War of the Spanish Succession Admiral Jennings makes another unsuccessful attempt to conquer the islands.

1706

History

1723	Santa Cruz de Tenerife displaces La Laguna as capital of Tenerife.
1778	The port of Santa Cruz de Tenerife is granted the right to trade with America.
1797	Nelson, with a force of eight warships, threatens the town of Santa Cruz de Tenerife. A few hundred British troops manage to land on the island but fail to take the town and are compelled to withdraw with heavy losses (see Baedeker Special p. 130).
1799	The German traveller Alexander von Humboldt (1769–1859) spends some time on Tenerife on his way to South America (see Quotations).
1822	Santa Cruz de Tenerife becomes capital of the whole of the Canary Islands.
1837	Gomera, Hierro, Lanzarote and Fuerteventura lose their status as *señoríos*.
1852	Queen Isabella II declares the Canaries a free trade area.
Late 19th c.	The cultivation and export of bananas becomes the mainstay of the Canarian economy.
1912	The islands are granted local self-government with the establishment of Cabildos Insulares (Island Councils).
1913	The Centre of Advanced Studies in La Laguna is raised to the status of a university.
1927	The Canary Islands are divided into two provinces, Santa Cruz de Tenerife (Tenerife, Gomera, Hierro and La Palma) and Las Palmas de Gran Canaria (Gran Canaria, Lanzarote and Fuerteventura).
1936	General Francisco Franco (1892–1975), commander of the military region of the Canaries, meets his senior officers in the Bosque de la Esperanza on Tenerife to plan the military coup that leads to the Spanish Civil War (1936–9).
1971	Eruption of the Volcán de Teneguía on La Palma (the most recent volcanic eruption in the Canaries).
1975	After Franco's death King Juan Carlos becomes head of state.
1976–8	Canarian separatists carry out repeated terrorist bomb attacks under their slogan "Fuera Godos" ("Goths Out", meaning Spaniards from the mainland). The attacks are supported by the Algerian government. Fortunately no one is seriously injured.
1977	On March 26th Los Rodeos airport on Tenerife is the scene of one of the world's worst aircraft accidents, in which 577 people are killed. Spain reacts quickly to the disaster, and the Reina Sofía Airport in the south of the island, which meets the highest standards of safety, is opened only a year later. Almost all international flights now use this airport.
1978	A new democratic constitution comes into force. Spain becomes a constitutional monarchy.
1982	The Canary Islands, together with the other sixteen autonomous regions of Spain, get their own regional constitution and elected representative bodies.

In June, in the presence of a number of heads of state, new observatories are opened on Tenerife and La Palma. Thirteen countries are involved in the research carried out in them.   1985

On January 1st Spain joins the European Economic Community. There is a special agreement on the position of the Canaries. .   1986

After years of debate the contract for the construction of Gomera airport is signed, and work begins in the course of the year. (After a number of interruptions to the work the airport was completed in 1999).   1991

The Canaries play a part in the celebrations of the 500th anniversary of the discovery of America. The fleet of boats that sails from Spain to San Juan de Puerto Rico calls in at the Canaries, just as Columbus did.   1992

The Canaries are fully integrated into the European Union.   1993
   Gomera applies to UNESCO to be recognised as a "biosphere reserve". (Garajonay National Park had already been listed in 1986 as a "natural treasure of mankind").

The Coalición Canaria, a nationalist grouping, is victorious in local and parliamentary elections, and forms a minority government under Manuel Hermoso.   1995
   At a meeting of European Union ministers on Gomera in October the Gomera Declaration is signed. It commits all EU countries to act against terrorism.

The Canaries lose their special status within the European Union.   1996

From November Los Rodeos airport in northern Tenerife is again used by international charter flights.   1998

Early Inhabitants

The name Guanches is frequently but erroneously applied to the indigenous inhabitants of the Canaries. Strictly, however, this term applies only to the inhabitants of Tenerife. The word Guanche in the old Canarian language means "son of Tenerife" (from *guan*, son, and *Achinech*, Tenerife). The original population of the other islands had different names: for example the inhabitants of Hierro were called Bimbaches. In this section, therefore, the early inhabitants of the Canaries as a whole are not referred to Guanches but as ancient Canarians.

Origins

There has for centuries been uncertainty about the origins of the ancient Canarians. When Europeans first reached the Canaries in the 14th and 15th c. they encountered a culture of herdsmen and farmers that appeared to have no contact with the outside world. Moreover the various islands in the archipelago differed from one another in development and culture. Scholars attempted to establish the origins of the population and when and how the islands had first been populated. There was also no clear understanding of the origins of the archipelago itself: it was supposed that at some stage the islands had split off from the African continent, and it was accordingly believed that some Africans had survived in the Canaries.

More recently it was suggested that the Canaries may have been settled by incomers from the Iberian peninsula. This theory was based on the existence of similar cultural features (megalithic petroglyphs, forms of religion) and of marine currents that would have enabled ships to sail easily from the Iberian peninsula to the Canaries.

Statue of a Guanche king in Candelaria

Prehistorians now believe that the Canaries were settled from North Africa. The evidence for this has been provided by the examination of skeletons, which show a relationship between the ancient Canarian and North African peoples, and on numerous similarities between Canarian and Berber cultures. It has also become possible, on the basis of a variety of studies and archaeological finds, to establish the period of settlement with greater precision. Carbon dating and comparisons with Berber cultures of the period suggest that the islands were settled from 500 BC at the earliest.

How the incomers reached the islands is still unknown, since no remains of boats have been found. They may have travelled on reed boats, which simply rotted away. But why did the Canarians give up seafaring, and why did they want to settle on the Canaries? Various theories have been put forward to explain their departure from Africa – perhaps the increasing aridity of the region, or the pressures of Roman occupation. It is believed at any rate that the settlers arrived in the Canaries in a series of waves and that there may have been a variety of reasons for these migrations.

Economy

The ancient Canarians were herdsmen and tillers of the soil. On land cleared from the forest they grew barley and wheat, and also pulses, without the aid of the plough. Their domestic animals were goats, sheep, pigs and dogs.

The staple food was *gofio* – roasted barley, ground into flour, mixed with honey and water and kneaded to form a dough, and then shaped into balls (a recipe that has survived to the present day; see p. 151).

Other important foodstuffs were goat's meat, milk and butter. Mushrooms and wild fruits were gathered in the forests. Seafood must also have featured on the menu, though without boats the ancient Canarians could fish only in coastal waters.

They lived mainly in caves, which suited the climatic conditions of the time. The interiors of the caves were often hewn smooth, and could have thatched reed ceilings; some caves were hewn from the rock. There were also occasional stone structures, particularly tombs, semi-underground dwellings, and straw-roofed wattle-and-daub huts.

Dwellings

The clothing of the ancient Canarians was simple. A common garment was the *tamarco*, a skin cloak made by stitching goatskins together with thorns from plants. The art of weaving was unknown, although there were sheep on the islands. Garments were also made of plaited palm fibres and bast.

Clothing

When the Spaniards conquered the islands in the 15th c. they had little difficulty in overcoming the inhabitants, who had only the most primitive weapons. They had no metal tools or weapons, and lacked even the polished stone axes of the neolithic period. The bow was unknown to them, and their only means of defence were stones, fire-hardened spears and wooden clubs. For close fighting they had pointed stone blades, so sharp that they could also be used for cutting up everyday objects.

Tools and weapons

That the ancient Canarians were not primitive cavemen is shown by their social structure. There were three classes of society: the king and his family, the nobles, and the rest of the population. There seems to have been no clear distinction between the second and third groups. Nobility was not hereditary but could be attained by personal qualities, and noble status had to be confirmed by the priests. On the individual islands there were independent tribal territories, each ruled by a king. (At the time of the Spanish conquest Tenerife was divided into ten tribal territories, each headed by a *mencey* or king). Inheritance was in the female line, but it was not a matriarchal society. A woman could not herself exercise royal authority, but her husband was authorised by her election to rule. In practice the system of inheritance in the female line must undoubtedly have given women a high status in society. There is also some evidence that women played a major part in religious rites. On Fuerteventura two women are said to have had the leading roles in legal and religious matters.

Tribal society

The ancient Canarians believed in a single all-powerful higher being. On the island of Tenerife it was the god Abora. He had an adversary in Guayote, who was confined in the crater of Mount Teide and punished the misdeeds of men with volcanic eruptions. An important part was played in the religious practices of the Canarians by sacred mountains and cave sanctuaries, where animal sacrifices and libations were made to the god.

Religion

To the ancient Canarians the world of the dead was closely bound up with the world of the living. Dwellings and burial places cannot always be clearly distinguished from one another, for both natural and artificial caves were used either for living in or for burial. Only on the island of Gran Canaria have burial mounds been found.

Burials

Early Inhabitants

An ancient Canarian mummy

The bodies of the higher classes were mummified by being anointed with goat's butter and preserved by the application of heat and smoke. The brain was never removed; nor, normally, the entrails. This, compared with Egyptian methods, was a very simple form of mummification, and the mummies did not last long without decomposing. Evidently the caves traditionally used for burial were repeatedly reoccupied. The mummies found in such caves and now displayed in the museums of Santa Cruz de Tenerife and Las Palmas de Gran Canaria are none of them very old.

Language

Only scanty remnants of the language of the ancient Canarians have survived into our day, mainly in the form of place names. They suggest that the Canarian tongue was related to the language of the Berbers. It may be, however, that Berber elements entered the language at some later date. The various islands had different dialects, though basic words were common to them all. It is uncertain whether the whistling language known as *el silbo* (see Baedeker Special p. 76) was peculiar to the island of Gomera or was also used on Tenerife.

When the Spaniards conquered the Canaries the native population had no written language, though many rock inscriptions have been found. The first such inscriptions were discovered in 1867 on La Palma (Cueva Belmaco). Then in 1870 a rock face was found on Hierro (Los Letreros) with inscriptions of different periods: a pictographic script that conveyed only ideas and concepts; a series of characters resembling an alphabetic script; and various forms transitional between the two. On Gran Canaria there are rock-cut spirals and concentric circles (petroglyphs) – nothing comparable been found on Tenerife and Gomera. The scripts have not so far been deciphered, and it is doubtful whether they can be, for souvenir hunters have broken off much of the rock faces bearing the inscriptions. It is also uncertain whether the inscriptions were the work of the Canarians themselves or of occasional visitors.

Art

Some handsome pieces of pottery, made without the use of a wheel, have survived from the pre-Hispanic period. Many of them have hollow handles that could also be used as spouts. They are mostly plain and undecorated, but some are patterned with nicks or notches. The forms vary from island to island: thus on La Palma stamped or impressed decoration was used, and on Gran Canaria the decoration was particularly elaborate.

Mention should also be made here of the *pintaderas* – seals in a great variety of patterns, usually made of pottery, rarely of wood. They were presumably used to mark objects with the owner's name. No two pintaderas with the same pattern have so far been found.

There were also figures of idols, presumably used in various cult ceremonies, which almost without exception have survived only in fragments. The only one of any artistic quality is the "Idol of Tara", perhaps the most celebrated relic of ancient Canarian culture, which was found on Gran Canaria. This clay figure with grotesquely fat limbs is thought to be female, though there are no indications of breasts. In total there are only scanty remnants of ancient Canarian art, all of modest artistic pretensions.

Cultural influences

In general the remains of ancient Canarian culture are characterised by their archaic simplicity; but there are also elements that appear to

36

belong to a higher cultural level. Thus wheat and barley were ground on a circular hand-operated mill found in antiquity throughout the Mediterranean region, in which the grain was introduced through an opening in the upper stone. Since this piece of relatively advanced technology is out of line with other ancient Canarian remains it is supposed that it was brought to the islands by other peoples. Similarly the rock inscriptions found on the islands may have been left by foreign visitors. It is certainly the case that the Canarians had sporadic contacts with other peoples before the coming of the Spaniards: for example Roman amphorae or fragments of amphorae have been found off the coasts of the Canaries.

Hand mill

Spanish conquest

After the Spanish conquest the culture of the ancient Canarians, their language and way of life, fell completely into oblivion. In consequence it was long believed that the conquerors had ruthlessly exterminated the native population. There is no doubt that large numbers of Canarians were enslaved and shipped away from the islands and that the population was decimated in the fighting with the invaders. Many, however, survived, and anthropology has revealed the survival of ancient Canarian ethnic characteristics in the modern population of the Canaries. There must, therefore, have been a very rapid mingling of the two races after the Spanish conquest. The ancient Canarians became rapidly assimilated and adopted the way of the life of the Spaniards – not surprisingly, for Spanish culture was much superior to their own.

Famous People

Jean de Béthencourt (1359–1425)

Jean de Béthencourt, a Norman, was entrusted by Henry III of Castile with the task of conquering the Canaries. His lieutenant was Gadifer de la Salle, with whom he had taken part in a "Crusade" against Tunis in 1390. The two men assembled an expeditionary fleet, which sailed from La Rochelle in 1402. When Béthencourt at last saw the first islands in the archipelago he named them in delight, bare and rocky though they were, Alegranza (Joy) and Graciosa (the Beautiful). Soon afterwards the adventurers landed on Lanzarote and were able to capture it in a relatively short time. Then Béthencourt returned to Spain for reinforcements, and Henry bestowed on him the title of king of the Canary Islands: whereupon Gadifer, offended,

took no further part in the enterprise. In consequence Béthencourt was solely responsible for the conquest of Fuerteventura, which was achieved in 1405. Soon afterwards he also took Hierro. Thereafter he settled the two islands with peasants from Normandy and Spain, and the native population was rigorously converted to Christianity.

In 1406 Béthencourt appointed his nephew Maciot de Béthencourt viceroy of the islands and returned to France, where he died in 1425 in his castle in Granville.

Beatriz de Bobadilla (late 15th c.)

Beatriz de Bobadilla, a lady of the Spanish Court, played a part in the destinies of the Canaries as mistress or wife of men who took part in the conquest of the islands.

As mistress of King Ferdinand of Aragon she attracted the wrath of his wife Isabella of Castile, who took the first opportunity to get rid of her rival. Hernán Peraza the Younger, who was suspected of having murdered the conqueror of Gran Canaria, was pardoned on condition that he married Beatriz de Bobadilla and took her with him to Gomera. The couple were ruthless in their treatment of the native population, who reacted violently, and Hernán Peraza was killed during a rising in 1488.

Thereupon Beatriz de Bobadilla, with her children, took refuge in the Torre del Conde in San Sebastián de la Gomera. The governor of the island of Gran Canaria came to her assistance, the rebellion was repressed and its ringleaders executed.

As ruler of Gomera Beatriz several times received Columbus (see entry), and when he called in at Gomera on his second voyage of discovery she greeted him with fireworks and an artillery salute. Whether she had a liaison with Columbus cannot be certainly established, but there is no doubt about her next love affair: in 1498 she married Alonso Fernández de Lugo (see entry), conqueror of Tenerife and La Palma.

This seductive lady is still not forgotten

on Gomera, and her portrait occupies a place of honour in the parador high above San Sebastián.

Christopher Columbus (in Spanish Cristóbal Colón, in Italian Cristoforo Colombo), a native of Genoa, visited the Canaries several times on his voyages of discovery.

Christopher Columbus (1451–1506)

Columbus went to Lisbon in 1476 hoping to get assistance for his project of seeking a western route to India; then, proving unsuccessful, applied to Spain in 1485. It was not until 1492, however, that Ferdinand of Aragon and his wife Isabella of Castile signed an agreement with Columbus making him viceroy of any lands he discovered and granting him 10 per cent of the expected profits.

On his first voyage of discovery (1492–3) Columbus put in at Las Palmas (Gran Canaria), where he had his ships overhauled and took on supplies of water and provisions. At the end of August he set out for Gomera; and his logbook records that when sailing past Tenerife he observed an eruption of Mount Teide. During his stay on Gomera he met Beatriz de Bobadilla (see entry); but whether he had a liaison with her, as rumour had it, is uncertain. That there may have been some truth in the story is suggested by the fact that Columbus also spent some time on Gomera on his second (1493–5) and third (1498–1500) voyages. His visits have earned Gomera the style of "Isla Colombina".

On his fourth crossing of the Atlantic (1502–4) Columbus again took on supplies on Gran Canaria. On his return from this voyage he was a sick man, and he died in Valladolid in 1506.

Born on Tenerife in 1750, Tomás de Iriarte is one of the few Canarian personalities who have made a name for themselves outside the islands. He became known as a translator – he put Horace's "Ars Poetica" into German, for example – and also as a writer. He is famed for his "Fábulas Literarias", in which he pilloried literary shortcomings and attempted to improve the taste of the public at large, as well as for his didactic poem "La Música". In his plays he censured the idle lives led by the nobility and praised the industry shown by the lower classes.

Tomás de Iriarte (1750–91)

Tomás de Iriarte's literary talents were recognised at an early age. When only 13 years old he left the Canary Islands and went to live with his uncle in Madrid, where he completed his education. He initially worked as a translator for the Secretary of State and as an archivist from 1776. As a member of the famous literary circle, the Fonda de San Sebastián, he came into contact with the leading Spanish writers of his day.

Iriarte died in Madrid on September 17th 1791. Today there is a street in Puerto de la Cruz named after him, and the family house where he was born has been restored and is open to visitors.

The Andalusian nobleman Alonso Fernández de Lugo played a leading part in the conquest of the Canaries. He entered into an agreement with Ferdinand of Aragon and Isabella of Castile under which he was given the right to grant land and water rights on the Canary Islands. For his part he was required to raise the resources for the conquest of La Palma and Tenerife.

Alonso Fernández de Lugo (1456–1525)

On May 1st 1492 de Lugo, who had previously taken part in the conquest of Gran Canaria, landed on Tenerife with a thousand men; but after some initial successes he suffered an annihilating defeat in the

Barranco de Acentejo. In 1492–3 he conquered the island of La Palma without difficulty; then in the autumn of 1494 he again landed on Tenerife and by 1496 had brought the whole island under his control. In the same year he founded La Laguna and made it his capital. In 1498 he married Beatriz de Bobadilla (see entry). He showed great skill in the government of the islands, but there are differing views about his character. He is sometimes seen as an adventurer who treated the native population with great harshness and whose motives for action were his debts and his greed for money. De Lugo's tomb is in the Santa Iglesia Capital in La Laguna.

César Manrique
(1920–92)

Visitors to the Canaries will frequently come across the work of the architect, painter and sculptor César Manrique, a native of Lanzarote. The buildings and developments for which he was responsible, including the Costa de Martiánez, the lido and seafront promenade in Puerto de la Cruz, have left a distinctive mark on the landscape of the Canaries. After some early exhibitions of his work in the Canaries Manrique moved in 1945 to Madrid, where he studied at the Academy of Fine Art. Thereafter he achieved further success in the field of abstract painting, and his work was exhibited not only in Spain but in many cities in Europe, Japan and the United States. In 1965, now with an international reputation, he went to New York to take up a post in the International Institute of Art Education. In 1968 he returned to Lanzarote, where he founded the Museum of Contemporary Art.

Subsequently he was concerned in numerous building projects in the Canaries, particularly on Lanzarote and Tenerife. Basing himself on native architectural traditions, he sought to preserve the landscape as it is; architecture, he thought, should be in harmony with its setting. He saw it as his principal task to save his native island of Lanzarote from overbuilding. He did not fully achieve this goal, but it is due in no small measure to his efforts that the worst environmental crimes have been avoided and Lanzarote still presents an attractive picture to the visitor. Manrique was killed in a motor accident in September 1992. He is buried in Haria on Lanzarote.

Culture

Prehistory

Little is left of the art of the ancient Canarians. Apart from a few pieces of pottery and animal figures visitors will find no artistic evidence of the indigenous culture of the archipelago (see Early Inhabitants).

Vernacular houses

In the interior of the island there are still some traditional single-storey cottages. The living room can be large but much of the family's life is spent in the patio, which is gay with plants and flowers and at least partly roofed over. As a rule the houses face south, and accordingly need no shutters to protect the windows from wind and rain. Single-storey houses in towns usually have a narrow, rather cramped plan; two-storey houses have an outer staircase of wood or stone, a small balcony or – in rare cases – an entrance lobby. In the Canaries even mansions are almost always relatively small, differing very little in structure from two-storey houses in towns. The central feature of the house is the shady patio, often with a luxuriant display of flowers, from which a staircase (usually on the left-hand side) leads to the rooms on the upper floor. Almost all houses are limewashed, reflecting the sun and keeping the temperature down, as well as repelling insects, which instinctively avoid a white background since it shows up their protective colouring. The houses are typically cube-shaped and are roofed with red tiles.

The most striking feature of Canarian traditional architecture is its use of wood, in the elaborately carved green, white or cinnamon-coloured balconies, galleries, windows and doors, which were always regarded on the islands as signs of prosperity. There are two types of balcony: those that have a balustrade of lath-turned pillars and above this are open, and those that, following Arab models, are totally enclosed by a lattice screen. There are also various hybrid forms.

Architecture

In the centuries following the Spanish conquest numbers of churches and modest public buildings were erected, closely following European and particularly Spanish architectural and artistic traditions. Gothic influences are only occasionally found in the Canaries, but there are many examples of Renaissance architecture. Following ancient architectural forms, they make a clear distinction between the different storeys of a building (Town Hall, Santa Cruz de la Palma). The Mudéjar style, which shows a mingling of Moorish with Gothic or Renaissance forms, was developed in Spain by the Mudéjars (the "Moors who were allowed to stay"), but also by Christian architects influenced by the Moorish style. Its main characteristics arze horseshoe arches, stalactitic vaulting and stucco ornament. The Mudéjar style developed into plateresque, which came into vogue in Spain at the end of the 15th c. In this style the façades of buildings were covered with a profusion of intricate ornament. A particular variant of the style developed in the Canaries, and many buildings were given ceilings of Canary pine, richly carved and sometimes painted in many colours.

In the 17th c. the baroque style came to the Canaries. An example is the Iglesia de Santa Catalina in Tacoronte. In addition many churches were equipped with baroque furnishings and works of art. The neoclassical style that came in during the second half of the 18th c. left its mark mainly on the façades of buildings, which were strictly articulated and, in comparison with baroque architecture, given little in the way of sculptural decoration; an example is the town hall of La Orotava. The characteristic feature of 19th c. architecture is the mingling of a variety of styles modelled on the buildings of the past.

Since the mid-20th c. there has been a regular building boom in the

The central point of a Canarian house is the patio, usually with a luxuriant growth of greenery and often surrounded by decorated wood balconies

Canaries, particularly on Tenerife. Innumerable large hotels have been built all over the island; new tourist resorts such as Playa de las Américas have been created, and the process is still continuing. These developments, often of dubious architectural quality, have given rise to some controversy on the islands, and some attempts have been made to give new developments a more human face. Particularly notable in this respect has been the work of the Canarian architect César Manrique (see Famous People).

Woodcarving

Throughout their history the Canaries have been notable for fine wood-carving. In most of the major churches in the archipelago there are statues in wood by the greatest Canarian sculptor Luján Pérez (1756–1815) and his pupil Fernando Estévez (b. 1788 in La Orotava). Mention has already been made of the richly decorated wooden ceilings to be found in both sacred and secular buildings.

Literature

Tomás de Iriarte (1750–91; see Famous People) is one of the few Canarian writers who have made a name for themselves in the outside world. He gained an international reputation with his "Fábulas Literarias", in which he sought to improve the taste of the public.

No less well known on the islands is the name of the poet and dramatist Angel Guimerá (1849–1924). The theatre in his home town of Santa Cruz is named after him.

Also worthy of mention is the chronicler and historian José de Viera y Clavijo (1731–1813), whose "Notes on the History of the Canaries" and "Dictionary of the Natural History of the Canaries" are still important sources of information for students of Canarian history.

Folk traditions

The fiestas of the Canaries are essential features in the life of the islanders. As a rule these are of religious origin and are held in honour

of one of the island saints. They usually begin with a religious procession, which is followed by more secular diversions. Music features
largely in these celebrations. The songs, passionate in rhythm and
melody, are usually accompanied by the *timple,* a small stringed
instrument.

The costumes worn in the fiestas are mostly modern creations. Only
the wide-brimmed hat and the numerous underskirts worn by the
women are traditional features.

In almost every place of any size there is a ring for Canarian wrestling
contests *(lucha canaria),* 9–10 m (30–33 ft) in diameter. The contest is
between two wrestlers, each belonging to a twelve-man team. The
winner is the first to achieve a fall.

Traditional sports

The *juego del palo,* a contest like singlesticks but played with two
sticks, calls for extraordinary dexterity. Each contestant has to attack his
opponent and ward off his blows, moving the body as little as possible.

Quotations

Homer

But to thee is assigned, O beloved of Zeus, Menelaus,
Not the destiny of death in Argos, mother of horses;
But the gods will lead thee one day to the end of the earth,
To the Elysian fields, where the dark-skinned Rhadamanthys
Dwells, and men are blessed with an ever tranquil life.
There is no snow, no winter storm, no pouring rain;
And there is ever heard the murmur of the softly breathing West,
Which Ocean sends to bring men gentle coolness.

"Odyssey" (8th c. BC). Whether the "Elysian fields" described by Homer are to be identified with the Canary Islands is uncertain.

Plutarch

There are two islands, separated from one another by a narrow strait, ten thousand stadia from Africa; they are called the Isles of the Blessed. Seldom watered by moderate showers of rain, most commonly by gentle dew-bringing winds, they offer not only a good rich soil to be tilled and planted but also wild fruits sufficient in quantity and flavour to nourish an idle people without work or effort.

These islands enjoy a fortunate climate in consequence of the mingling and the barely perceptible change of the seasons; for the north and east winds blowing from our region of the earth are dispersed and die down when they emerge into this expanse of infinite space, while the sea winds from the south and west sometimes bring in moderate rain from the sea, but for the most part caress the islands with their gentle breath and make them fertile. And so there has been disseminated even among the barbarians the firm belief that these are the Elysian fields, the dwelling place of the blessed, of which Homer sang.

"Life of Sertorius" (1st–2nd c. AD)

Christopher Columbus

As we were passing Tenerife we observed an eruption of the volcano. The smoke and flames, the glowing masses of lava, the muffled roaring from the earth's interior caused panic among the crew. An evil omen, they thought, it must surely be. I told them about Etna and other volcanoes, but found only deaf ears. They believed that the volcano had erupted because we had undertaken this voyage. This caused me worry enough, but I was still more disturbed by the news brought by a ship coming from Ferro (Hierro). It reported that three Portuguese caravels were cruising in the vicinity, with orders to take me prisoner and so put an end to my enterprise.

The way from La Rábida to Córdoba is long, from Palos to Lisbon still longer; and yet the king of Portugal already knew that I had put to sea. He no longer needs me now that Diaz has found the eastern route to India, and so he wants to bar the western route to me. If I succeed – and I shall succeed – in winning the sea and reaching territories where no other vessels dare to go João's caravels will return to Lisbon empty-handed. Time, which has always run too fast for me, is now running too slowly. It will take another three weeks to make the "Pinta" seaworthy.

"Logbook" (August 9th 1492). On his first voyage of exploration (1492–3) Columbus, sailing past Tenerife, observed an eruption of Mount Teide.

**Leonardo Torriani
Italian Architect**

In these Canary Islands there were three different methods of fighting, with three different kinds of weapon: the two which have already been mentioned and a third, the thin stones called *tavas* which they used for letting blood. These they employ to wound one another in hand-to-hand fighting.

When two Canarians challenged one another to a fight they made their way to the spot used for this purpose, a small area of higher ground with a flat stone on each side, just big enough for a man to stand on. Each of them stood on his stone with three stones to throw at his opponent and wound him, and with the cudgels called *magodo* and *amodeghe*. They began by throwing the stones at each other, dexterously avoiding them without moving their feet. Then they stepped off their stones and had at each other with the cudgels, each striving to gain an advantage over the other, just as it is with us; and when they came hand to hand they wounded one another with the three sharp stones which they held between the fingers of the left hand. Then when one of the two was ready to admit defeat he cried out in a loud voice *"Gamá, gamá"*, which in our language means "Enough, enough!". Thereupon the victor ceased to fight and the two men became friends. Before challenging one another to fight they had first obtained permission from a chieftain called a *sambor* and this permission had been confirmed by a *faicagh* (priest). Both the chieftain and the priest, as well as the relatives of the two men, were present at the fight.

"The Canary Islands and their Inhabitants" (1590)

To speake somewhat of these Ilands, being called in olde time Insulae Fortunatae, by the meanes of the flourishing thereof, the fruitfullnesse of them doeth surely exceed farre all other that I have heard of: for they make wine better than any in Spaine, they have grapes of such bignesse, that they may bee compared to damsons, and taste inferiour to none: for sugar, suckets, rasins of the Sunne, and many other fruits, abundance: for rosine and rawe silke, there is great store, they want neither corne, pullets, cattell, nor yet wilde foule: they have many camels also which being young are eaten of the people for victuals, and being olde, they are used for caryage of necessaries.

Richard Hakluyt

"Principal Navigations ..." (1598–1600)

Tenerife, situated as it were at the gateway of the tropics and yet only a few days' sail from Spain, already displays much of the splendour with which nature has endowed the lands between the tropics ... Anyone who has a feeling for the beauty of nature will find on this delightful island a remedy even more powerful than the climate. No place in the world seems to me more likely than Tenerife and Madeira to banish melancholy and restore peace to a troubled spirit ... The coast is fringed with date palms and coconut trees; higher up banana plants stand out from dragon trees, whose stem is quite properly likened to the body of a snake. The hillsides are planted with vines clinging to tall trellises. Blossom-covered orange trees, myrtles and cypresses surround chapels which piety has erected on isolated hills. Everywhere the fields are enclosed by hedges of agave and cactus. Countless cryptogams, particularly ferns, clothe the walls, which are kept moist by small springs of clear water. In winter, when the volcano is covered with ice and snow, an eternal spring prevails here. In summer, towards evening, the sea wind brings agreeable coolness.

Alexander von Humboldt
German scientist and geographer

[Ascent of Teide] We settled down on the outermost rim of the crater and looked first to the north-west, where the coasts are decked with villages and hamlets. The mist at our feet, continually driven this way and that by the wind, offered us an ever-changing spectacle. A level layer of clouds between us and the lower regions of the island was pierced here and there by the little currents of air which the earth's surface, warmed by the sun, sent up to us. The harbour of Orotava, the vessels anchored in it, the gardens and vineyards round the town were visible through an opening which seemed to become bigger every moment. From these lonely regions we looked down into an inhabited world, relishing the sharp contrast between the barren flanks of the peak, its steep slopes covered with volcanic detritus, its plantless plateau and the smiling aspect of the cultivated land; we saw how the vegetation was distributed into zones according to temperature, declining with increasing height. Below the summit lichens are beginning to clothe the shining flows of lava. A violet (*Viola cheiranthifolia*), closely related to Viola decumbens, grows at heights of up to 3390 m (11,120 ft) on the slopes of the volcano. *Retama* bushes, covered with flowers, grow in the little valleys carved out by rainwater and blocked by the lateral eruptions. Below the *retama* follows the region of the ferns, which in turn are followed by the tree heaths. Forests of laurels, rhamnus and strawberry trees lie between the heaths and the area planted with vines and fruit trees. A rich green carpet extends from the level of the brooms and the zone of Alpine plants to the groups of date palms and bananas, against whose feet the ocean seems to wash ... In vain we prolonged our stay on the summit, waiting for the moment when we should be able to see the whole archipelago of the Blessed Islands. We saw at our feet Palma, Gomera and Grand Canary, but soon the hills of Lanzarote, which at sunrise had been clear, were again shrouded in dense mist.

"From the Orinoco to the Amazon" (1889)

Suggested Routes

The routes suggested in this section will take you through some of the most beautiful parts of Tenerife. Places that are the subject of a separate entry in the Sights from A to Z section of the guide are printed in **bold** type; other places may be found by reference to the Index. The general course of a route can be seen from the marginal references.

Route 1: circuit of Tenerife

Puerto de la Cruz is taken as the starting point of this itinerary, but of course it is possible to start from any point on the route. In general, however, it is best to begin in the west of the island, where the roads are not so good and visibility is important. A tour of Santa Cruz de Tenerife or La Laguna, on the other hand, is still of interest in the evening, and thereafter the northern and southern motorways make it easy to get back to any particular resort.

If only a single day can be devoted to this itinerary this will allow only a short time in any of the places on the route and will give only a first brief impression of the beauty and interest that Tenerife has to offer.

Leave ★★**Puerto de la Cruz** on the expressway running west. Road 820 is soon reduced to two lanes, but is still a good road. At ★★**Icod de los Vinos** follow the signs to the town centre. The principal attraction here is the oldest and finest dragon tree on Tenerife. 6 km (4 mi.) further on, lying directly on the sea, is ★**Garachico**, one of the prettiest little towns on the island.

Only if you start very early in the morning will you have time to fit in a side trip to the Teno Hills: otherwise you will have to leave this for another occasion. From Garachico take the road that runs west by way of **Los Silos** to **Buenavista,** where a very narrow road turns south and winds its way up, with many curves and sharp bends, into the Teno Hills (★Macizo de Teno), offering a succession of magnificent views; unfortunately there are few stopping places. In 13 km (8 mi.) the road comes to ★★**Masca**. There is room for parking outside this charming little town, which can then be explored on foot. From here it is only 4 km (2.5 mi.) to Santiago del Teide, where you return to the main route.

From the west end of Garachico a road runs up to Tanque and just beyond this rejoins road 120. Plenty of time must be allowed for the next stretch of road, which snakes its way up through a lonely upland region to reach its highest point at the Erjos Pass (1117 m (3665 ft)) and then continues through increasingly barren country to **Santiago del Teide**. Just beyond the south end of this little town take a road on the left signposted to Arguayo. Here you can visit the Centro Alfarero, where pottery is produced without the aid of the potter's wheel. Then on by way of Chio and **Guía de Isora** to **Adeje**, where you can enjoy a walk through this unspoiled mountain village. The landscape to the south of Adeje has changed dramatically in recent years, with the continuing development of tourist centres along the coast. If you have not yet seen **Playa de las Américas** and **Los Cristianos** it is worth while taking a stroll along the promenade that links the two resorts.

For the next section of the route it is best to take the motorway. Road 822, which runs parallel, is winding and has no particular scenic beauties to offer. The motorway runs past the Reina Sofía Airport, which is

Detour to the Teno Hills

Routes on Tenerife

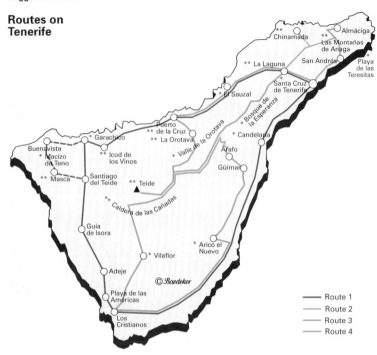

- —— Route 1
- —— Route 2
- —— Route 3
- —— Route 4

now used by almost all international flights, and continues to ★**Candelaria**, the most important pilgrimage centre in the Canaries. The next place of interest on the route is the island's capital, ★**Santa Cruz**. If you have already seen this busy city, or want to visit it later, you should turn off into the Autopista del Norte, which runs north-east to ★★**La Laguna**. This quiet university town has preserved its characteristic townscape and is little affected by tourism. From here it is 35 km (22 mi.) back to Puerto de la Cruz on the Autopista del Norte.

Route 2: south of Tenerife to the Caldera de las Cañadas

A trip to the Caldera de las Cañadas and Mount Teide will be one of the most memorable impressions of your visit to Tenerife. The route suggested here (180 km (110 mi.)) runs through all the different vegetation zones on the island.

The quickest route from the tourist centres of **Playa de las Américas** and **Los Cristianos** in the south of Tenerife to the Caldera de las Cañadas is on the recently improved road by way of Chayofa, **Arona** and ★**Vilaflor**. From the Mirador de San Roque, at the north end of Vilaflor, there is a fine view of Tenerife's highest village. The road then continues to climb through aromatic pine plantations, passing the Zona Recreativa Las

The snow-capped peak of Mount Teide can be seen from the starting point of this route, Playa de las Américas

Lajas, with restaurants and picnic spots that are crowded with Canarians at weekends. Beyond this, after numerous curves and sharp bends, the road comes to the Boca de Tauce (2046 m (6713 ft)), the gateway to the ★★Caldera de las Cañadas. From here a road goes off on the right into the lunar landscape of the **Parque Nacional del Teide**. The vegetation consists mainly of unspectacular ground cover, with occasional shrubs. The road runs in an almost straight line over a wide plain, the Llano de Ucanca. 7 km (4.4 mi.) beyond the Boca de Tauce a side road goes off on the left to Los Roques, the most striking rock formation in the National Park. A well laid out footpath at Los Roques affords magnificent views of the grand landscape. Refreshment is available in a cafeteria in the nearby parador, which also has a visitor centre offering background information on the National Park. 4 km (2.5 mi.) further on a signpost points the way to the cableway up ★★Mount Teide. The cableway operates only when weather conditions are favourable, and long waits are to be expected. Beyond this the road continues past more striking rock formations shimmering in a variety of colours. At the Montaña Blanca is the starting point of a route to the summit of ★★Mount Teide. It is also worth stopping at the visitor centre (Centro de Visitantes) near El Portillo.

Attached to it is a small botanical garden that gives an overview of the flora of the National Park. At El Portillo the route leaves the National Park and follows road 824, on the right, signposted to La Laguna and Santa Cruz. This ridge road, the Carretera Dorsal, runs along the crest of the hills that separate the northern and southern halves of the island, through the ★**Bosque de la Esperanza**. The dense growth of trees in this forest area is made possible by the clouds and mist brought by the trade winds. Soon, on the right of the road, can be seen Tenerife's two observatories, the Observatorio de Izaña and the Observatorio del Teide. (If you want to see the visitor centre associated with the observatories it is advisable to check its opening hours before setting out). Further along the road there are magnificent views on either side (provided that they are not obscured by cloud). 18 km (11 mi.) beyond El Portillo a road goes off on the right to **Arafo**, an attractive village set amid orchards and vineyards, which is reached after another 18 km of curves and narrow bends. 4 km (2.5 mi.) south-east of Arafo is **Güimar**, famed for its mysterious pyramids, now the central features of the Parque Etnográfico Pirámides de Güimar. If you are not tired of winding roads you can continue on road 822; alternatively, there is the motorway, which runs roughly parallel to it. To the right of the road are bare hill ridges; to the left, far below, can be seen the blue sea. Although there is hardly any rain in this area, the land is extensively cultivated, in small and sometimes terraced fields. The modest little town of **Fasnia** need not detain you long, but it is worth spending some time in **Arico**, particularly the district of ★Arico el Nuevo with its typically Canarian little houses. The return to Los Cristianos and Playa de las Américas is on the motorway.

Route 3: Valle de la Orotava and Mount Teide

An early start is advisable for this trip (125 km (78 mi.)), since a dense blanket of cloud always almost gathers over Mount Teide in the course of the day, obscuring the view of the mountain.

From ★★**Puerto de la Cruz** take one of the roads that run south to ★★**La Orotava**, from which road 821 runs up to the Caldera de las Cañadas. The first section of the road, through the ★★**Valle de la Orotava**, is lined with luxuriant banana plantations, which soon give place to fields of vines, vegetables and fruit. At Aguamansa (altitude 1000 m (3280 ft)) the vegetation changes again to forests of laurels and pines and a profusion of tree heaths.

Walk to the Caldera and Los Órganos

1 km (0.6 mi.) beyond the parking area for walkers at Aguamansa a road goes off on the left to the Caldera, a small subsidiary crater, which you can drive or walk round; the walk takes about 10 minutes. You can walk from here to Los Órganos (The Organ Pipes; 1.5 km (1 mi.)), rock columns formed from the lava.

Further up is the Mirador Marguerite, another good starting point for walks. The road runs past the Montaña Roja (1800 m (5906 ft)) and at El Portillo (2020 m (6628 ft)), the "gateway" to the Caldera de la Cañadas, is joined by the road from La Laguna. The route continues on road 821, coming just beyond El Portillo to the visitor centre of the **Parque Nacional del Teide**. The road now runs through the lunar landscape of the ★★Caldera de las Cañadas, climbing only slightly. Passing the Montaña Blanca, it continues through scenery of almost surreal aspect. If weather conditions are favourable the ascent of ★★Mount Teide by cableway is not only the high point of this trip but one of the outstanding experiences of a visit to Tenerife.

Now return to El Portillo and turn right into the Carretera Dorsal (road 824), which runs along the crest of the hills through the ★**Bosque de la Esperanza**, offering scenery very different from that on the road up through the Valle de la Orotava. 6 km (3.7 mi.) beyond El Portillo a road goes off to the two observatories on Mount Izaña. (If you want to see the visitor centre associated with the observatories it is advisable to check its opening hours before setting out). The Carretera Dorsal continues past numerous *miradores* (viewpoints), among the finest of which are the Mirador de Ortuño (1804 m (5919 ft)) and the Mirador Pico de las Flores, from which there are superb views of the La Laguna plateau and the Montañas de Anago. Soon after Pico de las Flores a road goes off on the right to Las Raíces, where General Franco met the officers of the Tenerife garrison to plan his military coup in mainland Spain. Beyond

Seafront promenade, Puerto de la Cruz

this is the little town of La Esperanza. The road now emerges from the forest and runs through an intensively cultivated farming area. 6 km (3.7 mi.) north of La Esperanza, at ★★**La Laguna**, it runs into the Autopista del Norte, which runs west back to Puerto de la Cruz. From the motorway a side trip can be made to ★**El Sauzal**, whose attractions include its beautiful parks and the gardens and the Casa del Vino, with a museum of wine, a restaurant and a tasting centre). From there it is a short distance on the motorway to Puerto de la Cruz.

Route 4: Through the Montañas de Anaga

This route (85 km (53 mi.)) runs through the still largely unspoiled landscape of the ★★**Montañas de Anaga**. It requires good weather for its full enjoyment: when the hills are shrouded in dense cloud much of the scenery is obscured. See also the entry on the Montañas de Anaga in the Sights from A to Z section of the guide.

The starting point of the tour is ★★**La Laguna**, which is easily reached from both the north and the south of the island by motorway. The road runs up through the Bosque de las Mercedes to the summit ridge of the Anaga Hills, with the possibility of rewarding side trips to the hill village of ★★Chinamada and Almáciga on the north coast. From there the route runs back to El Bailadero and continues south to **San Andrés**, near which is an attractive bathing beach, the ★Playa de las Teresitas.

**Sights
from A to Z**

Sights from A to Z

Adeje

B 4

Altitude: 250 m (820 ft)
Population (district): 13,000

Adeje is one of the more attractive towns in southern Tenerife, and a popular starting point for walks in the Barranca del Infierno (Gorge of Hell). The huge tourist centres of Playa de las Américas and Los Cristianos are only a few kilometres away, and as a result Adeje is rarely free from swarms of day trippers. The town is now well equipped to cater for them, with numerous pavement cafés where walkers can refresh themselves before or after their trip into the Gorge of Hell.

Adeje is the administrative centre of the small district of the same name. The district has a 16 km (10 mi.) coastline, the Costa Adeje, that is now fringed by hotels and apartments with a total of some 60,000 beds for visitors. The income from tourism has enriched many of the town's citizens and enabled the municipality to spend lavishly on road building, parks and gardens, housing and cultural facilities.

History In pre-Hispanic times Adeje was the seat of a tribal king. The Spaniards also chose this as the site of one of their first settlements on Tenerife, since the stream that flows down through the Barranco del Infierno supplies the area with sufficient water all year round. In 1497 Cristóbal de Ponte was granted authority over the little town, and in 1555 his son Pedro de Ponte was given the right to build a *casa fuerte* (fortified house) here to protect the settlement from pirate raids. At that time a large proportion of the inhabitants gained their living from growing sugar cane, and this remained so until the late 19th c., when other agricultural products came to the fore.

The old **town centre** is now surrounded by much modern building but it has remained relatively quiet and peaceful. The hub of the town's life is the main street, which is lined with Indian laurel trees and simple white houses.

Iglesia de Santa Úrsula

In the main street is the Iglesia de Santa Úrsula, an aisled church built in the 17th–18th c., with a beautiful painted coffered ceiling. Above the apse are two balconies once reserved for the nobility, protected from the public view by wrought-iron screens. The church has a fine figure of the Virgen del Rosario attributed to Tenerife's finest sculptor, Fernando Estévez (1788–1854).

Convento de San Francisco

In the town centre is a Franciscan friary, the oldest parts dating from the 16th c. The Tenerife government plans to house the Museum of Religious Art (Museo de Arte Sacro) here.

Casa Fuerte

A few hundred metres up a side street near the church is the Casa Fuerte, a fortified mansion built in the mid-16th c. to give protection against

◀ *A trip to the Parque Nacional del Teide is a must for visitors to Tenerife. A path running past Los Roques, a curious rock formation, offers wide views of Mount Teide and the lunar landscape of the Caldera de las Cañadas*

pirate raids. The complex also includes residential apartments occupied by the de Pontes, one of the most powerful families on the island (see History, above). There were also a sugar mill, storerooms and accommodation for a large number of slaves. For many years the house was used as a tomato packing plant. There are plans to restore the building.

★Barranco del Infierno

The Barranco del Infierno (Gorge of Hell) is a huge gorge immediately north-east of Adeje. It is reached by turning off the main street at the church of St Ursula into the road to the Casa Fuerte and, just before reaching the house, taking a road on the right that ends at the mouth of the gorge.

The path through the *barranco*, which is easy to follow, leads into one of the most beautiful stretches of scenery on Tenerife. At first there is only the sparse vegetation characteristic of the southern part of the island, bur further up the gorge the vegetation is increasingly luxuriant. The *barranco* owes its rich growth of plant life to the stream that flows through it. Since the water is carried down into the valley in artificial channels, it does not appear until lower down the gorge. Further up the valley the path, which is well maintained, crosses the stream several times (though after heavy rain it is impassable). At the head of the valley a waterfall plunges down from a height of 80 m (260 ft), forming a tiny lake of crystal-clear water. The waterfall is not particularly impressive in itself, but it is an unusual phenomenon in the Canaries that have few springs and perennial watercourses.

The walk up the gorge (8 km (5 mi.) round trip) takes little more than 2 or 3 hours (without breaks), starting from the entrance. Stout footwear is essential. The difference in height between Adeje and the waterfall is about 300 m (1000 ft). Since this is one of the most popular excursions on the island, you are unlikely to find yourself alone. There are particularly large numbers of visitors at weekends.

Arafo   D 2

Altitude: 510 m (1675 ft)
Population (district): 4500

The little town of Arafo lies 20 km (12 mi.) south-west of Santa Cruz, near the pilgrimage centre of Candelaria.

Arafo is noted for its musical and cultural traditions, and the ceremonies at the end of August in honour of its patron saint attract large numbers of visitors.

Arafo is an attractive little **village** surrounded by orchards and vineyards. The village church (with fine carved woodwork in the interior) is of only local importance.

Surroundings

To the west of Arafo is the Montaña de las Arenas (1582 m (5191 ft)), also known as the Volcán de Arafo. In a series of eruptions in 1705 and 1706 masses of lava flowed down towards the sea.

Montaña de las Arenas

Arico   C/D 3/4

Altitude: 575 m (1885 ft)
Population (district): 5000

The Viña Vieja Hotel in Arico, an old mansion house, offers a typical Canarian atmosphere

The village of Arico, 45 km (28 mi.) south-west of Santa Cruz, takes in a number of communes, the most important of which are Lomo de Arico, Arico el Nuevo and Arico Viejo. The most interesting is Arico el Nuevo, a pretty hill village that has preserved some typical Canarian architecture. The inhabitants live by farming, but attempts are being made to develop tourism.

Lomo de Arico

The most prominent feature of Lomo de Arico is the baroque church of San Juan Bautista. Begun in 1590, it was given its present form in the mid-18th c. Its most precious treasure is a Gothic figure of the Virgin of Abona.

★Arico el Nuevo

Arico el Nuevo has no spectacular art treasures, but it is an attractive hill village of closely packed little houses. Most of the houses are white-washed, with green shutters and doors. Visitors can absorb the atmosphere of the village from a bench in the shady square in front of the church.

Arico Viejo

Adjoining Arico el Nuevo on the north is Arico Viejo. In spite of its name *(viejo,* old), it cannot compete with Arico el Nuevo (New Arico), which is protected as a national monument.

Surroundings

Poris de Abona

6 km (3.7 mi.) from Arico, on the coast, is the fishing village of Porís de Abona, round which a number of apartment blocks and holiday bungalows have been built. There are facilities for bathing, but no sandy beaches. These are to be found at Punta de Abona (2 km (1.2 mi.) south) and Punta del Rincón (2.5 km (1.6 mi.) north).

Arona   B 4

Altitude: 632 m (2074 ft)
Population (district): 30,000

Arona, 10km (6 mi.) north of Los Cristianos, is the chief place in its district, which also takes in the Costa del Silencio, Los Cristianos and part
of Playa de las Américas (see entries), the major tourist centres in
southern Tenerife. It ranks, therefore, as the wealthiest commune on the
island.

The houses of this little **town** are scattered over the hillside on both
sides of the main road. The attractive square in the centre of the town,
with the 17th c. parish church (magnificent retable), bears witness to a
degree of prosperity. The new Ayuntamiento (Town Hall), in traditional
Canarian style with artistic wooden balconies, was built in the late 1970s.

Surroundings

High above Arona is the Roque del Conde (1003 m (3291 ft)), a flat-   **Roque del Conde**
topped hill from which there are fascinating panoramic views. To climb
the hill, leave Arona on the road to the village of Vento, from which a
path leads up to the summit (9 km (5.6 mi.) round trip). The plateau was
formerly used for the growing of grain; it is now carpeted with flowers
in spring.

The "Atlantis project", originally conceived in 1984 and now in course of   **Mariposa**
development under the name of Mariposa at Túnez, to the east of Arona,   **(Atlantis)**
is an unusual holiday settlement designed by the Luxembourg architect
Leon Krier. It was conceived as a retreat for the interchange of ideas
between artists, philosophers, writers and thinkers from all over the
world. The original plans were for a town in classical Greek style with
accommodation for some 200 residents, but for various reasons the imi-
tation temples were never built. The first houses on the site, which
covers 2.7 ha (6.7 acres), were completed in 1982. It is planned to con-
vert the project into a foundation to which the public will have access.

Bajamar   D 1

Altitude: sea level
Population: 2800

Bajamar (meaning down by the sea), at the foot of the Anaga Hills in
north-eastern Tenerife, is one of the oldest tourist settlements on the
island. This is a favourite place for a restful holiday or for a longer stay.

Numbers of hotels, apartment blocks and holiday bungalows extend
along the coast and the gentle slopes above the **resort**. Because of the
heavy surf sea bathing is not to be recommended, but there are sea-
water swimming pools along the promenade, and the hotels have their
own pools. The main street is lined with cafés, restaurants, shops and
banks.

Surroundings

3 km (2 mi.) north-east of Bajamar on the coast road is Punta del   **Punta del Hidalgo**
Hidalgo, an old fishing village that has been transformed by the building

of large hotel complexes but nevertheless, like Bajamar, is still pleasantly quiet. The rocky coast offers good fishing; for bathers and sunbathers there are sea-water swimming pools.

The main street ends in a circular area, near which is a viewpoint
affording fantastic views of the coastal scenery (otherwise difficult of
access) of the Anaga Hills. From here signs point the way to a footpath
leading to the troglodytic village of Chinamada (see Montañas de
Anaga).

★Bosque de la Esperanza   B 9

The Bosque de la Esperanza (**Esperanza Forest**) extends along the
Cumbre Dorsal, the ridge of hills that run north-east from the gigantic
crater of Las Cañadas and descend on the north to the plateau of La
Laguna. It is best reached from La Laguna on the Carretera Dorsal (ridge-
way), which runs south-west from the town to the Caldera de las
Cañadas. The forest begins soon after the little town of La Esperanza, at
an altitude of about 700 m (2300 ft).

Huge Canary pines and eucalyptus trees grow in the Bosque de la
Esperanza. The forest lies in the misty trade-wind zone that makes
possible the dense growth of trees. Moisture condenses on the long
needles of the pines and on the other plants, seeps into the volcanic
rocks and accumulates in underground cavities floored with impermeable rock.

Further west, towards the Caldera de las Cañadas, the Carretera Dorsal
offers a succession of magnificent views – provided always that visibility
is not reduced by the morning mists. The finest **viewpoints** are the

The two observatories on Mount Izaña, against the backdrop of Mount Teide

On fine days there is a magnificent view from the Punta de Teno of the cliff coastline of north-western Tenerife

Mirador Pico de las Flores (1310 m (4300 ft); views of the La Laguna plateau and the Anaga Hills), El Diabillo (1600 m (5250 ft); views on both sides of the ridge) and the Mirador de Ortuño (1804 m (5920 ft); view of La Victoria).

2 km (1.2 mi.) south of La Esperanza a side road goes off on the left to **Las Raíces** Las Raíces (The Roots), where on June 17th 1936 General Franco assembled the officers of the Tenerife garrison to plan his military coup in mainland Spain (July 17th–18th 1936). There is a commemorative stone.

Observatorio de Izaña · Observatorio del Teide

The road along the Cumbre Dorsal continues to climb. At about km 32, on the left, can be seen two white buildings, the Observatorio Meteorólogico de Izaña and the Observatorio Astronómico del Teide, situated on Mount Izaña at an altitude of 2367 m (7766 ft). The clear air in this area offers excellent conditions for the recording of meteorological data and for astronomical observation.

The astronomical observatory, a European Community project, was opened in 1985. Since then it continued to acquire the most modern types of telescope and astrophysical instruments.

Attached to the observatories is a **visitor centre** that supplies information on the work of the observatories, their history, the various telescopes and other instruments and current research projects. Open Fri. 10am–2pm.

Buenavista   B 6

Altitude: 122 m (400 ft)
Population (district): 5500

Buenavista (Buenavista del Norte) lies at the foot of the Teno Hills in
north-western Tenerife, 35 km (22 mi.) from Santa Cruz. It is the chief
place in the district of the same name.

Buenavista is still largely unspoiled by tourism, apart from the first
new apartment blocks in the surrounding area. The mayor of the little
town, however, regularly makes headlines in the island press with
ambitious new building projects. First the old lighthouse on the Punta de
Teno was to be converted into a hotel; then in 1997 there was a proposal
for a leisure park with a museum and an underwater observation cham-
ber. It remains to be seen whether the Ventana del Mar (Window on the
Sea) project will be carried out. If it is, this will mark the end of the
unspoiled beauty of this stretch of coast.

Town There are a number of handsome 17th and 18th c. houses round
the main square, in which is the church of the Virgen de los Remedios
(begun 1513; chapels added in the late 16th c.). The church was almost
completely destroyed by fire in 1966, and its art treasures, including an
ornate retable and a painting of St Francis by the 17th c. artist Alonso
Cano, were lost.

Surroundings

★Mirador de Don
Pompeyo

6 km (4 mi.) from Buenavista on the Punta de Teno road is the Mirador
de Don Pompeyo, a viewpoint with a magnificent prospect of the
impressive rocky coast and Buenavista itself, surrounded by banana
plantations.

★Punta de Teno

4 km (2.5 mi.) further on the road comes to the Punta de Teno. (On
stormy days beware of falling rock). From here – the most westerly point
on Tenerife – the view extends on clear days to the island of La Palma on
the horizon. There is a lighthouse here, the Faro de Teno, but it is many
years since it was occupied by a lighthouse keeper. Nowadays, however,
the area is by no means empty of people. Until the late 1980s it could be
reached only on a rough gravel track and was visited only by a few
tourists and anglers, but now that there is a made road the Punta de
Teno attracts a stream of visitors.

Candelaria   D 2

Altitude: sea level
Population (district): 12,000

20 km (12 mi.) south-west of Santa Cruz, on the Autopista del Sur, is the
little town of Candelaria, the most important pilgrimage centre in the
Canaries. Thousands of Canarians come to Candelaria every year on
February 2nd, and in even larger numbers on August 14th, 15th, to do
honour to the Virgin of Candelaria, patroness of the archipelago.

After passing through the modern housing developments round the
town visitors come to the attractive and still unspoiled old **town centre**,
with narrow little streets of whitewashed houses climbing the slopes of
the hill. The central feature of the old town is the Iglesia de Santa Ana,
Candelaria's baroque parish church (18th c.), whose principal treasure is

Basílica de Nuestra Señora de la Candelaria

a 17th c. crucifix. For Canarians, however, the most important church in the town is the Basílica de Nuestra Señora de la Candelaria, which stands beside the sea on the edge of a large plaza. After visiting the basilica it is worth taking time to look round the idyllic little harbour.

The Basílica de Nuestra Señora de la Candelaria, a modern church completed in 1958, houses the most venerated object in the Canaries, the image of the Virgen de la Candelaria. The legend has it that in pre-Hispanic times, at the end of the 14th c., Guanche shepherds found a figure of the Virgin that had been washed ashore to the south of Candelaria. They tried to throw stones at the image, but found that their arms were paralysed. Impressed by this miracle, they took the statue to their king, the *mencey* of Güimar, and the figure, now credited with miraculous powers, was set up in a cave and became an object of devotion. After the Spanish conquest of Tenerife a Dominican friary was built beside the cave, and this soon became the most important place of pilgrimage on the island.

There is another wondrous legend about the theft of the image. Henchmen of the ruler of Lanzarote stole it and took it to a monastery on their island. But the Virgin was displeased, and each morning turned her face to the wall. When the statue was turned round again the same thing happened on the following morning. Since the chapel was locked every

★Basílica de
Nuestra Señora
de la Candelaria

61

evening, there were clearly supernatural forces at work, and it was finally decided to return the statue to Candelaria. During a storm tide in 1826 the monastery was largely destroyed, and the statue was washed out to sea again. The present statue was carved by Fernando Estévez in 1830. The story of the Virgen de la Candelaria is commemorated by a marble monument near the church. Open Mon.–Fri. 7.30am–1pm, 3–7.30pm (summer 8.30pm), Sat., Sun. pub. hols. 7.30am–8pm.

Guanche statues

On the seaward side of the square in which the basilica stands are nine large statues of the Guanche kings *(menceys)* who reigned on Tenerife before the Spanish conquest. The present bronze figures were set up here in 1993, replacing older sandstone figures. They were the work of the Canarian sculptor José Abad, who based his representations on the descriptions of the kings in poems written in the late 16th c. by Antonio de Viana. They are given different attributes: thus Pelinor is armed with a sling, another Guanche king with a lance.

Surroundings

Las Caletillas
Las Arenitas

3 km (2 mi.) north of Candelaria are two small tourist centres, Las Caletillas and Las Arenitas. They consist mainly of high-rise hotels, and, lying close to the industrial centre of Santa Cruz, are not particularly attractive. There are two bays with beaches of dark sand, and Las Arenitas also has freshwater and sea-water swimming pools.

Costa del Silencio   C 4

The Costa del Silencio extends along the southernmost tip of Tenerife, a few kilometres west of the Reina Sofía Airport and close to the little fishing village of Las Galletas. Although called the Coast of Silence, it is no longer quite as quiet as it once was.

There are no sandy beaches on this stretch of coast, and bathing is possible only in a few rocky coves, some of which are reached on flights of steps running down to the sea.

There are a number of holiday developments along the Costa del Silencio, centred on the holiday village of Ten Bel (Ten for Tenerife, Bel for Belgica). The apartment blocks and holiday bungalows of this complex are scattered about in the hilly countryside amid lush vegetation. Like other holiday centres, Ten Bel is well provided with leisure and sporting facilities. There are numerous sea-water swimming pools to make up for the lack of a beach.

El Médano   C 4

Altitude: sea level
Population: 1500

El Médano is Tenerife's premier resort for surfers. Thanks to the winds that constantly blow here this former fishing village has developed since the 1970s into a popular destination for surfers from far and wide. Numerous international championships have been held here. El Médano lies close to the Reina Sofía Airport, at the foot of the Montaña Roja (Red Hill; 171 m (561 ft)).

Resort First impressions of El Médano are not particularly favourable: multi-storey hotels and apartment blocks, and between them gorge-like streets that have little appeal. But things are very different on the

The beach, El Médano

seafront. The plaza and the short promenade are favourite meeting places; and here you will see not only holidaymakers, as in other resorts on Tenerife, but local people as well. There is a kind of family atmosphere about the place. In spite of the hotels and apartment blocks that have been built in recent years El Médano has not been totally taken over by tourism. This may partly be because of the strong winds that blow here, often carrying drifting sand, and this may put off the sun worshippers.

El Médano owes its name (The Dune) to its beach of pale sand, the longest and finest on the island, extending to the south-west of the resort for almost 2 km (1.2 mi.). Sloping gently down to the sea, it is suitable for children and non-swimmers.

★Playa del Médano

Surroundings

From El Médano the coast road runs west to the fishing village of Los Abrigos, noted for the good fish restaurants dotted along the main street; many of them offer a fine view of the sea.

Los Abrigos

North-west of Los Abrigos is the golfing resort of Golf del Sur, which has a 27-hole golf course, together with a hotel, holiday homes and apartments, many of them in traditional Canarian village style. It is unexpected to find such expanses of green turf in such an arid and barren landscape – watered during the night by thousands of sprinklers. There are also facilities for a variety of other sports – surfing, sailing, tennis, riding – that compensate for the lack of a sandy beach.

Golf del Sur

★El Sauzal   D 2

Altitude: 322 m (1056 ft)
Population: 6500

El Sauzal, on the north-east coast of Tenerife, has been able to preserve its original character unspoiled, but with its interesting wine museum, its beautiful public gardens and a viewpoint offering tremendous views it is now attracting increasing numbers of day trippers.

The central feature of the **town**, whose houses climb in tiers up the hillside, is the main square, with the Iglesia de San Pedro, a church with a Moorish air. A broad flight of steps leads up to the modern town hall, built in traditional Canarian style. In recent years great efforts have been made to beautify El Sauzal, with luxuriant gardens round the town hall and in other streets and squares. In additions to the sights described below, it is worth while, one morning, looking in to the large market hall.

★Casa del Vino
La Baranda

The Casa del Vino (House of Wine) is at the entrance to El Sauzal, coming from the motorway. Here you can learn about the history of winemaking on Tenerife, sample the products of the five wine-growing areas on the island, buy wine, drink it in the bar and enjoy Canarian cuisine in the restaurant. The Casa del Vino occupies a 17th c. country house. Open Tue.–Sat. 11am–8pm (wine tasting and sale until 10pm), Sun. 11am—6pm.

Las Tosquillas
Garden

From the El Sauzal motorway signs direct to the nearby Las Tosquillas Garden. The speciality of this small and lovingly tended garden is its collection of bromeliads, of which it has more than 80 different species. The paths in the garden are shaded by these plants, which belong to the pineapple family, forming a kind of roof over them. They need no earth, but are hung on strings or trellises and acquire the moisture they require from dew. They put on a magnificent display during their flowering season in April. But the garden is well worth visiting at other times of year, when you can see its 50 different species of palm and enjoy the luxuriant greenery from shady seats in the garden. Open daily 9am–5pm.

Mirador La
Garañona

There is a fantastic view of the cliff coastline of north-eastern Tenerife from the Mirador La Garañona, in the lower part of El Sauzal. Round the viewpoint is a small and beautifully planted garden. The café here is a popular resort of local people at weekends, but during the week you will often have the magnificent scenery to yourself.

Parque Los
Lavaderos

From the main square of El Sauzal signs point the way to the Parque Los Lavaderos, only a few hundred metres away. Laid out in terraces, the gardens display typically Canarian flora and offer superb views. Open summer 8am–9pm; winter 8am– 7pm.

Fasnia   D 3

Altitude: 400 m (1300 ft)
Population (district): 2500

The little town of Fasnia, the chief place of its district, lies near the east coast of Tenerife, 40 km (25 mi.) south-west of Santa Cruz, from which it is easily reached on the Autopista del Sur. It was founded in the 17th c. The population live by farming, growing fruit, vegetables and above all wine in terraced fields.

Surroundings

Montaña de
Fasnia

Fasnia's principal landmark is the Montaña de Fasnia (406 m (1332 ft)), just outside the town. On the summit is a white chapel dedicated to Nuestra Señora de los Dolores, built as a thanksgiving for the town's escape from destruction in an eruption of the Volcán de Fasnia (see below). From the little chapel there are wide views of the coast.

Volcán de Fasnia

North-west of Fasnia is the Volcán de Fasnia (2176 m (7139 ft)), which last erupted in 1705 when the flow of lava stopped just short of Fasnia. The ascent of the hill should be attempted only by experienced climbers.

Garachico: a promenade runs along the rugged coastline of dark lava

★Garachico   B 2

Altitude: 10 m (33 ft)
Population (district): 6000

Garachico lies on the coast 25 km (15 mi.) west of Puerto de la Cruz. Its characteristic landmark is the Roque de Garachico, a striking rock that emerges from the sea just offshore. Its numerous historic buildings – in 1994 the Canarian government declared the whole town centre a historic site – and its picturesque situation attracts many visitors.

History Garachico was founded in 1496 by a Genoese, Cristóbal de Ponte. Thanks to its harbour, from which much of Tenerife's wine was exported, it rapidly developed into a prosperous trading town. The Italian architect Leonardo Torriani, who inspected the town's fortifications in 1589, declared: "Although this town has no more than 400 houses, it is the wealthiest on Tenerife and has a larger trade than any other town on the island." The town's prosperity was brought to a sudden end in 1706, when the Volcán de Negro erupted and the harbour and almost the whole of the town were buried under masses of lava. The town was rebuilt on the peninsula formed by the lava flows, but never recovered its earlier importance.

Today Garachico is a friendly and typically Canarian little **town**. Its most important buildings, apart from the Castillo de San Miguel, are grouped round the pleasant shady square in the centre of the town. Many of them have been restored in recent years.

The Castillo de San Miguel was built in 1575 to protect the harbour, and survived the 1706 volcanic eruption unscathed. At one time it was held by

Castillo de San
Miguel

65

Garachico

The Iglesia de Santa Ana in Garachico's attractive square

the Count of Gomera. Above the massive gateway are coats of arms and inscriptions. The castle now houses a small private natural history collection (shells, fossils, minerals and rocks from all over the world). From the castle roof there are beautiful views of the sea. Open daily 10am–6pm.

Puerta de Tierra

From the castle a street runs south to Plaza Juan González de la Torre, in which, surrounded by a small garden, is the Puerta de Tierra, the old harbour gate, excavated from the lava that engulfed it.

Iglesia de Santa Ana

The Iglesia de Santa Ana, originally built in 1509, was so badly damaged in a fire resulting from the volcanic eruption of 1706 that it was completely rebuilt between 1714 and 1721 on the foundations of the earlier church. It contains two figures by Luján Pérez of SS Joachim and Anne.

Bolívar Monument

On the raised Plaza de Arriba in front of the church is a statue (erected in 1970) of Simón Bolívar (1783–1830), leader of the Latin American independence movement.

Convento de San Francisco

The Convento de San Francisco, a Franciscan friary, was founded in 1525, and suffered heavy damage in the 1706 eruption. The conventual buildings, apart from the church, are now occupied by the Casa de Cultura, the venue of various cultural events. It also houses a museum, including displays illustrating the importance of Garachico's harbour in the 16th and 17th c., and a natural history collection. Also of interest are the two beautiful cloisters. Open Mon.–Fri. 9am–7pm, Sat. 9am–6pm, Sun. 9am–2pm.

Palacio de los Condes de la Gomera

On the south side of the plaza is the Palacio de los Condes de la Gomera, built in the late 17th c. It was partly destroyed in the 1706 eruption.

On the eastern edge of the town centre is the former Convento de Santo Domingo, a Dominican friary established in the 17th c. The church now houses the **Museum of Contemporary Art** that displays work by contemporary Spanish architects. Open daily 10am–1pm, 3–6pm.

Museo de Arte Contemporáneo

Surroundings

The finest view of Garachico is to be had from the Mirador de Garachico above the town (restaurant), on road 820 from Icod to Santiago del Teide. From Garachico take the road that snakes its way up past the village of Tanque to join road 820, and then turn left in the direction of Icod.

Mirador de Garachico

There are wide views of the coastal scenery of north-western Tenerife from the Mirador Lomo Molino, where there are extensive facilities for visitors, including a large restaurant. It is reached from the road to Tierra del Trigo, which branches off road 820.

Mirador Lomo Molino

The Puerta de Tierra in the centre of Garachico is the starting point of a 5.5 km (3.4 mi.) trail (steep in places) that runs up to the Arenas Negras recreation area (picnic spots, barbecue sites). It follows Calle del Sol and the Camino de las Piteras to the Ermita de los Reyes, from which a paved bridle track winds its way uphill, with a succession of fine views of Garachico. Finally it comes to the village of San Juan del Reparo, on the road from Icod to Santiago del Teide. Turn right along this for 100 metres and then left into Calle Arguayo (500 metres before the Garachico Restaurant). Continue along the track, the first section of which is asphalted, and in 400 metres follow the paved track, enclosed by stone walls, that leads to the hamlet of Barrio de la Montañeta. The track continues to the Ermita de San Francisco de Asís. Near this little pilgrimage chapel (to the right of road TF 2228) take a narrow path that becomes broader and then runs into the road again. Cross the road and continue on the path, which climbs through dense forest. The last stretch of the trail is on a wide forest track to the Arenas Negras recreation area.

Garachico
Arenas Negras trail

Gomera (La Gomera)

Area: 378 sq. km (146 sq. mi.)
Population: 20,000
Chief place: San Sebastián de la Gomera

The island of La Gomera, 30 km (19 mi.) west of Tenerife, can be reached by ferry in just under 90 minutes; and by hydrofoil (passengers only) it takes only about half an hour to get from Los Cristianos to San Sebastián de la Gomera. It is quite easy, therefore, for holidaymakers on Tenerife to take a trip to Gomera, and many travel agencies on Tenerife offer organised tours by ship and bus – though there is no difficulty about making the trip on your own. From Los Cristianos there are several sailings daily by ferries and hydrofoils (see Practical Information, Ferries). You can then hire a car in San Sebastián and explore the island, returning to Tenerife with the last ferry of the day. But it is a pity to devote only a single day to Gomera. It is better to do as increasing numbers of visitors now do and arrange to spend some time on the island. Its rugged hills, deep gorges and beaches of dark sand will fascinate all nature lovers.

Until recently Gomera's only means of contact with the outside world was the port of San Sebastián. With the opening of its new airport the island is now more easily accessible for holidaymakers.
    The construction of an airport had long been under consideration but

Airport

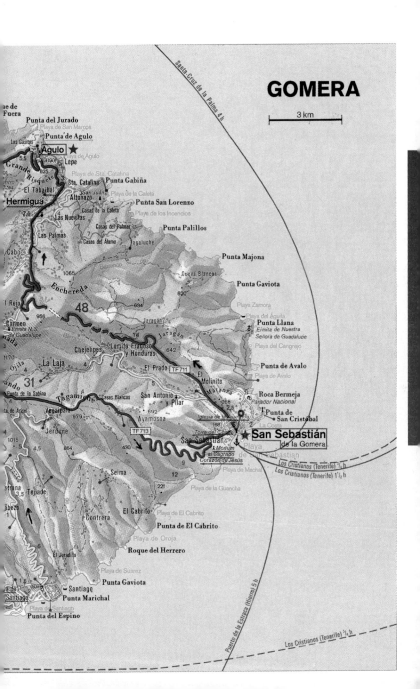

GOMERA

3 km

e de
Fuera
Punta del Jurado
Playa de San Marcos
Punta de Agulo
Las Casitas
★ Agulo
Playa de Agulo
Lepe
Grande
Risquete
Sta. Catalina
Punta Gabiña
Playa de Sta. Catalina
El Tabaibal
San Juan
Altonazo
Playa de la Caleta
Hermigua
Punta San Lorenzo
Casas de la Caleta
Playa de los Incencios
Las Nuevitas
Casas del Palmar
Punta Palillos
Las Palmas
Casas del Alamo
Tagaluche
Cabo
Punta Majona
1065
Carranco
Enchereda
Cueva Blancas
48
620
Punta Gaviota
634
Playa Zamora
I Rejo
956
Jaragán
Playa del Águila
Carmen
Ermita N.S.
de Guadalupe
Jaragán
Punta Llana
Ermita de Nuestra
Señora de Guadalupe
Chejelipes
Lomito Fragoso
y Honduras
642
Playa del Cangrejo
La Laja
El Prado
TF 711
Punta de Avalo
Ojila
El
Molinito
Playa de Avalo
31
Tagamiche
Casas Blancas
San Antonio
y Pilar
Matanza
Punta de la Sabina
Vegaipala
979
692
Roca Bermeja
Parador Nacional
ta de Arsel
Ayamosna
Iglesia de la Asunción
Punta de
San Cristóbal
Jerdune
TF 713
(68)
★ San Sebastián
1015
864
430
San Sebastián
de la Gomera
Seima
Torre del
9
La Costa
Los Cristianos (Tenerife) 1/4 h
Tejiade
12
Playa de San Sebastian
Playa de Machal
Los Cristianos (Tenerife) 1 1/2 h
abezo
221
Monum.
al Sagrado
Corazón de Jesús
Playa de la Guancha
Contrera
El Cabrito
Playa de El Cabrito
Punta de El Cabrito
Playa de Oroja
El Jeradino
Roque del Herrero
Playa de Suarez
Santiago
Punta Gaviota
Santiago
Punta Marichal
Playa de Santiago
Punta del Espino
Puerto de la Estaca (Hierro) 5 h
Los Cristianos (Tenerife) 3/4 h
Santa Cruz de la Palma 4 h

the project was delayed by protests against the impact on the island's unspoiled landscape. Finally in 1991 work began on the first phase of the development, but by 1996 only the runway had been completed. The second and third phases were completed in 1999. The new airport cannot, however, handle international flights because the runway is too short for large aircraft.

Name

The name Gomera may possibly be derived from the Gumara, a Berber tribe that still exists in Morocco. The name is first mentioned on a map dated 1339 by Angelino Dulcert, a Majorcan. There is also a second plausible explanation for the name – that the Majorcans named it after the Spanish word for rubber *(goma)*, because they thought that the mastic shrub *(Pistacia lentiscus)*, the dried resin of which can be used as an adhesive, came from there.

Topography

The island's greatest length from north to south is 23 km (14 mi.) and from east to west 25 km (16 mi.). These figures, however, give a misleading impression of the distances to be covered. Since the interior of the island is broken up by *barrancos* (deep gorges), the road from north to south follows a slow and winding course. Many of the imposing gorges open out in their lower reaches into wide valleys. Scattered about in these valleys and in the hills, which rise to 1487 m (4879 ft) in Mount Garajonay, are numbers of little villages and hamlets. To many visitors approaching Gomera on the ferry from Los Cristianos on Tenerife it seems a bare and rocky wilderness – an impression created by the sheer cliffs, up to 900 m (2950 ft) high, which ring the island, with only a few coves and beaches to provide relief. The realisation that the interior of the island is covered with a lush growth of vegetation comes later.

Although Gomera, the second smallest of the Canaries (after Hierro), is built up from volcanic rocks, like the other western Canaries, it differs from them in showing little in the way of volcanic landscape forms. This indicates that the last volcanic activity on the island occurred a very long time ago, probably as much as a million years ago.

Gomera ranks equal with La Palma in the abundance of its water supply, with numerous springs and perennial watercourses in the interior and on the north and west coasts.

Climate

Like the other western Canaries, Gomera lies under the influence of the moist trade winds. Most of the rain falls in the north and west of the island; the east is drier, and it seldom rains in the south. In the centre of the island the annual rainfall is some 600 mm (24 in.).

Flora

The relatively high rainfall and the island's natural water supplies foster a lush growth of vegetation in the interior. Nowhere else in the Canaries are there so many palm groves as on Gomera. The Canary palm grows wild mainly in the lower regions in the north and west. The interior of the island is covered with dense woodland. Here too are tree heaths and laurels (see p. 000), which sometimes grow to a height of 20 m (65 ft). The lichens that hang from the trees give the area something of the air of a primeval forest. Pines flourish in the highest regions, round Mount Garajonay. But while this lush vegetation grows in northern and central Gomera, low-lying regions in the south and east have only a sparse plant cover. In these areas only drought-loving plants such as the spurges can flourish.

Population

Gomera has suffered an sharp decline in population in recent years. It now has just under 20,000 inhabitants, compared with almost 30,000 in 1940. Evidence of this alarming decline is given by the almost depopulated settlements, particularly in the west and south of the island, and

◀ *Luxuriant vegetation in the interior of Gomera*

the villages in which families without men predominate. The explanation for the decrease in population lies in the poor economic
prospects that have led many people to migrate to the larger Canary
islands or to South America.

Economy

The island's principal source of income is still, as in the past, agriculture.
The fertile volcanic soil and the rainfall in the north of the island provide
favourable conditions for the growing of subtropical and tropical fruits.
While the fruit and vegetables mainly required for local consumption are
grown by dry farming methods, the bananas and tomatoes grown for
export require irrigation. In the arid south, however, the wells required
to provide an adequate water supply can be afforded only by large farming units. Many places, particularly in the north of the island, are almost
wholly dependent on the growing of bananas – though increasing areas
of land are now being turned over to the cultivation of avocados, mangoes and pawpaws for export.

Over the last ten years or so stock farming has increased in importance. There are few cattle because of the lack of grazing, but the numbers of pigs, sheep and goats have almost tripled. Stock farming on
Gomera, however, is still unable to meet the island's demands for meat,
milk and milk products.

The island's fisheries have been declining for years. In the early eighties catches were still sufficient to supply two fish-processing plants, but
now they are not even enough to meet local demand.

Tourism

Since the 1970s tourism has begun to make a contribution to Gomera's
economy. Initially the island, especially the Valle Gran Rey, was the
resort of adherents of the "alternative society", but it was not long
before it was discovered by individual travellers and the large holiday
firms. In the 1980s Playa de Santiago developed into the island's second
holiday centre. Gomera now has around 4500 beds for visitors – a high
proportion of them in private houses and apartment blocks. The island's
government plans to increase this number to 8000 over the next few
years.

History

Exact knowledge of the history of Gomera dates only from the early 15th
c., when the Norman adventurer Jean de Béthencourt, sailing in the
Spanish service, landed on the island (1404). He established a small settlement but was unable to occupy the whole island. A Spaniard,
Fernando Ormel de Castro, came to Gomera in 1438 but – for reasons
that are still not understood – withdrew without achieving anything. In
the mid-15th c., however, Hernán Peraza the Elder succeeded in conquering the island and establishing his authority, and in 1472 Gomera
was officially made subject to the Spanish crown and given the status of
a *señorio* (feudal fief). In 1487 the native population rose against
Spanish rule, murdering Hernán Peraza the Younger; but Spanish authority was soon restored. Thereafter a relationship of peaceful coexis-
tence between Spaniards and natives was established, and the two
races gradually merged. The island remained a *señorio* until 1812.

San Sebastián de la Gomera

The island's chief town and port, San Sebastián de la Gomera (San
Sebastián for short), lies on the east coast at the mouth of the Barranco
de la Villa. The town's modest little white houses fill the sheltered bay
and climb up the steep and barren hillsides above it. The population of
the town, including the adjoining communes, is 6200. It is a quiet little
place, with the atmosphere of a village rather than a town; but when the
ferry comes in from Los Cristianos (Tenerife), it livens up. For most visitors, however, San Sebastián is only a staging post.

San Sebastián has featured only briefly in history, when Columbus put in here on his voyages of discovery to take on provisions and water. Gomera likes to recall this glorious chapter in its past, which earned it the nickname "Isla Colombina".

The hub of the town's life, a few hundred metres from the harbour, is the Plaza de las Américas. The pavement cafés round the square, shaded by palm trees, are designed to cater mainly for tourists. The most eye-catching feature of the square, on its east side, is the modern town hall, in traditional Canarian style, with its clock tower.

Plaza de las Américas

The town's two main streets, Calle Real (still sometimes referred to by its earlier name of Calle del Medio) and Calle Ruiz de Padrón, start from the square. A tour of San Sebastián's principal sights can best start from Calle Real, the first section of which forms the Plaza de la Constitución. Local people like to meet their friends, particularly in the afternoon and evening, under the tall old bay trees.

The first building on the right of Calle Real is the 17th c. Casa de Aduana (Custom House), which also served as a warehouse and a prison. In the patio is a well known as the Pozo de Colón (Columbus's Well), from which Columbus is said to have drawn the water he required to supply his ships. There is a commemorative tablet with the Spanish inscription, "With this water America was baptised".

Pozo de Colón

Some 200 metres along Calle Real, set back from the street, is the Iglesia de la Asunción (Church of the Assumption), to which Columbus is said to have come for a final prayer before setting out into the unknown. The foundation stone of the church was laid in the 15th c.; the nave aisles were added in the 16th c. The church burned down several times, however, and the present building dates mainly from the late 18th c.

Iglesia de la Asunción

Notable features of the interior are the wooden baroque altarpiece, the statue of Nuestra Señora de la Asunción (18th c.), and a figure of Christ on the Cross by Luján Pérez.

The left-hand doorway, the Puerta del Perdón (Doorway of Pardon), has a special interest of its own. This doorway proved to be ill named. After the repression of the rising in which the governor of the island, Hernán Peraza, was killed his widow Beatriz de Bobadilla held a service of reconciliation, promising that all who passed through the Puerta del Perdón and thus confessed their guilt would be pardoned; but the promise was not kept and the rebels were executed. The present doorway is not the original, which was destroyed by fire in 1618.

Another building in Calle Real (No. 56) is associated with Columbus: the 17th c. Casa de Colón (restored 1979). Every year, around September 6th, this is the scene of various cultural events and exhibitions – part of the Fiestas Colombinas in honour of Columbus.

Casa de Colón

Beyond this is the Ermita de San Sebastián, a chapel built in the mid-15th c. in honour of the town's patron saint. It was largely destroyed in pirate raids in 1571 and 1618, and only the side doorway with its pointed arch survives from the original building. The chapel contains an early 18th c. statue of San Sebastián.

Ermita de San Sebastián

Now turn back along Calle Ruiz de Padrón, which runs parallel to Calle Real, and before returning to Plaza de las Américas bear right to reach a park in which stands the Torre del Conde (Tower of the Count). This tower, in Castilian style, was built by Hernán Peraza the Elder in 1447 as part of the town's defences. Soon afterwards it provided a safe refuge for Beatriz de Bobadilla after the murder of her husband. In the 16th and 17th c. the tower, the walls of which were strengthened in 1587, served for the safe keeping of booty brought back from America by the Conquistadors. This, of course, made the tower a target for pirates, but it was never taken.

Torre del Conde

The Torre del Conde, San Sebastián de la Gomera's principal landmark

The tower houses a collection of historic maps of the Canarian archipelago.

Parador Nacional Conde de la Gomera

High above the town stands the Parador Nacional Conde de la Gomera, one of the finest hotels in the the Canary Islands. It is reached by a narrow street that branches off Calle Real just beyond the Iglesia de la Asunción. Although it was built only in 1973 and enlarged in 1985, it has all the atmosphere of an old Canarian country house, and the impression is reinforced by the historical paintings in some of the rooms.

Beaches

Bathing in sight of the harbour does not appeal to everyone, and so the Playa de San Sebastián, a beach of dark sand that is skirted by the promenade, is frequented mainly by local people. A more attractive beach, with fine sand, is the Playa de la Cueva, which is reached from the harbour by way of a tunnel though the steep wall of the gorge. One of the finest beaches on the island, the Playa de Avalo, lies 6 km (3.7 mi.) north of San Sebastián and is reached on the road running past the parador: soon after the parador turn left into the Camino del Lomo del Cavo. The first section of this road is asphalted, but it soon becomes an unsurfaced track running down to the beach. At weekends the beach, partly sand and partly shingle, is usually crowded with local people, but during the week it is relatively unfrequented.

★★Parque Nacional de Garajonay

In 1978 the hilly region in central Gomera, round Mount Garajonay, the island's highest peak (1487 m (4879 ft)), was declared a National Park, covering about a tenth of the island's area, and in 1986 it was recognised as a World Heritage Site by UNESCO. Its special interest lies in the forests of laurels that four million years ago covered the whole Mediterranean area but now are nowhere to be found in such abundance as here. They have been able to survive on Gomera thanks to the temperate oceanic climate, and no doubt also because the steep hillsides in the centre of the island are not suitable for agriculture and have therefore not been cleared by man. There is, however, a constant danger of forest fires. The laurel forests of Gomera have now less than half their original extent.

Flora The hills in the centre of Gomera range between 800 and 1000 m (2625 and 3300 ft) – high enough to draw down moisture from the trade winds. Most of the rain falls in winter, but there are also many days of mist and cloud in summer. The high rainfall enables an evergreen forest with 16 different species of laurel (only two of them suitable for use as a culinary spice), wax myrtles and tree heaths to flourish. Some of the laurels are up to 20 m (65 ft) high, from many of which hang lichens. The trunks of the trees are covered with moss. Other typical plants found in this dense expanse of forest – which is called the Bosque del Cedro, though there are no longer any cedars here – are ivy, ferns, various herbs and mushrooms. Altogether some 450 species of plants have been recorded, including 34 that are endemic to Gomera and eight that are found only in the National Park.

Fauna There are numerous species of birds, notably the blue–grey Canary pigeon and the dark brown laurel pigeon, which are found only found in the laurel forests of the Canaries. Blackbirds, robins, bluetits, chaffinches and Canary finches can frequently be seen and heard.

At the northern entrance to the National Park is the **Centro de Visitantes** (visitor centre; see p. 79) that provides information on the flora, fauna and the ecology of the National Park, and may also organise guided walks through the laurel forest (tel. 922800993). Attached to the visitor centre is a botanic garden that offers a general survey of the varied flora of the Canaries. Open Mon.–Sat. 9.30am–4.30pm.

The National Park has an excellent network of roads, but by far the best plan is to explore the dense forest on foot. The National Park administration has laid out a number of well **waymarked trails**, starting from the parking areas within the park. 2 km (1.2 mi.) from the Laguna Grande rest area on the road to San Sebastián, for example, there is a parking area from which one trail runs down into a beautiful part of the Bosque del Cedro and another runs up Mount Garajonay (1487 m (4879 ft)), the highest point on the island, from which there are magnificent views over the western Canaries. 2 km (1.2 mi.) further, at the Pajarito road junction, is another parking area from which a forest track runs up to the summit of Mount Garajonay (3.5 km (2.2 mi.)).

Sights on Gomera

Other places of interest on the island are described below in the form of a circular tour starting from San Sebastián. Although the distances involved are not great it takes quite a long time to get from place to place on the island's winding roads: at least two days should, therefore, be allowed for the tour. Visitors on a day trip to Gomera from Los Cristianos (Tenerife) should limit themselves to part of the route. A good plan, for example, would be to take the road from San Sebastián via Hermigua to Agulo, return to Hermigua on the same road and then, 7 km (4.4 mi.) beyond this, take a narrow side road that goes off on the right and climbs 4.5 km (3 mi.) to La Zarcita road junction, from which a magnificently engineered scenic road runs past the Roque Agando to return to San Sebastián.

Whistle Language

Devotees of the Marx Brothers' films will remember how Harpo, the dumb one, communicates with his brothers: by gestures, blasts on a hooter, playing on a harp – and whistling. Although in the films this means of communication serves only for the amusement of the viewers, there are people in the world who do actually communicate by whistling. Among them are the Mazatec Indians in the Mexican state of Oaxaca, who whistle to their friends over short distances; but in a few other areas in the world there are people who communicate by whistling over considerable distances. One such place is the island of Gomera.

Pedro the goatherd was overjoyed. That morning his granddaughter had given birth to a stout, healthy girl, making him a proud great-grandfather. Of course his old friend Manolo, who, like him, had herded goats for more than 60 years round the hill of La Fortaleza de Chipude in southern Gomera, must be told the joyful news. Pedro laid two fingers of one hand in V-formation on the tip of his tongue, held up the other hand in a horn shape and began to whistle. The message arrived safely, although the recipient was herding his goats in a village 2 kilometres away, for Pedro soon heard a whistle from the far side of the hill. He sat down on a stone, smiling: Manolo had not only congratulated him on his new great-granddaughter but had promised to celebrate the occasion with a good bottle of wine.

Pedro and Manolo had communicated by means of *el silbo* (the whistle), an elaborate whistling system found only on Gomera. It is sometimes called a whistle language, but it is not a language in the normal sense of the word. It merely imitates the sounds of speech, though with considerable limitations, for whistling has only two variants: high or low notes on the one hand, long or short notes on the other. Linguistic study has established that the whistle "language" consists only of six sound groups – two groups of vowels, light (e, i) and dark (a, o, u), and four groups of consonants, plosives that may be light or dark, voiced or unvoiced. With only six sound groups, therefore, *el silbo* can give only a rough approximation to normal language, and accordingly the vocabulary of the *silbadores* is restricted to the major concerns of everyday life. In spite of this practised *silbadores* are able to carry on conversations of some length. There are, of course, "dialects" of the whistle language, though these are understood all over the island: in northern Gomera, for example, the whistling is slower and more measured than in the south. It is equally difficult, if not more difficult, to understand the whistling, and training of the hearing is therefore one of the most important points in learning *el silbo*. Only those who have learned it from their earliest youth can become expert in its use.

The origins of *el silbo* are not known, though it is believed that the whistle language was used by the earliest inhabitants of Gomera. And of course when the origin of something is not known the most fantastic theories are put forward. Thus the early Spanish chroniclers reported that the whistle language had been developed by the natives after the Spanish conquerors had torn out their tongues as a punishment. And then there is an explanation derived from a heart-rending love story. On either side of the Barranco Juan de Vera lived two clans who were bitter enemies. Both clans grazed their livestock on the fertile land in the valley bottom, taking care to avoid any contact with one another. One day, however, a goatherd named Tamuyo encountered the beautiful Azamota, a member of the enemy clan, also herding her goats, and the two fell

again; but it is said that the herds of Gomera developed their whistle language from the song of the nightingale.

The *silbo* has probably been able to survive on Gomera for so long because of the geographical pattern of the island. The whistling could be heard over the gorges of Gomera, no matter how deep they were, and could carry further than shouting – up to more than 10 km (6 mi.), depending on wind conditions. A message could be passed from one whistler to another, so that information could be transmitted all over the island within a very short time. The whistle language was used during the Spanish Civil War (1936–9), when *silbadores* from Gomera were stationed along important sections of the front to convey information – though the enemy was always able to decode such

El silbo: the whistler inserts two fingers of one hand into his mouth, bringing his lips to a point or stretching them wide according to the pitch required. The other hand is shaped into a horn to add resonance

madly in love. This attracted the displeasure of both clans. Azamota was forbidden to leave her parents' house, and Tahuyo was allowed to herd his goats only in the immediate neighbourhood of his village. Full of longing, he kept gazing over the gorge to the village in which Azamota lived, and when his pain and sorrow became unendurable he began, in his despair, to imitate the song of the Canary nightingale. Then one day his singing was heard and answered from the other side of the gorge. He could bear it no longer, stole out of his village and carried off Azamota from her village. The two of them were never heard of

messages, since there were Gomeran *silbadores* on both sides.

Nowadays the *silbo* is threatened with extinction, replaced by more modern means of communication. In 1982, in order to preserve it, UNESCO added it, on the application of the Spanish government, to the World Heritage List, and this has already produced results. Since 1994 the whistle language has been taught in schools on Gomera, and the development of tourism has also given a fresh lease of life to this traditional means of communication. A display by *silbadores* is now regularly included in organised tours of the island.

Gomera

Mirador de la Carbonera

From San Sebastián de la Gomera the Carretera del Norte runs north-west through a barren landscape; then, beyond the Tunel de la Cumbre, the scene changes and the road continues through luxuriant vegetation.

From the Mirador de la Carbonera, a short distance beyond the tunnel, there is a wide prospect of the lush green interior of the island. The view takes in the Barranco de Monte Forte and, in the distance, the white houses of Hermigua.

★Hermigua

Hermigua (pop. 2100), the third largest place on the island, is surrounded by terraced banana plantations. Its houses extend down the gorge to the Playa de Hermigua. The most notable feature of the little town is the 16th c. Iglesia de Santo Domingo de Guzmán, which originally belonged to a Dominican friary. It contains a fine image of Nuestra Señora de la Encarnación by the 19th c. Spanish sculptor Fernando Estévez. In Plaza de San Pedro is a small private ethnological museum. Also of interest is the craft exhibition of Los Telares that has a number of rooms containing spinning and domestic equipment of earlier times but is mainly devoted to the display and sale of fabrics woven on old looms, plus beautiful local pottery.

★Agulo

3 km (2 mi.) north-east of Hermigua, at the foot of formidable rock walls, lies Agulo, which is worth visiting if only for the sake of the fine view of the old town on its low hill that can be had from the main road, against the majestic backdrop of Mount Teide, almost always cloud capped. A prominent feature of this little town of medieval aspect is the Iglesia de San Marcos, built in 1939. Its four dazzling white towers have something of an Arab air.

Playa de Hermigua. on Gomera any patch of fertile and reasonably level land is brought into cultivation

The pretty little town of Agulo, seen against the majestic backdrop of Mount Teide

Las Rosas

The road now continues on its winding course to the hamlet of Las Rosas, with a restaurant of the same name.

From here a road runs south-east to the visitor centre of the Garajonay National Park (see p. 74).

Vallehermoso

The next stop on the tour is Vallehermoso, with its striking landmark, the Roque Cano (Dog Rock; 646 m (2120 ft)), the vent of a volcano that has been laid bare by erosion. From Vallehermoso a short side trip (4 km (2.5 mi.)) can be made to the Playa de Vallehermoso. The heavy surf sometimes makes bathing hazardous here. There is a promenade constructed within the last few years.

★Los Órganos

A few kilometres north-west, on the bay of La Playita, are Los Órganos (The Organ Pipes). This imposing stretch of cliffs, over 80 m (263 ft) high, made up of large numbers of basalt columns resembling organ pipes regularly arranged on different levels, can be seen only from the sea. There are boat trips to Los Órganos from Valle Gran Rey and Playa de Santiago.

★Valle Gran Rey

The road winds down by way of the village of Arure, which was probably one of the main settlements on the island in pre-Hispanic times, into the Valle Gran Rey (Valley of the Great King), with the village of that name. There is a fine view of this long valley with its terraced fields, its profusion of palms and its scatter of little houses from a Mirador (with restaurant) designed by César Manrique.

It was in the Valle Gran Rey that tourism on Gomera began to develop in the 1970s with an influx of adherents of the "alternative" culture. Increasing numbers of ordinary tourists have since come and the valley has perhaps lost some of its wildness as a result, but it remains incredibly beautiful and still attracts many individual tourists.

At the mouth of the valley are the villages of Calera, La Playa Calera and Vueltas, each with its own distinctive atmosphere. Calera, perched on the hillside amid banana plantations, is one of the most beautiful villages in the Canaries. La Playa Calera, with numerous apartment blocks built since the 1980s, has developed into a tourist centre. From La Playa the main road runs along the coast by way of La Puntilla to Vueltas, whose harbour now shelters yachts as well as fishing boats. Round the harbour are restaurants and bars.

To continue the circuit of the island, return to Arure and take a road on the right to Las Hayas, where there is a choice between two roads running through the Garajonay National Park. The more northerly route, which is somewhat shorter, runs past the Laguna Grande rest area, affording beautiful views. The other road runs by way of El Cercado and Chipude; it is even more winding than the other road, but also has beautiful views. The two roads join just beyond Igualero.

El Cercado

El Cercado has a number of workshops producing native pottery made in the traditional way without the use of a wheel. Beyond Chipude a road goes off on the left to the Garajonay National Park (see p. 74).

Igualero

The road continues, with many sharp bends, to the highest village on Gomera, Igualero (altitude 1300 m (4265 ft)). From the Mirador de Igualero there is a magnificent view of the Fortaleza de Chipude (1241 m (3024 ft)), a flat-topped hill to the west.

Playa de Santiago

Beyond Igualero a road winds its way down through an arid and almost treeless landscape to the new airport, continuing to Playa de Santiago, the sunniest place on the island, a little fishing town that has developed into the island's second tourist centre after Valle Gran Rey. Its principal attraction is the well designed Tecina hotel complex. There are also

The Fortaleza de Chipude, a massive flat-topped hill, dominates south-west Gomera

Roque de Agando

some small apartment blocks, and round the harbour are a number of restaurants.

Pajarito

The main road continues through the National Park to the Pajarito road junction. The parking area here is the starting point of a number of waymarked trails (see p. 182).

Roque de Agando

The road to San Sebastián soon comes to a viewpoint from which there is a magnificent view of the Roque de Agando (1250 m (4100 ft)), a striking crag that is the remains of a volcanic vent. When volcanic activity ceased the vent filled up with lava, and this hard rock has survived the passage of millions of years, while the softer surrounding rock has been worn away by erosion.

Degollada de Peraza

There is another viewpoint at the Degollada de Peraza, a pass named after Hernán Peraza the Younger, who married Beatriz de Bobadilla (see Famous People). He is believed to have been murdered in 1488 in a nearby cave by the father of his lover, a Guanche princess.

Monumento al Sagrado Corazón de Jesús

Shortly before the road reaches San Sebastián the Monumento al Sagrado Corazón de Jesús (Monument to the Sacred Heart of Jesus) can be seen on a hill on the right. This is a 7 m (23 ft) high figure of Christ on a tall plinth, erected in 1958. From here there are good views of San Sebastián and the island of Tenerife.

Granadilla de Abona   C 4

Altitude: 654 m (2146 ft)
Population (district): 18,500

The little town of Granadilla de Abona lies in a fertile region in the south of Tenerife, some 10 km (6 mi.) north of the Reina Sofía Airport. It is an important road junction, situated at the intersection of the main north–south road with a road running from east to west, and one of the island's largest agricultural centres. Vegetables, potatoes, corn and vines are grown in the area.

In the Granadilla district, near the coast, is a wind-energy plant that came into operation in 1990. There are five generators that supply power to 3000 homes.

Although it is the chief place in southern Tenerife Granadilla has little to offer the visitor. It is a modest little town, with its unpretentious houses and shops lining the main road, but it has no buildings of particular interest.

Guía de Isora   B 3

Altitude: 612 m (2008 ft)
Population (district): 13,000

The little town of Guía de Isora in western Tenerife, near the holiday settlement of Los Gigantes, owes its prosperity to its abundant supplies of
water. Situated outside the area of influence of the moist trade winds, it
was previously restricted to a very modest development of agriculture;
but with the help of irrigation from its circular storage tanks it now has
flourishing crops, mainly of tomatoes and bananas.

Iglesia de la
Virgen de la Luz

The most important building in this trim little town is the Iglesia de la
Virgen de la Luz, which stands in the plaza. This Renaissance church
with Mudéjar features was restored in its original style in the 1950s. It
contains a number of works (including the figure of the Virgen de la Luz)
by the Canarian sculptor Luján Pérez.

Güímar   D 3

Altitude: 289 m (948 ft)
Population (district): 15,500

Güímar, 25 km (15 mi.) south-west of Santa Cruz, is the chief place in
the fertile Valle de Güímar. In pre-Hispanic times this was the seat of
a Guanche *mencey* (king), and numerous Guanche burial places and
dwellings have been found in caves in the area. Güímar hit the headlines in the summer of 1990, when the well-known Norwegian zoolo-
gist and ethnologist Thor Heyerdahl discovered pyramids in the Valle
de Güímar that he believed might have been Guanche cult sites. The
pyramids can now be seen in the Parque Etnográfico Pirámides de
Güímar.

Parque
Etnográfico
Pirámides de
Güímar

This neat and busy little **town** is laid out on a spacious scale. Above the
main street is the Iglesia de San Pedro Apóstol, which has a fine statue
of St Peter, the town's patron saint..

One of the newest tourist attractions on Tenerife is
Güímar's Pyramid Park, established on the initiative of
Thor Heyerdahl and the Canarian shipowner Fred Olsen.
The park, in the upper part of Güímar, is signposted from the
town centre. A path runs round the site, which has an area of 6.5
ha (16 acres). The tour starts from the museum, the exhibits in
which are designed to support Thor Heyerdahl's theory of early
transoceanic contacts. In Heyerdahl's view it was not mere
chance that similar advanced cultures developed in the Near
East and South America. There are astonishing parallels not
only in the practice of building pyramids but also in pottery
forms. There must therefore, he thinks, have been contacts between the peoples on either side of the Atlantic
long before Columbus. That it is possible to cross the
Atlantic in simple reed boats has been several times
demonstrated by Heyerdahl himself: in 1970, for
example, he crossed the Atlantic with an international
crew in "Ra II", a 14 m (46 ft) long papyrus boat (of
which there is a full-size reproduction in the Pyramid
Park). In Heyerdahl's view the Tenerife pyramids provide
a link between the pyramids of Egypt and South America.
The theory is developed in a video film shown in the visitor centre.

*Reed boat in
the Pyramid
Park museum*

A pre-Hispanic cult site or just a pile of stones? The pyramids of Tenerife are still a riddle.

Seven pyramids have been brought to light in the park. The island government and many archaeologists see nothing spectacular in these stepped pyramids formed of small stones, believing that they were built up after the Spanish conquest when fields were cleared of stones. Heyerdahl and his supporters, however, do not accept that the pyramids were constructed in this casual way. The pyramids consist of between four and seven steps or platforms, each one smaller than the one below. The stones used in their construction are different from the stones used in field walls: they are angular blocks hewn from lava rock, the corner-stones are carefully dressed, and the steps are very precisely laid. A flight of smaller steps runs up each pyramid, always on the west side, and the roof is made up of smaller stones. It has not been possible to establish when the pyramids were constructed. Park open daily 9.30am–6pm.

Surroundings

The best view of Güímar and its valley is to be had from the Mirador de Don Martín, above the town to the south-west on the road to Fasnia. In the background can be seen Santa Cruz and the Anaga Hills.

Mirador de Don Martín

There are also panoramic views from the summit of the Volcán de Güímar (276 m (906 ft)) to the east of the town, near the Autopista del Sur. The crater of the volcano is 300 m (984 ft) in circumference and 60 m (197 ft) deep.

Volcán de Güímar

4 km (2.5 mi.) east of Güímar is the fishing village of Puerto de Güímar. Although the coast in this area is not particularly inviting, a number of apartment blocks and hotels have been built here. There is an artificially

Puerto de Güímar

built up sandy beach. The harbour is now used by yachts as well as fishing boats.

★Icod de los Vinos   B 2

Altitude: 235 m (771ft)
Population (district): 22,500

Icod de los Vinos lies some 20 km (12 mi.) west of Puerto de la Cruz in a fertile valley above the coast. As its name indicates, the town, founded in 1501, is famous for its wine. Most visitors, however, come to Icod to see the oldest and finest dragon tree in the Canaries.

The old part of the **town**, round the Iglesia de San Marcos, is trim and attractive. The gardens in the square in front of the church and round the dragon tree contribute to its charm.
A shady avenue runs past the church to the newer part of the town, which during business hours is a scene of hectic activity, with people and cars thronging the narrow streets.

★★Drago
Milenario

Formerly the busy main road ran past the Drago Milenario (thousand-year-old dragon tree). There is now a bypass, and the dragon tree stands in beautifully kept gardens, with a visitor centre.
The dragon tree was long believed to be anything between a thousand and three thousand years old, but botanists now estimate its age as a few hundred years, and certainly not more than 500 or 600. Since the dragon tree forms no annual rings its age can be estimated only by the number of forks in the branches; but the branches fork at very irregular intervals, so that any estimate of age can only be very approxi-

Drago Milenario: the "thousand year old dragon tree" of Icod

Iglesia de San Marcos

mate. (See Facts and Figures, Flora and fauna). At any rate the Icod dragon tree is the oldest example of the species in the Canaries. It stands over 16 m (50 ft) high and has a girth of some 6 m (20 ft).

Close to the dragon tree is the Mariposario del Drago, a **butterfly park**. In a hall luxuriant with tropical and subtropical plants multi-coloured butterflies from all over the world flutter about freely. All stages of the butterflies' development can be observed here, and background information is provided by a video show in the basement. Open daily 9.30am–6pm.

Mariposario del Drago

Above the gardens surrounding the dragon tree stands the Iglesia de San Marcos. Built in the 15th–16th c. and thereafter several times enlarged, it has a handsome Renaissance doorway. The ceiling of the church, made from the heartwood of the Canary pine, dates from the late 15th c. Other features of interest are the baroque altarpiece with its beaten silver ornament, the rococo woodcarving in the Capilla de Ánimas, several 17th–19th c. statues and a silver filigree crucifix from Mexico.

Iglesia de San Marcos

From the square in front of the Iglesia de San Marcos a flight of steps and a narrow little street lead up to the tree-planted Plaza de la Constitución. Among the trees is a botanical rarity, an eight-branch washingtonia (a species of palm).

Round the square are houses with typically Canarian balconies. Further up the street is another handsome dragon tree.

Plaza de la Constitución

Surroundings

The road running north from Icod ends in 3 km (2 mi.) at the little fishing port of San Marcos, with a number of restaurants bordering the well kept beach of black sand to tempt the visitor. It is a picturesque scene – if one or two new tower blocks can be ignored – with rugged cliffs fringing the little bay.

San Marcos

2 km (1.2 mi.) east of San Marcos is the Cueva del Rey, a cave that was used by the Guanches for burials. It can be visited only with a local guide.

Cueva del Rey

Near Icod, in the El Amparo district, is the world's longest known volcanic cave. It has not yet been decided whether parts of the Cueva del Viento should be made accessible to the public. The cave was discovered in stages. In 1970 it was assumed that it was only 6.2 km (3.9 mi.)

Cueva del Viento

85

long. Thereafter several more galleries were discovered, and since the mid-1990s the length has been put at 18 km (11 mi.). No plants can exist in the complete darkness, but insects have adapted to their surroundings by mutation, as the result of which some no longer have eyes but possess instead unusually long legs and antennae. Almost 150 different species of insect have been identified in the cave.

★★La Laguna E 1/2

Altitude: 550 m (1805 ft)
Population: 127,000

La Laguna (officially San Cristóbal de la Laguna), the largest and most important town on Tenerife after Santa Cruz, lies in the fertile Aguere plain in the north-east of the island. For centuries La Laguna had the only university in the Canaries and was accordingly the undisputed intellectual centre of the archipelago. The people of Tenerife were not pleased when Gran Canaria got its own university in Las Palms in 1990; but La Laguna's university still, of course, plays an important part in the life of the city, which, as a bishop's see, is also the religious centre of the province of Santa Cruz de Tenerife.

History The town was founded in 1496 by the conqueror of Tenerife, Alonso Fernández de Lugo, who made it his residence and the administrative capital of the whole archipelago. A factor in the choice of the site may have been the small lake (now dried up) from which the town takes its name. La Laguna rapidly developed into the political and intellectual centre of the Canaries, a status that it retained until superseded by Santa Cruz in 1723.

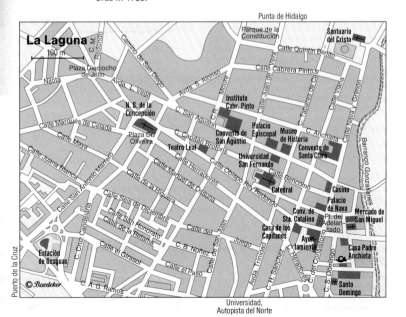

Universidad,
Autopista del Norte

Handsome mansions in Plaza del Adelantado

The first university was founded by Augustinian canons in 1701; the present Provincial University dates from 1817. La Laguna has been an episcopal see since 1818.

La Laguna is often thought of as the most Spanish **town** in the Canaries. It has preserved its original grid plan and numerous handsome burghers' houses and noble mansions, impressive examples of the Spanish colonial style of the 16th and 17th c. These features are found in the historic centre of the town. Since the mid-20th c. La Laguna has experienced a substantial growth in population, and its modern suburbs continue to expand. Nevertheless it has much more of a small-town atmosphere than one would expect in a university city of over 100,000 inhabitants.

You can walk round the main sights of La Laguna in one or two hours – or rather longer if the museums are included. It is easier to find a parking place, and the streets are quieter, during the lunch break, when the town seems to go to sleep, coming to life again in the late afternoon. Earlier in the day, too, the town is a lively and attractive place: this is the time to look into the market hall in Plaza del Adelantado.

A good starting point for a tour of La Laguna is the shady Plaza del Adelantado (where there is an information kiosk). The name of the square (*adelantado*, governor) recalls Alonso Fernández de Lugo (see Famous People), who made La Laguna his capital. In the centre of the square is a fountain of white marble with lions' heads. Round the square, which has been much altered in the course of the centuries, are a number of handsome houses with carved wooden balconies and doorways bearing coats of arms.

The most magnificent secular building in the square (and in the whole

Plaza del
Adelantado

Palacio de Nava

87

La Laguna

of La Laguna) is the Palacio de Nava (No. 1), a typical example of Spanish colonial baroque dating from the late 16th c. It belonged to the Nava y Grimón family, one of the most influential families on the island.

Convento de Santa Catalina

On the south side of the Palacio de Nava is the Convento de Santa Catalina, a plain white building that was given its present aspect around 1700. The striking tower was added in 1717. Here, hidden behind wooden lattice screens, the nuns could catch a glimpse of the busy life in the square without being seen.

Ermita de San Miguel

On the east side of the square, beside the market hall, is the little Ermita de San Miguel, a chapel that dates from the earliest days of the town. It is now used for art exhibitions.

Casa Padre Anchieta

In the south-west corner of the square is the Casa Padre Anchieta, birthplace of the Jesuit José de Anchieta (1534–97), who emigrated to Brazil in 1553 and made his name as a missionary as well as a writer and historian (see p. 90).

Iglesia de Santo Domingo

A little way south of the Casa Padre Anchieta is the Iglesia de Santo Domingo, formerly the church of a Dominican friary. In plateresque style, it was built in the 16th–17th c. It has modern frescos by Mariano de Cossio (1890–1960) that are in stark contrast to its older works of art. Adjoining it is a garden containing a dragon tree that was partly destroyed by lightning but is still impressive.

Ayuntamiento

Now return to Plaza del Adelantado and from there take Calle Obispo Rey Redondo, the town's main shopping street and promenade. The building at the corner of the street is the Ayuntamiento (Town Hall), with a neoclassical façade of 1822. It contains murals illustrating the history of the island.

Casa de los Capitanes

Adjoining the Town Hall is the Casa de los Capitanes, built between 1624 and 1631. In the 18th c. it was the residence of the military governors of the island. The building has a very beautiful and typically Canarian patio. It is now used for art exhibitions.

★Santa Iglesia Catedral

Further along Calle Obispo Rey Redondo is the cathedral. A small chapel built here in the early 16th c. was latter much enlarged and rebuilt, and in 1813 was given a neoclassical façade. By the end of the 19th c. it was in a state of ruin, and in the early 20th c. was completely rebuilt, but retaining the neoclassical façade. One of the towers was added in 1916. Although the exterior is relatively plain there are some major treasures of art in the interior. Among them are the metal screen between the choir and the Capilla Mayor, the tabernacle (by Luján Pérez) and the marble pulpit (1767). In the chapel of the Virgen de los Remedios is a magnificent baroque retable. The altarpieces are by the Flemish painter Hendrik van Balen (1575–1632), Van Dyck's master. Behind the high altar is the simple tomb of Alonso Fernández de Lugo (see Famous People), who initiated the building of the original chapel.

Teatro Leal

Also in Calle Obispo Rey Redondo is the Teatro Leal, built in 1915, whose façade has art-nouveau features. It was closed in 1991 due to dilapidation. Since it proved also to be too small, the city authorities decided both to restore and enlarge the theatre; it is planned to be reopened in 2000.

★Iglesia de Nuestra Señora de la Concepción

At the west end of Calle Obispo Rey Redondo is the Iglesia de Nuestra Señora de la Concepción, the oldest church in the town, built between 1502 and 1543. The tower, which has Mudéjar features, was added about 1700. In subsequent centuries it underwent much alteration. It now ranks as a national cultural monument. The church's timber ceiling, a feature characteristic of the Canaries, dates from the 16th c. Finely carved, too, are the cedarwood pulpit, one of the finest in Spain, and the choir stalls. At the other end of the church is the high altar, of beaten silver. The 15th c. font of glazed tiles was used in the baptism of Guanche chieftains. Other features of interest are Luján Pérez's Mater Dolorosa and the figure of Nuestra Señora de la Concepción by Fernando Estévez.

The return to the starting point of the tour can be by way of Calle San Agustín. A few hundred metres along this street, on the left, is the Instituto Cabrera Pinto, a handsome building with a fine bell tower that once formed part of an Augustinian priory. Between 1742 and 1747 the first university in the Canaries was housed here. It has a particularly beautiful inner courtyard.

Instituto Cabrera Pinto

Beside the Institute is a former Augustinian house (now much dilapidated), the Convento de San Agustín. Its church was burned down in 1963, leaving only the tower, built of dark stone.

Convento de San Agustín

Still further east is the 17th c. Palacio Episcopal (Bishop's Palace), with a fine baroque façade. It was built between 1664 and 1681 as the residence of a noble family; later it became a casino patronised by the upper classes; and finally it was purchased by the Bishop of Tenerife in the 19th c.

Palacio Episcopal

The Tenerife Historical Museum was established in a late 16th c. mansion, the Casa Lercaro, in 1993. The exhibits illustrate the island's history from the Spanish conquest until its recent past. Among the museum's major themes are the conquest of Tenerife, its Christianisation, and its social development and economy. It has a fine map collection, displayed in a separate room, with the earliest maps of the Canary archipelago. Open Tue.–Sat. 10am–5pm, Sun. 10am–2pm.

★Museo de Historia de Tenerife

Santuario del Cristo, La Laguna

La Orotava

Universidad de San Fernando	On the opposite side of the street (No. 23) is the Old University, dating from the 18th c. It now houses archives and a library.
Santuario del Cristo	Calle San Agustín finally runs into Calle Viana, which runs north to the Santuario del Cristo, a pilgrimage church in a Franciscan friary that has the most venerated figure of Christ in the Canaries, carved by a 15th c. Seville sculptor and brought to Tenerife by Alonso Fernández de Lugo in 1520.
Convento de Santa Clara	The return to Plaza del Adelantado is along Calle Nava y Grimón. In this street is the Convento de Santa Clara, occupied by Clarissine nuns.
Casino	A few paces beyond this is the Casino, an elegant building dating from the turn of the 19th c. It contains function rooms and reading rooms.
University	On the south side of the city, near the Autopista del Norte, is the New University, surrounded by gardens. The buildings date from the mid-1950s and accommodates some 20,000 students. In contrast to other university towns, the students frequent not the old town centre but the Barrio Nuevo, an undistinguished quarter to the north-east of the university. Here, along Calle Heraclio Sánchez and its side streets and Avenida Trinidad, there are numerous bars and cafés.
★Museo de la Ciencia y del Cosmos	Below the University, in Via Lactea, is the Museum of Science and the Cosmos, opened in 1993. Visitor's can experience more than 60 scientific experiments, tricks and models. The museum's major attractions include a planetarium, a lie detector, and a "skeleton mirror" in which you can see your own skeleton. Visitors can send messages into outer space by means of parabolic antennae on the roof of the museum. Open Tue.–Sun. 10am–8pm.
Monumento José de Anchieta	Nearby, in the motorway roundabout, is a monument commemorating José de Anchieta, a native of La Laguna who became the first Christian missionary in Brazil (see p. 88).

Surroundings

Viewpoints	There are superb views of La Laguna and the surrounding valley from the Cruz del Carmen and the Mirador Pico del Inglés on the fringes of the Anaga Hills (see Montañas de Anaga), from the Mirador Pico de las Flores, and many other viewpoints along the road from La Laguna to the Caldera de las Cañadas (see Bosque de la Esperanza).

★★La Orotava   C 2

Altitude: 345 m (1132 ft)
Population (district): 36,000

La Orotava, the chief place in the beautiful Orotava valley (see Valle de la Orotava), is one of the most attractive and most typical towns in the Canaries, whose climate allows a highly productive agriculture.

The most important event in La Orotava's year is the Corpus Christi celebrations, when the square in front of the Town Hall is decorated with elaborate designs in polychrome lava ash from the Caldera de las Cañadas. Every year since 1847 new works of art, on varying themes, have been created. Preparations begin four weeks or so before the procession, which takes place a week after the actual date of Corpus Christi.

Through traffic is diverted round the historic centre of the town. Visitors arriving by car should park in the newer parts of the town round

Plaza de la Paz or Plaza San Sebastián and make their way to Plaza de la Constitución on foot.

History La Orotava was founded in the early 16th c., soon after the conquest of the island, and rapidly grew into a thriving little settlement, second only to La Laguna in importance. In 1648 it was granted the status of town by a decree of Philip IV. Some years earlier it had acquired a port, Puerto de la Orotava (now Puerto de la Cruz; see entry), which was part of La Orotava until 1813.

Although the **town** has expanded considerably in recent years, it has preserved much of the old centre with its handsome public buildings. On a stroll through the narrow and sometimes steep streets visitors will come across many noble mansions with handsome façades and finely decorated balconies. La Orotava has been classified by the European Union as an important heritage site.

From the floral Plaza de la Constitución there is a superb view over the roofs of the town to the coast that has earned it the name of the "balcony of La Orotava".

Plaza de la Constitución

On the north-east side of the square are the church and former monastery of San Agustín, founded in 1694. The church contains several fine retables.

Iglesia de San Agustín

Above Plaza de la Constitución, reached by way of a small park, is the Liceo de Taoro. Although it is now a private club, visitors are usually allowed into the public rooms (lounges, bar, gaming rooms, library).

Liceo de Taoro

Further north is the **Convento de Santo Domingo**, a Dominican friary founded in the late 16th c. when an influential local family gave a suitable building to the order. The building at Calle Tomás Zerolo 34 was erected in the 17th and 18th c. It was occupied by Dominicans until 1835.
In 1991 the Museo de Artesanía Iberoamericana was opened in part of the former monastery. It displays arts and crafts from Spain and many countries in Latin America. There is a fine collection of musical instruments, including traditional Canarian instruments such as the *timple,* as well as pottery, textiles, basketwork and woodwork. Open Mon.–Fri. 9am–6pm, Sat. 9am–2pm.

Museo de Artesanía Iberoamericana

Opposite the Convento de Santo Domingo is the Casa Torrehermosa, an 18th c. mansion that now displays and sells typically Canarian crafts.

Casa Torrehermosa

The tour continues along Calle Viera and Calle Cologán, which lead up to one of the most impressive churches on the island, the Iglesia de Nuestra Señora de la Concepción, built between 1768 and 1788 on the foundations of an earlier 16th c. church destroyed in an

★Iglesia de Nuestra Señora de la Concepción

Exhibits in the Museo de Artesanía Iberoamericana

Puerto de la Cruz, Santa Cruz

La Orotava

Puerto de la Cruz

Puerto de la Cruz, Santa Cruz

La Luz

Cañadas del Teide

La Perdoma, Los Realejos

Calle R. Drago
Calle Talinaste
Carretera TF 211
Calle César Manrique
Calle F. M. Perdomo
C. San Felipe
C. O. S.
C. Dr. S.
Pereza González
Rodríguez
Plaza La Paz
Av. de Franchi
C. R. Mora
C. Isla de Cuba
C. Santo Domingo
C. S. J. Bosco
C. Leonor
Pnal. Monteverde
Calle Tomás Zerolo
Urarra
Plaza San Sebastián
Estación de Guaguas
C. Dom. H. González
Monteverde
C. B. Toter
Santo Domingo
Calle Nicandro González Borges
Calvario
Avda. Obispo Benítez
Casa Torrehermosa
Calle Juan Patrón
Avda. E. L. Moreno
C. Gen. Grimaldi
C. Viera
C. Tomás Zerolo
C. Prosates
Avda. Sor Soledad Cobián
C. Colgán
C. Barreda
C. M. Barreda
San Agustín
C. I. García
Plaza de la Constitución
Liceo de Taoro
N. S. de la Concepción
Calle San
Casa Monteverde
C. del Escultor Estévez
San Agustín
A. C. Toter
Palacio Municipal
Barranco de Araujo
Mausoleo
Colegio
Hijuela del Botánico
Jardín Victoria
Aventura Carrera Blanco
Casas de los Balcones
El Pueblo Guanche
C. Hermano Apolinar
Calle León
Casa de Molina
C. San Francisco
Plaza San Francisco
Calle J. C. Cantillo
Hospital de la Santísima Trinidad
Calle San Juan
M
San Juan
Calle Nueva
EL FARROBO
Soriola
Fórmula Bethencourt
Barranco de
Calle Sarazat
C. Dr. Meneses
C. Dr. Domingo González García
M
M
M
Calle Calvo
C. Centella
M
M
Plaza Cruz Verde
Calle Perafitu
Barranco Araujo
C. La Canceta
Calle Reina
C. Estopa
Calle Candelaria
M
M = mill
200 m
© Baedeker
Plaza de la Piedad

The finest view of La Orotava town centre is from Plaza de la Constitución

earthquake in 1705. With its large and massive dome and two small towers it is a masterpiece of baroque architecture, with some rococo features. It was declared a national monument in 1948; but in spite of this it was allowed to fall into increasing dilapidation, until in 1994 it was threatened with collapse. It is at present being restored.

Notable features of the interior are the beautiful choir stalls, the statues of the Mater Dolorosa and St John by Luján Pérez, the baroque retable of the Virgen de la Concepción and above all the alabaster and marble high altar by the Italian sculptor Giuseppe Gagini, preserved from the earlier church. The church treasury contains a number of liturgical utensils made of precious metals that originally belonged to St Paul's Cathedral in London.

Diagonally opposite the church, in Calle Colegio, is the Casa Monteverde, a 17th c. mansion that shows both baroque and Renaissance features. A plaque on the building commemorates Leonor del Castillo, who initiated the practice, followed since 1847, of laying carpets of flowers and sand in front of the Town Hall during the Corpus Christi celebrations.

Casa Monteverde

A few paces above the church is the neoclassical Palacio Municipal (Town Hall), built between 1871 and 1891. It has very little in the way of decoration apart from the pediment that displays the town's coat of arms (in the centre of which is depicted the oldest and largest dragon tree in the Canaries, blown down in a storm in 1868) as well as allegorical figures representing municipal authority, agriculture, history and education.

Palacio Municipal

The square in front of the Town Hall is the focal point of the town's Corpus Christi celebrations (see pp. 90 and 148).

Las Montañas de Anaga

El Pueblo Guanche

In Calle del Escultor Estévez (No. 17) is a small Guanche museum (El Pueblo Guanche – Museo Etnográfico). It occupies the upper floor of a typical Canarian house, on the ground floor of which are a souvenir shop and a restaurant. The museum offers a comprehensive survey of the indigenous population of the Canaries – their origins, culture and way of life. Open Mon.–Sat. 9.30am–7.30pm.

★Casas de los Balcones

From here it is a short distance to the Casas de los Balcones in Calle San Francisco – two houses, joined together, built between 1632 and 1670, with fine decorated balconies of traditional Canarian type. On the ground floor is a shop selling craft products; but even if you have no intention of buying anything it is worth going through to see the beautiful inner courtyard with its luxuriant greenery. Here too visitors can watch the making of traditional hemstitch embroidery, basketwork and the rolling of cigars.

Casa de Molina

Opposite the Casas de los Balcones is the Casa de Molina (also known as the Casa de la Alfombre or Casa del Turista), a plain Renaissance building dating from 1590 that also sells souvenirs and local craft products. From the terrace in the rear part of the building there is a beautiful view of the Orotava valley. Here too you can watch the creation of the patterns from polychrome volcanic sands, like those displayed in front of the Town Hall during the Corpus Christi celebrations.

Hospital de la Santísima Trinidad

100 m above the Casas de los Balcones is the Hospital de la Santísima Trinidad. This former monastery has been occupied by a hospital since 1884. From the terrace (open to the public) there is a magnificent view of the Orotava valley. At the entrance to the hospital is the "revolving cradle" in which foundling children were formerly deposited.

El Farrobo

Further south is the deprived district of El Farrobo. In the steep Calle Dr Domingo González García there are a number of 17th and 18th c. mills. Some are still in operation, but they are now electrically driven.

Iglesia de San Juan

From Plaza de la Piedad Calle San Juan runs down to the 18th c. Iglesia de San Juan, in a pretty little square. It contains two sculptures by Luján Pérez and one by Fernando Estévez, a native of the town. In the square is a bust of President Rómulo Betancourt of Venezuela (1908–81).

Hijuela del Botánico

Further down is the Hijuela del Botánico (Daughter of the Botanic Garden), an offshoot (established in 1923) of the world-famous Botanic Garden in Puerto de la Cruz (see entry).

Jardín Victoria

To the east of the Hijuela del Botánico is the Jardín Victoria, a terraced garden dominated by the mausoleum of Diego Ponte del Castillo erected in 1882, an eclectic monument in Carrara marble. Ponte del Castillo was in fact buried in consecrated ground and the mausoleum is empty. From the garden there is a fine view of the old town of La Orotava.

Surroundings

Casa Tafuriaste Museo de Cerámica

4 km (2.5 mi.) west of the town centre of La Orotava, in the Las Candias district, is the Casa Tafuriaste, a typical Canarian house built about 1600. Next to the owner's workshop is an exhibition of ceramics; a video presentation shows how pottery is made. Open Mon.–Sat. 10am–6pm.

★★Las Montañas de Anaga   E/F 1

The Montañas de Anaga (Anaga Hills) occupy the whole of the north-east tip of Tenerife. On the south side of this rugged range of hills is the La Laguna plateau.

The Anaga range runs in a north-easterly direction, with a series of peaks of around 1000 m (3300 ft), the highest of which is Mount Taborno (1024 m (3360 ft)). The hills fall steeply down on both sides, cut here and there by deep *barrancos* (gorges).

Geologically, the Anaga Hills are one of the oldest parts of the island, as is shown by the topography of the area. In the course of many million years the original lava flows have been eroded away, leaving only the harder rocks (basalt). As a result the hills as we see them today are rugged and bizarre, looking from a distance forbidding and inaccessible. This first impression, however, is modified when, closer up, the slopes are seen to be covered with luxuriant green. Since the Anaga Hills lie within the area of influence of the north-easterly trade winds, and accordingly are frequently shrouded in mist, they are well provided with water. At lower and medium heights there are dense forests of bay trees, which at higher levels give place to heath and scrub.

Only part of the range is well served by roads. A good road runs from La Laguna along the crest of the hills by way of Las Mercedes to the village of Chamorga, from which there are narrow and sometimes very winding roads to the remote little villages in the Anaga Hills. It is not possible, however, to drive round Tenerife's north-eastern tip, and many of the farms are still well off any road accessible to cars. There are a number of bays with beaches that can only be reached from the sea.

These conditions naturally have their effect on the population of the area. Some of the inhabitants have abandoned their modest holdings to seek employment in the towns; others remain, living without the amenities of modern civilisation in their little cottages and existing on the produce of their small terraced fields; most of them also keep goats, which can be seen everywhere grazing on the steep hillsides.

Population

Suggested route through the Anaga Hills

The trip through the Anaga Hills that is described here – travelling at a leisurely pace, including one or more side trips and perhaps a short walk, with a lunch break in Taganana – will take a full day. The scenery of the Anaga Hills is seen at its best only on clear days (which are relatively rare).

Leave La Laguna on the ridge road that runs north-east through the Anaga Hills. Soon after the village of Las Mercedes it comes to an important ecological feature of Tenerife, the Bosque de las Mercedes, a bay-tree forest that reaches up to the higher levels in the range. In addition to four species of bay tree the forest contains briers, bayberries and strawberry trees.

★Bosque de las Mercedes

Shortly after Las Mercedes the road comes to the Mirador Jardina, from which there is a fine view of the La Laguna plain – a beautiful landscape of green hills with the outlying districts of the town of La Laguna in the background. If the trade winds have already enveloped the hills in cloud this is the point offering the best prospects of a view.

Mirador Jardina

The road now winds its way up through the Bosque de las Mercedes to the Cruz del Carmen (920 m (3019 ft)). On clear days there is a magnificent view of Mount Teide from here. At the viewpoint there is a chapel of the early 17th c. with a much venerated figure of Nuestra Señora de las Mercedes. There are also a rest area, a restaurant, and a tourist office offering maps, brochures and advice on walks and climbs in the Anaga Hills.

Cruz del Carmen

1.5 km (0.9 mi.) beyond the Cruz del Carmen a road (1 km (0.6 mi.)) goes off on the right to the Mirador Pico del Inglés (960 m (3150 ft)), from

★★Mirador Pico del Inglés

95

which there are breathtaking views of the whole Anaga range, with the island of Gran Canaria on the horizon.

★★Chinamada

The village of Chinamada, near the north coast of Tenerife, has only been connected by road with the outside world since 1993. The road branches off the main ridge route shortly after the access road to the Mirador Pico del Inglés. A more rewarding way to the village is on foot, along the walk described below (p. 98). Its few small houses are scattered over the rolling countryside, lying at a height of about 600 m (2000 ft). At first glance the houses of Chinamada look little different from those of other villages: it is only on a closer view that they are seen to be cave dwellings hewn from the hillsides. Yet, As fitted out and furnished by their occupants, these sometimes large homes can be surprisingly comfortable.

Mirador del Bailadero

The ridge road now comes to the Mirador del Bailadero (759 m (2490 ft), the last viewpoint on the crest of the Anaga Hills. There are wide views on both sides of the range. To the north, far below, can be seen the village of Taganana. To the south is the little town of San Andrés (see entry), backed by the brilliant blue of the sea. There are two modest bars offering refreshment.

The road then continues for another 10 km (6 mi.) to Chamorga.

Taganana

Rather than continuing to Chamorga, however, it is much more rewarding to take a side road that winds its way down to the village of Taganana, near the north coast of Tenerife. As the road approaches Taganana it offers a succession of fine views of the picturesque little place. Sugar cane was formerly grown here, but Taganana is now famed for its excellent wine. The church has a Flemish triptych dating from the first half of the 16th c. There are bathing beaches (rock and shingle)

Mirador Pico del Inglés: a fascinating panorama of the Anaga Hills

Taganana, perched on the steep slopes of the Anaga Hills, where agriculture is possible only in tiny terraced fields

below Taganana, at Playa de San Roque and Playa de Benijo. There are a number of modest restaurants serving freshly caught fish.

On the coast 3 km (2 mi.) north-east of Taganana is the village of Almáciga, which has a 17th c. chapel dedicated to the Virgen de Begoña, patroness of the Basque country.

Almáciga

Now return to El Bailadero and continue south on a road that runs down, with endless curves and sharp bends, to San Andrés (see entry).

San Andrés

★★Anaga Hills

The Anaga Hills offer perhaps the best walking country on Tenerife. The walks described below run through lonely and unspoiled country. Along the ridge road, on both sides, there are signposts pointing to attractive walks.

Walks

The following routes are waymarked. For fuller information consult the green ICONA walking map (Zone 1), obtainable from tourist information offices (see Practical Information, Information).

This 20 km (12 mi.) circular route is one of the finest walks in the Anaga Hills. Since it involves wide differences in level and much climbing, it should be undertaken only by walkers with stamina and endurance. It takes about 7 hours; by stopping at Chamorga the time is reduced to 4 hours. From Almáciga the route runs parallel to the coast and comes in about an hour to the hamlet of El Draguillo (alt. 170 m (558 ft)) – a marvellous walk through dense forest. From there the return to Almáciga is on the same route as on the way out.

Almáciga–Faro de Anaga–Chamorga –Almáciga

97

Los Cristianos

Parque Forestal de Anaga–Cabezo del Tejo–Parque Forestal de Anaga

This circuit begins at the rest area 2 km (1.2 mi.) west of El Bailadero. After a steep climb to Mount Chinobre (910 m (2986 ft)) the route continues to Mount Anambro (864 m (2835 ft)) and then descends to the Cabezo del Tejo viewpoint (670 m (2198 ft)). The return route is on the Pista Forestal. Time 2 hours.

El Bailadero–Almáciga

This short but sometimes very steep walk starts from the El Bailadero viewpoint and runs down to the village of Almáciga, with superb views of the rugged hills.

Casa Forestal–Taganana

From the Casa Forestal (Forester's House) on the ridge road 4 km (2.5 mi.) west of El Bailadero follow the waymarking to Vueltas de Taganana. After climbing to the Cruz de Taganana the path runs down to Taganana. Until the early 1960s this winding track was the only way to get to Taganana. Time about 1 hour.

Las Carboneras–Chinamada–Punta del Hidalgo

This walk, which passes the troglodytic village of Chinamada (see p. 96), takes 2–3 hours. The best starting point is the village of Las Carboneras (alt. 620 m (2034 ft)). It can, of course, be done in the reverse direction, but this is more strenuous, with some steep climbing.

Los Cristianos

B 4

Altitude: sea level
Population: 5000

Along with Playa de las Américas (see entry), Los Cristianos forms a

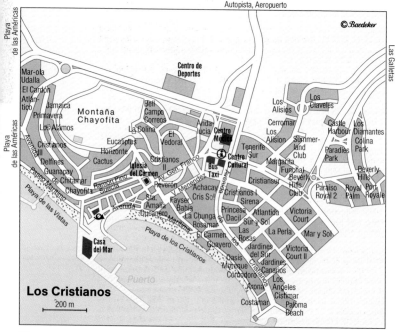

Yachts, fishing boats and ferries share the harbour of Los Cristianos

huge tourist centre on the south coast of Tenerife. The town lies in a
sheltered bay 15 km (9 mi.) west of the Reina Sofia Airport. Thanks to its
beautiful climate, with almost perpetual sunshine, this former little fishing village has developed rapidly into a vast resort.

Los Cristianos offers a wide choice of leisure activities. Almost all the
larger hotels have a swimming pool and tennis courts, and there are
facilities for water-skiing, hiring pedalos or joining organised boat trips.
Particularly popular are dolphin and whale photo-safaris, deep-sea fishing trips and excursions to the neighbouring island of Gomera (see
entry). Car ferries and hydrofoils ply several times a day between Los
Cristianos and San Sebastián de la Gomera, from which fast boats take
visitors to Valle Gran Rey. There are also ferries from Los Cristianos to
Hierro and La Palma (though the distances to be covered puts these
islands out of range of a day trip). Los Cristianos tends to be quiet in the
evenings, but there is always something going on in the neighbouring
resort of Playa de las Américas.

Town Approaching Los Cristianos, the visitor sees at first only huge
apartment blocks and hotels, laid out on wide – sometimes almost too
wide – streets. Since it hardly ever rains here and the surrounding
country is barren and desolate, first impressions may be unfavourable.
This first impression, however, is deceptive. The hotels and holiday
bungalows are set in luxuriant gardens and most of the streets are
lined by palms. Moreover, unlike many resorts in the Canaries, Los
Cristianos has preserved the historic town centre. This contains no
major buildings, but the little pedestrian zone with its shops and restaurants and the plaza near the harbour have an atmosphere all their own.
Sitting in one of the cafés, visitors soon forget the passage of time, for
there is always something to see – the arrival or departure of the
Gomera ferry, the fishermen returning with their catch, the elegant

yachts, and even the dogs that are an essential element in the street scene.

Centro Cultural

At the end of Avenida General Franco is the Centro Cultural, whose theatre is also used for film shows and other events. Here too are a library and the tourist office.

Beaches

Unlike other coastal resorts on Tenerife, Los Cristianos has a large sandy beach: sloping gently down to the sea and sheltered by the harbour pier, it is safe for children.

Another beach, the Playa de las Vistas, has recently been constructed to the west of the harbour, offering an unobstructed view of the sea. Along the beaches runs a spacious paved promenade leading to the adjoining resort of Playa de las Américas.

Surroundings

Chayofa

4 km (2.5 mi.) north of Los Cristianos is Chayofa, one of the most attractive holiday villages on the island, with many comfortable holiday houses built by upmarket European visitors. The houses are surrounded by luxuriant gardens, in striking contrast to the bare surrounding hills. Since Chayofa lies considerably higher than Los Cristianos it is usually cooler and more agreeable here than on the coast. There have been a number of other holiday developments in this area in recent years, notably the Las Águilas del Teide complex, with a hotel and a restaurant.

★Parque
Ecológico Las
Águilas del Teide

Just before Chayofa on the road from Los Cristianos a side road goes off to the Parque Ecológico Las Águilas del Teide (Ecological Park of the Eagles of Teide). The park, established in 1994, covers 7.5 ha (18.5 acres) and contains a varied range of flora and fauna. A particular attraction is the demonstration of birds of prey. Feeding time for the crocodiles and penguins always attracts large audiences. Before the park was opened environmental protection bodies objected strongly to the title of "ecological park", arguing justifiably that many of the plants and animals to be seen here are not native to the Canaries. Visitors who are not concerned about such considerations will find this beautifully laid out park a pleasant and interesting place to spend a few hours. Shows are also put on in the evening under the title "La Isla Mágica". Open daily 10am–7pm; shuttle service from hotels in Los Cristianos and Playa de las Américas.

★Parques
Exóticos

A few kilometres north-east of Los Cristianos, close to the motorway to Santa Cruz, are the Parques Exóticos. There is a shuttle service from hotels in Los Cristianos and Playa de las Américas; visitors travelling by car should leave the Autopista del Sur at exit 28.

Since 1985 extensive gardens have been laid out in this barren upland region, and numerous varieties of cactus and other drought-loving species have been established. Many of the plants, which are arranged according to their country of origin, are rare or unusual in form. Numerous species of animals have been introduced, giving the Parques Exóticos their alternative name of Cactus and Animal Park. Another attraction is Amazonia, a large dome containing an "Amazonian rain forest" in which butterflies and birds fly freely. There are over 100 hummingbirds alone.

On entering the park visitors are given a brochure with full information about the various species of plants and animals. Open daily 10am–6pm.

Tenerife Zoo

Near the Cactus Park is another leisure park, the Tenerife Zoo. The main attractions are the monkeys, and the orang-utan, which is a particular favourite with visitors. The children will also like the llamas, ponies and

Cactuses from all over the world flourish in the Parques Exóticos near Los Cristianos

parrots. Among other attractions are camel rides. Open daily 10am–6pm; free shuttle service.

Jardines del Atlántico

To get to the Atlantic Gardens, leave the Santa Cruz–Los Cristianos motorway at the Valle de San Lorenzo exit and head for Valle de San Lorenzo; then take a road on the right signposted to the Jardines del Atlántico, a banana plantation. Visitors are taken round the park by a guide who describes the various plants; apart from bananas they include avocados, pawpaws and coffee. Before the tour a short video film provides information about the country and the people, and a glass of banana liqueur is served. Open daily 10am–6pm; free bus services from hotels in Los Cristianos and Playa de las Américas.

Los Realejos   C 2

Altitude: 260–420 m (850–1380 ft)
Population (district): 33,000

Los Realejos, 5 km (3 mi.) west of Puerto de la Cruz, consists of an upper town, Realejo Alto, and the lower town, Realejo Viejo. It was here that the last Guanche chiefs submitted to the Spanish conquerors in 1496. The town's main source of income is agriculture, supplemented by tourism; there are two holiday villages, La Romántica I and II, within its territory.

The houses of the **town** extend up the slopes of the hill, surrounded by luxuriant banana plantations. Realejo Alto has a small nucleus of older houses; Realejo Bajo consists mainly of new building. There are three notable churches.

Los Silos

★Iglesia de
Santiago Apóstol

The oldest church on Tenerife is the Iglesia de Santiago (St James, Spain's patron saint) in Realejo Alto. It was built in 1498 on the spot where the conqueror of the island, Alonso Fernández de Lugo, had set up his *realejo* (camp) in 1496. Most of the present church, however, dates from the 17th c. The tower, added in the 18th c., contains a bell presented by Ferdinand of Aragon (1452–1516) and his wife Isabella of Castile. The octagonal coffered ceiling of the Capilla Mayor is a fine example of Mudéjar style.

Iglesia de la N. S.
del Carmen

Higher up in Realejo Alto is the Iglesia de la Nuestra Señora del Carmen. In front of it is a statue of the Canarian writer and historian José de Viera y Clavijo (1731–1812), who was born in Los Realejos. His "Noticias de la Historia de las Islas Canarias" remains a classic history of the archipelago.

Iglesia de la N. S.
de la Concepción

The Iglesia de la Nuestra Señora de la Concepción in Realejo Bajo has a fine 17th c. timber altar and a jasper font.

Surroundings

La Romántica

Near the rocky coast a few kilometres east of Los Realejos are the holiday developments of Romántica I and II. The scenery is certainly romantic, though the effect is spoiled by a number of modern tower blocks. Most of the holiday bungalows and apartments have views of the bizarre rocks along the coast and the ever restless sea. Because of the heavy surf bathing is usually possible only in the swimming pool. The plaster is beginning to peel off some of the buildings in Romántica I; Romántica II is much trimmer.

La Guancha

10 km (6 mi.) west of Los Realejos is the village of La Guancha, formerly famed for its pottery. There is now a craft school that has established a considerable reputation. The village church, which dates from the 17th c., is notable for its fine woodcarving and its baroque altar.

Los Silos   B 2

Altitude: 111 m (364 ft)
Population (district): 5600

Los Silos lies in north-west Tenerife, 6 km (3.7 mi.) west of Garachico and 2 km (1.2 mi.) from the coast. It was originally planned to establish a holiday centre here, but the project never passed the early stages. As a result the sea-water swimming pool near the village is used almost exclusively by local people.

The modest houses of the **village** cluster round an attractive shady plaza and a typical village church. The church contains a 17th c. figure of the Cristo de la Misericordia that is attributed to Juan de Mesa.

★★Masca   A 3

Altitude: 650–800 m (2130–2625 ft)
Population: 150

Masca is an extraordinarily pretty village in the Teno Hills in north-west Tenerife. Until the early 1960s this remote little village could be reached

The Barranco de Masca in the Teno Hills ▶

only on mule tracks, but it is now in contact with civilisation and attracts swarms of visitors. It is linked with Buenavista and Santiago del Teide by a narrow and winding hill road that is in good condition but runs above some alarmingly steep rock faces. If you are travelling by car you should leave it on the main road above the village, which offers little room for parking. There are regular bus services to Masca as well as many organised excursions: there are few travel agencies without a trip to Masca on their programme. By about 4 o'clock in the afternoon most of the coaches have left the village and quietness settles down on the valley, now occupied only by the local people and a few walkers and independent travellers.

The **village** of Masca, set amid high hills, consists of a number of separate parts spread over the surrounding hillsides. All round it, wherever the geography of the valley permits, are terraced fields. The main crops are potatoes and wheat, together with small quantities of fruit and vegetables. With a plentiful water supply, the countryside is green and gay with flowers. The houses are unusual, built on two levels against the slope of the hill, with a flight of wooden steps leading up to the entrance. They usually consist only of a single room. Some of the houses are abandoned, the inhabitants having left for the towns or emigrated to other countries to seek a better living; others have been converted into restaurants (most of them with magnificent panoramic views). Many of the villagers have beehives on the steep hillsides.

Surroundings

★Macizo de Teno

The Teno Hills, like the Anaga Hills (see Montañas de Anaga), are composed of basalt and present a rugged and inaccessible appearance. They rise to around 1000 m (3300 ft), falling steeply down on the north. Unlike the Anaga Hills, however, the Teno Hills – with the exception of the Barranco de Masca – offer little scope for walkers.

★★Barranco de Masca

The Barranco de Masca is one of the most attractive and botanically one of the most interesting areas in the Teno Hills. A walk through the gorge opens up a region of wildly beautiful scenery. On a hot day the climb to the top of the gorge and back again (with a height difference of 600 m (2000 ft) between Masca and Playa de Masca) is a fairly strenuous undertaking but not beyond the scope of a fit and experienced walker. The ascent is particularly difficult in wet weather. It is essential to wear stout footwear and carry plenty of water. The descent of the gorge takes about 3 hours, and the return to Masca takes about the same. To avoid this double effort, the best plan is to join an organised walk, which will usually have arrangements for picking up the walkers by boat at Playa de Masca.

The walk begins at the little church in Masca. The route runs down to the left of the church to reach a lower part of the village situated on a hill ridge. Just beyond the first houses a path on the left runs down into the Barranco de Masca (beware of loose rock and stones) to cross the gorge on a small bridge. Beyond this point you are unlikely to miss the track if you keep on going downhill. The path keeps changing from one side of the gorge to the other and the rock walls of the gorge draw ever closer together, opening up only near the end of the gorge. The walk ends on the Playa de Masca, a beach that is part rock and part sand. It is more difficult to follow the route on the way up, since there are a number of side valleys opening off the gorge. At some critical points there are arrows or piles of stones to mark the way.

Parque Nacional del Teide   B/C 3

The Parque Nacional del Teide (Teide National Park), in the centre of

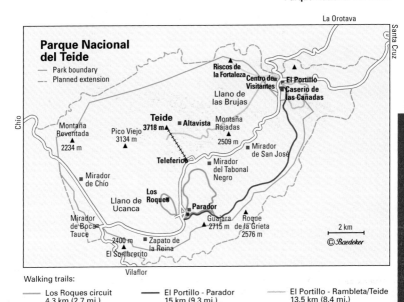

La Orotava

Santa Cruz

Parque Nacional del Teide

— Park boundary
-- Planned extension

Chio

Riscos de la Fortaleza
Centro de Visitantes
El Portillo
Caserío de las Cañadas

Llano de las Brujas

Teide 3718 m ▲
Altavista ■
Montaña Rajadas

Montaña Reventada
2234 m ▲

Pico Viejo
3134 m ▲

2509 m ▲
Mirador de San José ■

Teleferico ▲

Mirador del Tabonal Negro ■

Mirador de Chío ■

Los Roques

Llano de Ucanca

Parador ▲

Mirador de Boca Tauce

Guajara
2715 m ▲
Roque de la Grieta
2576 m ▲

2400 m ▲
Zapato de la Reina ■
El Sombrerito ▲

Vilaflor

2 km

© *Baedeker*

Walking trails:

Los Roques circuit 4.3 km (2.7 mi.)	El Portillo - Parador 15 km (9.3 mi.)	El Portillo - Rambleta/Teide 13.5 km (8.4 mi.)
Parador circuit 11 km (6.8 mi.)	El Portillo circuit 7 km (4.3 mi.)	El Portillo - La Fortaleza 5.3 km (3.3 mi.)

Tenerife, is a immense lunar landscape that is a must for every visitor. The park is bounded on the north by Mount Teide and on the south, east and west by the steep rock walls of the Caldera de las Cañadas. The Parque Nacional del Teide, the third of Spain's National Parks, was established in 1954. The whole area of the park lies above 2000 m (6560 ft). It is planned to be expanded to 18,500 hectares (45,700 acres), and will then be the fourth largest park in Spain.

Climate

Climatic conditions in the National Park are very different from those prevailing in the rest of the island. The strong sunlight produces unusually high daytime temperatures (in summer up to 40°C (104°F)), that fall sharply at night. The relative humidity of the air is low (under 50 per cent, in summer sometimes below 25 per cent). Annual precipitation is about 400 mm (16 in.), mostly in the form of snow during the winter months.

Flora

Considering the altitude and the unfavourable soil conditions in the National Park, its flora is remarkably rich. Some 45 species grow here, including some that are found only in this area.
    The commonest shrubs on the great expanses of pumice and volcanic soils are the Teide broom, with white and pink flowers, and the yellow-flowered goat's clover. With a little luck you may find (perhaps near the Parador Nacional) one of the most striking plants in the Canaries, *taginaste rojo*, with flowering stalks up to 2 m (nearly 7 ft) high. Among other species common here are *hierba pajonera* (yellow flowers), the Teide daisy (white flowers) and the stock-like *alhelí de las Cañadas* (crimson flowers). It is only very rarely and in the highest regions of the Montaña Blanca and Mount Teide that the Teide violet, discovered by Alexander von Humboldt, can still be found; it flowers in late spring.

The Caldera de las Cañadas – an arid landscape

Fauna

The fauna shows less variety. Apart from small numbers of cats and rabbits that have gone wild and the Canary lizard there are only various species of birds (ravens, partridges, rock doves, Canary chaffinches). Insects are well represented, with some 400 species, predominantly endemic.

Environment

With some 3.25 million visitors annually, the Parque Nacional del Teide is the most visited National Park in Spain. Visitor numbers have increased dramatically over the last decade: in 1989 the total was only 1.5 million. Around 80 per cent of all visitors to Tenerife make an excursion to the National Park. The sensitive ecosystem round Mount Teide cannot cope with an influx on this scale, and the question of restricting the number of visitors has been under consideration for some years. One possibility that has been discussed is the introduction of an admission charge.

Visitors should always keep to the marked paths; and they should bear in mind that the stones and rocks, as well as the plants and animals, are all protected.

★★Caldera de las Cañadas

The Caldera de las Cañadas is a gigantic volcanic crater with a diameter of some 16 km (10 mi.). It is bounded on the north by Mount Teide and on the east, south and west by high rock walls rising 500 m (1650 ft) above the plain. Within the crater are great expanses of *malpaises* (scoria), and further expanses of such lava fragments cover smaller volcanoes and overlie earlier lava flows. The rock displays a wide range of colouring, from almost black to shades of red. The varied hues result from the oxidisation of manganese in the rock; the most recent beds of lava with a manganese content are black. There are also extensive areas of obsidian, a brilliantly black rock, and areas in which light-coloured pumice predominates.

A caldera is a volcanic crater of unusual width that has been enlarged by collapse and erosion. It is supposed that where Mount Teide now stands there was once a much larger volcanic peak, of which there remain only the high rock walls surrounding the Caldera de la Cañadas. The present huge caldera came into existence when the centre of this earlier volcano collapsed after the ejection of a molten lava flow or as the result of an earthquake. The time when this occurred cannot be accurately established, but it is probable that the caldera was formed in the late Tertiary period, perhaps 3 million years ago. The pressure exerted by the collapsed masses of rock forced the remaining magma upwards, creating fresh cones of lava on the bottom of the caldera. This is thought to have been the origin of Mount Teide and probably also of the earlier Pico Viejo.

There are good roads leading to the Caldera de las Cañadas from north, south, east and west. The northern approach road runs past the entrance to the caldera at **El Portillo**, a group of houses with a first aid station.

Near here is the National Park's **Centro de Visitantes** (Visitor Centre). The exhibition rooms are entered through a reproduction of a lava tunnel. With the help of computers, video presentations, graphics and a variety of other exhibits the exhibition illustrates the origins of the caldera and Mount Teide and the geology, flora and fauna of the National Park. Guide books can be bought at the sales counter on the ground floor. Open daily 10am–4pm.

Attached to the Visitor Centre is an interesting **botanic garden** that introduces visitors to the flora of the National Park and will help them to identify the plants they see in the park.

View of Mount Teide from the Llano de Ucanca. Only plants that can stand extreme variations in temperature – mainly various species of spring-flowering broom – can survive in this stony waste

The Visitor Centre can provide information about **walks** in the National Park. The main trails are shown on the map p. 105.

Montaña Blanca

Visitors who prefer to explore the Caldera de las Cañadas by car come, 8km (5 mi.) beyond El Portillo, to the Montaña Blanca (2750 m (9023 ft)), on the right of the road. The White Mountain takes its name from its mantle of light-coloured lapilli rocks (a mixture of phonolites and pumice). This is the starting point of the shortest route up Mount Teide (see p. 109). During a walk through this area you will encounter the so-called *huevos del Teide* (eggs of Mount Teide) – rounded fragments of rock that lie scattered about on the ground. They are believed to have been ejected from the crater in the form of molten lava, which then hardened on exposure to the air.

Soon after this the access road to the cableway up Mount Teide (signposted) is passed.

Parador de Cañadas del Teide

The Parador de Cañadas del Teide offers attractive accommodation in the National Park. There are also a **Centro de Visitantes** (visitor centre; open daily 9.15am–4pm), a cafeteria, and a stall selling souvenirs, books and maps.

★Los Roques

Opposite the access road to the Parador is a road going off to Los Roques de García, or Los Roques for short, perhaps the most impressive rock formation in the Caldera de las Cañadas. These rocks, like the rock walls round the caldera, are probably a remnant of the original giant volcano, left after its collapse. The most impressive formation is the 30 m (100 ft) high Roque Chinchado (Tree of Stone). It is possible to clamber some way up the rock, but it is at least as rewarding to follow the path that has been laid out round the rock, on which you will encounter various species of plant that are endemic to Mount Teide.

★Llano de Ucanca

From Los Roques there is a view to the west of the Llano de Ucanca, a wide plain. A small lake is usually formed here by snow melt at the end of winter.

Los Azulejos

The rocks known as Los Azulejos, a few hundred metres south-west of Los Roques, have long been famed for their greenish colouring, caused by iron hydrates in the rock.

Zapato de la Reina

Because of its shape – it resembles a ladies' high-heeled shoe – this rock rising up out of the Llano de Ucanca to the south of the road to Boca de Tauce is known as the Zapato de la Reina (Queen's Shoe).

★★Mount Teide (Pico del Teide)

Almost everywhere on Tenerife the Pico de Teide (3718 m (12,199 ft)), Spain's highest mountain, dominates the horizon, provided always that it is not shrouded in cloud; and for passengers flying to or from Tenerife or sailing between the islands it long remains a landmark. It is of particularly majestic effect in winter when it is capped with snow. The name Teide comes from the Guanche word *echeide*, hell. The Guanches believed that Mount Teide was the seat of the god Guayote, who punished the misdeeds of men with volcanic eruptions.

Mount Teide rears 1500 m (4900 ft) above the Caldera de las Cañadas. In spite of appearances it is not a single regular cone: in fact the real summit, El Pilón, is some 150 m (490 ft) higher than the Rambleta, a crater with a diameter of 850 m (2800 ft).

The north side of Mount Teide falls steeply down towards the coast. On the south-western and eastern slopes are two outlying spurs, marking subsidiary craters – to the south-west the Pico Viejo (3135 m (10,286 ft)), o the east the Montaña Blanca.

The last **volcanic activity** in this area occurred in 1798, when for three months lava poured out of vents on the Pico Viejo. The vents are known as Las Narices del Teide (The Nostrils of Teide). Teide is now in a solfatara stage, with only residual volcanic activity. Sulphurous vapours at a temperature of 86°C (189°F) are emitted from the crater and the slopes of El Pilón.

One of the first ascents of Mount Teide was by Alexander von Humboldt in June 1799. In those days the ascent involved a strenuous climb from the Orotava valley; nowadays it is possible to enjoy the spectacular view from the summit without undue exertion. There are four good roads leading to the **cableway station** at the foot of Mount Teide (alt. 2356 m (7732 ft)), providing rapid access from all parts of the island. When wind conditions permit (and in winter they frequently do not) the cableway runs daily 9am–5pm (last ascent 4pm); there are usually long queues.

It takes some 15 min. to reach the Rambleta (3555 m (11,664 ft)). To protect the environment visitors are not permitted to stay there for more than an hour. If you want to make the ascent to the summit of El Pilón (30 min. climb) you must obtain a permit (free of charge on production of your passport) from the National Park offices in Santa Cruz (Calle Emilio Calzadilla 5, 4th floor, tel. 922290129; open Mon.–Fri. 9am–2pm).

If you have not obtained a permit you have the alternative possibilities of making for the Mirador Fortaleza on the northern edge of the Rambleta (500 m from the cableway station) or the Mirador Pico Viejo on the south-western edge of the Rambleta (1 km), from both of which there are magnificent views.

It is also possible even for those without mountaineering experience to ascend Mount Teide on foot from El Portillo (distance 13.5 km (8.4 mi.); see map p. 105). A shorter route starts near the Montaña Blanca (at km 40 on the road 8 km (5 mi.) south-west of El Portillo). From here the climb (with a height difference of 1400 m (4600 ft) to overcome) takes 4 hours, with another 2 hours for the descent; but it is worth taking two days, spending a night in the Altavista hut (alt. 3260 m (10,696 ft)) for the sake of seeing the magnificent sunset and sunrise from the summit. The hut has accommodation for 50 people; advance reservation essential (tel. 922239811). The climb should be undertaken only in good weather. In the event of high winds, mist or snow the last section of the climb in particular is hazardous. Proper protection against the sun is essential at any time of year, and warm waterproof clothing is required, particularly in winter. Sufficient food and drink must of course be taken.

Climbing Mount Teide

Playa de las Américas   B 4

Altitude: sea level

Playa de las Américas, a tourist resort on the south coast of Tenerife created in 1966, combines with Los Cristianos (see entry) to form the largest holiday complex in the south of the island. Today it is difficult to say where the one place ends and the other begins. But expansion is still continuing, and the hotel bed capacity, at present around 50,000, is due to increase still further.

Playa de las Américas is second only to Puerto de la Cruz in the range of entertainment and leisure facilities it offers. There are sporting facilities of all kinds, and in the evenings a vast number of restaurants, bars, discotheques and cafés with live music offer entertainment for (almost) all tastes until the early hours. Particularly popular, too, are the floor shows in the Pirámide de Arona and the folk events in the Pueblo Canario.

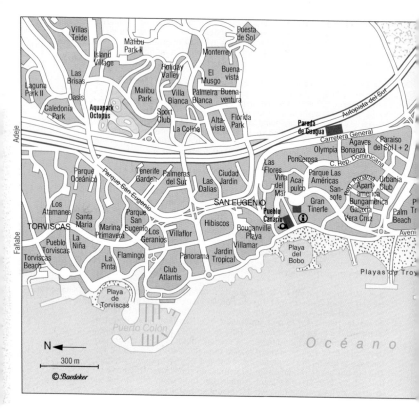

The **resort** of Playa de las Américas was developed on a virgin site, and
it has no historic buildings. The townscape is dominated by comfortable
hotels, magnificent apartment complexes, wide palm-fringed streets
and countless restaurants, cafés and shops. In the centre is the Pueblo
Canario, a complex of buildings in Canarian style that serves as the cultural centre of the town. The promenade, completed in the 1980s,
extends south to Los Cristianos. At its north end is the Puerto Colón
marina, with a modern statue of Columbus (in Spanish Cristóbal Colón).
The promenade continues to the Playa de Fañabé.

Many **beaches** have been artificially laid out at Playa de las Américas, but
this is barely sufficient, particularly during the main holiday season, for
the thousands of holidaymakers who come here. Long stone breakwaters prevent the sea from washing away the beautiful golden (or sometimes dark) sand.

Pirámide de
Arona

One of the most striking buildings in Playa de las Américas is the
Pirámide de Arona in the Mare Nostrum resort, which also includes five
five-star hotels with a total of 1000 rooms. This congress and entertainment centre was opened in 1996. It has a total of 28 rooms for meetings
and conferences, the largest of which can seat 2100 people. There are

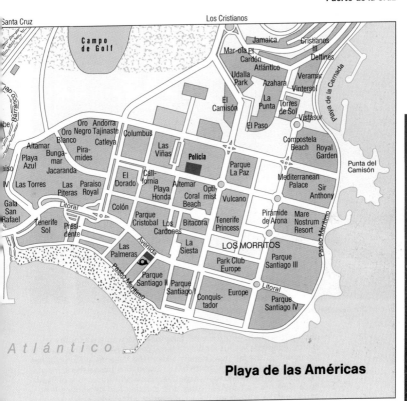

Playa de las Américas

floor shows every evening in the Pirámide de Arona. The complex also includes a gaming casino and a number of restaurants.

The Aguapark Octopus, in the northern part of the resort (exit 29 from the Autopista del Sur), offers a wide range of facilities for bathers. The principal attractions are the huge water slides and the two wild-water runs. There are free bus services from various hotels in Playa de la Américas and Los Cristianos, and there are also excursions to the Aguapark from northern Tenerife. Open daily 10am–6pm.

Aguapark
Octopus

There are a number of other leisure parks within reach of Playa de las Américas (see Los Cristianos).

Leisure parks

★★Puerto de la Cruz

C 2

Altitude: sea level
Population: 28,000

Visitors to Tenerife are faced with a choice: is their holiday to be in the

One of the beaches at Playa de las Américas

north or the south of the island? Most of those who elect for the north choose Puerto de la Cruz for their holiday centre. Although this resort at the mouth of the famous Orotava valley (see Valle de la Orotava) has more rain than the sunny south of the island, this makes the surrounding country greener and more beautiful. Among the attractions of Puerto de la Cruz are its beautiful parks and gardens and its various leisure parks, and there are many places of interest within easy reach.

Puerto de la Cruz was only a small fishing village until the mid-20th c., when it began to develop rapidly into an internationally known bathing resort. Puerto – as local people call it – now has a total of some 30,000 beds for visitors, making it Tenerife's second largest tourist centre (after Playa de las Américas, Los Cristianos). Unlike these southern resorts, however, Puerto de la Cruz has not been wholly taken over by tourism, and visitors can still see something of local Canarian life here.

History Puerto de la Cruz was founded at the beginning of the 17th c. as the port for La Orotava (see entry) and was originally known as Puerto de la Orotava. Most of the wine produced on Tenerife was shipped from here. As wine production fell so the importance of the little port diminished, and from 1813 it became known as Puerto de la Cruz. Because of the heavy swell in this coastal region the loading and unloading of ships always presented problems, and in the 19th c. imports and exports were increasingly shipped through Santa Cruz harbour.

The development into a modern tourist metropolis began at the end of the 19th c., when upmarket Britons began to discover its attractions and the first guest houses and hotels, of modest size, were built. The real tourist boom began only in the mid-20th c. (as late as 1951 there were still only 130 beds for visitors in Puerto de la Cruz).

Town Unlike other holiday towns in the Canaries, Puerto de la Cruz has contrived to preserve its own distinctive atmosphere. Here visitors will find attractive houses in traditional Canarian style, shady squares that, at least at weekends, are not frequented solely by tourists, and a seafront promenade of some architectural distinction. These factors, together with the agreeable climate and the luxuriant vegetation it fosters, make it easy to forget that Puerto de la Cruz lies on a rocky and inhospitable coast.

As there are only a few beaches of volcanic sand in or near Puerto de la Cruz, and the bathing there is dangerous because of the heavy breakers, there has been a great effort to lay out attractive new **beaches**. To the west of the town is the Playa Jardín, designed by César Manrique (see Famous People), a wide beach shaded by palms and gay with flowers, with a breakwater below sea level to reduce the strength of the waves. On the eastern edge of the town the Playa Martiánez has been improved, with new breakwaters and fresh supplies of sand. At the Lido San Telmo there are large sea-water swimming pools. For those who like to avoid the crowds there is the unspoiled Playa Bollullo, to the east of Puerto de la Cruz.

Centre of Puerto de la Cruz

The tour described in this section takes about 2 hours. The starting point is the promenade at the east end of the town, at the recently improved Playa Martiánez.

Car parking is difficult in Puerto de la Cruz, and you need a good deal of luck to find a parking place in the town centre (mostly with parking meters). There are usually sufficient places in the multi-storey car park at the Centro Comercial Martiánez, and there is also a car park by the Ayuntamiento in Plaza Europa. At present it is also possible to park free of charge on the site of the future Parque Marítimo.

The main attractions for holidaymakers are undoubtedly the bathing lido and the promenade on the Avenida de Colón, designed by the Lanzarote architect César Manrique and completed in 1977. Within the complex of the Lido San Telmo, or **Costa Martiánez** as this stretch of coast is also known, are a large artificial lake with islands of lava rock and several smaller swimming pools. At regular intervals one of the lava islands, to the great delight of the children, suddenly transforms itself into a huge fountain. A southern air is given to the complex by palms, exotic flowers and beautiful green lawns.

★★Lido San Telmo

For those who are not inclined to bathe, the promenade along the Avenida de Colón offers plenty of shady spots from which to watch the busy activity round the sales kiosks and stalls.

The chapel of San Telmo is at home on the seafront promenade. Built in 1626 by seamen and fishermen for their patron saint San Telmo (St Elmo), it was destroyed by fire in 1778 and rebuilt in 1780. A thorough restoration was carried out in 1968 and again in 1996. The much revered figure of San Pedro González Telmo was destroyed in the 1778 fire; the present statue dates from 1783. The coats of arms behind the altar show the emblems of the Dominicans and of seafarers.

San Telmo

The Plaza de los Reyes Católicos, adjoining the chapel of San Telmo, is named after the Catholic Monarchs, Ferdinand of Aragon (1452–1516) and his wife Isabella of Castile, during whose reign Tenerife was conquered by Spain. In the centre of the square is a bust of Francisco de Miranda (1750–1816), who fought for the independence of Venezuela from Spain. His parents came from Puerto de la Cruz (see Casa de Miranda, below).

Plaza de los Reyes Católicos

113

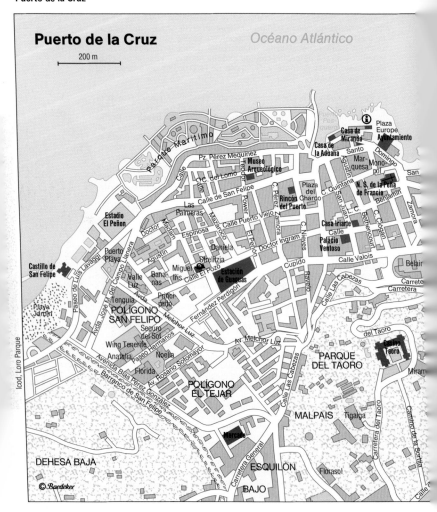

Puerto de la Cruz

200 m

Océano Atlántico

La Punta del Viento

The seafront promenade leads to the little square known as the Punta del Viento, from which there are fine views of the Lido San Telmo and the dark rocky coastline, often lashed by heavy surf.

Iglesia de Nuestra Señora de la Peña de Francia

Continuing along Calle Quintana (pedestrian zone), we come to the Plaza de la Iglesia, in which, surrounded by palms and flower beds, is the Iglesia de Nuestra Señora de la Peña de Francia, the town's most important church, built between 1681 and 1697; the tower was added at the end of the 19th c. It has a baroque retable by Luis de la Cruz, and among its other treasures are a number of statues – the Cristo del Gran Poder, by an unknown 18th c. sculptor, the 17th c. Virgen del Rosario

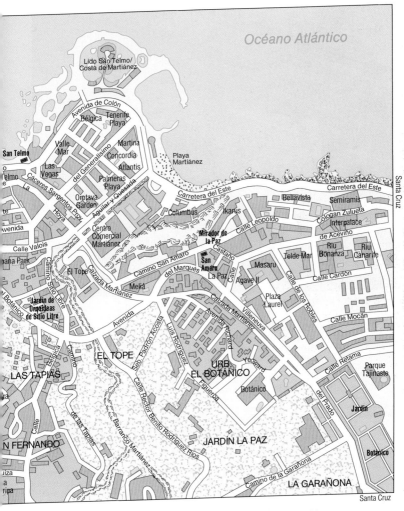

Océano Atlántico

Lido San Telmo/
Costa de Martiánez

Avenida de Colón

Bélgica

Tenerife
Playa

Valle
Mar

Martina

San Telmo

Concordia

del Generalísimo

Playa
Martiánez

Atlantis

Las
Vegas

Palmeras
Playa

Cáceres Sargentos Prov.

Aguilar y Quesada

Orptava
Garden

Columbus

Ikarus

Carretera del Este

Carretera del Este

Santa Cruz

Bellavista

Semiramis

Cólogan Zulueta

Calle Valois

Hoya

La

Centro
Comercial
Martiánez

Mirador de
la Paz

Calle Leopoldo

Interpalace
de Aceviño

ana Park

Camino Sitio Libre

El Tope

Calzada Martiánez

Camino San Amaro

Castaño

San
Amaro

del Marqués

La Paz

Meliá

Riu
Bonanza

Riu
Canarife

Telde Mar

Masaru

Agave II

Calle Cardón

Calle de los Robles

Jardín de
Orquídeas
de Sitio Litre

Calzada Martiánez

Villeneuva

Plaza
Laurel

Avenida Richard

Calle Mocán

Avenida

Botánico

EL TOPE

Seb. Padrón Acosta

Luis Rodríguez

Texward

URB.
EL BOTÁNICO

Figueroa

Calle Retama

Parque
Tajinaste

LAS TAPIAS

Calle Doctor Benito Rodríguez Ríos

Barranco Martiánez

Botánico

Jardín

N FERNANDO

JARDÍN LA PAZ

Botánico

Camino de la Garañona

LA GARAÑONA

Santa Cruz

and the Virgen de los Dolores and Santo Domingo, both by Luján
Pérez.

Further along Calle Quintana is the Iglesia de San Francisco, built
between 1599 and 1608, making it one of the oldest buildings in the
town. The beautifully planted little square in front of the church was laid
out in 1904. It is named after a local doctor, Víctor Pérez, who was com-
mitted not only to the care of his patients but also to the development of
tourism, which was just beginning in his day.

*Iglesia de San
Francisco*

From here it is a short walk along Calle San Juan to the mansion of the

Casa Iriarte

Puerto de la Cruz

The chapel of San Telmo on the promenade

noble Iriarte family, in which the writer Tomás de Iriarte (see Famous People) was born in 1750. With its beautifully carved balconies, it is a fine example of traditional Canarian architecture. It now houses a showroom selling embroidery and souvenirs. Visitors can also get some idea of the history of Puerto de la Cruz from the pictures on display here; and there is a small shipping museum. Every visitor should at least glance into the beautiful inner courtyard. Open Mon.–Sat. 10am–7pm.

Palacio Ventoso Casa Hermanos

Opposite the Casa Iriarte are two fine 18th c. buildings, the Palacio Ventoso and the Casa Hermanos. A little way south is the **Torre Ventoso**, with its four balconies, once originally part of the palace. Many wealthy merchants had tower houses of this kind from which they could watch ships entering and leaving the harbour.

Plaza del Charco

Now return along Calle San Juan to Calle Quintana, a little way along which is the Plaza del Charco, which has been the hub of the town's life since at least the 18th c. The tall Indian bay trees that shade the attractive square were first brought to Puerto de la Cruz from Cuba in 1852 and soon spread widely over the island.

Rincón del Puerto

The most notable of the buildings round the square is the Rincón del Puerto, on the west side. Built in 1739, it has been thoroughly restored in typical Canarian style. There are a number of restaurants in the inner courtyard with its profusion of flowers and characteristic wooden balconies.

La Ranilla

To the west of Plaza del Charco is the historic fishermen's quarter of La Ranilla, which still has many traditional buildings in its narrow streets. Many of them are now occupied by attractive restaurants, usually with beautiful inner courtyards. One of the finest streets in the area, Calle del Lomo, is now a pedestrian zone.

In Calle del Lomo is the Museo Arqueológico, housed in a 19th c. mansion. There is a small collection of material illustrating the history of the ancient Canarians, and there are periodic special exhibitions on various aspects of Canarian history and culture. Open Tue.–Sat. 10am–1pm, 5–9pm, Sun. 10am–1pm.

Museo Arqueológico

Continuing west along the coast, we pass a Moorish-style viewing pavilion, built on a lava crag in 1815. Beyond this is the Castillo de San Felipe, named after King Philip IV (1621–65), who ordered the foundation of Puerto de la Orotava, now Puerto de la Cruz. Built in the early 17th c., this little fort is the only building in the Canaries in pure Spanish colonial style. It is now used for exhibitions and cultural events.

Castillo de San Felipe

From the forecourt of the Castillo San Felipe there is a view of the Playa Jardín, a 1 km (0.6 mi.) long beach of dark sand. The designs for the beach and the gardens bordering it were by César Manrique. Breakwaters under the surface of the water break the force of the surf, so that bathing is entirely safe. The beach cafés and bars give the Playa Jardín something of a tropical air.
  At the west end of the Playa Jardín is the Loro Parque (see p. 120).

★Playa Jardín

Now return along the coast towards the town centre, past the site of the future Parque Marítimo, to be laid out on land reclaimed from the sea. The idea of creating the park, with a variety of leisure facilities, has been under consideration for many years, plans having been prepared by César Manrique in the early 1990s, but it was only in the summer of 1998 that the local press was able to report that work had begun.

Parque Marítimo

Immediately east of the park site is the Puerto Pesquero, the old harbour, now used only by a few fishermen. The two piers are the scene of bustling activity, particularly in the early morning. The shorter of the two was built in 1720, the other more than a century later.

Puerto Pesquero

The oldest surviving building in Puerto de la Cruz is the Casa de la Real Aduana, on the harbour, built in 1620. From 1706 to 1833 it served as the Custom House.

Casa de la Real Aduana

At the end of Calle Santo Domingo is the Casa de Miranda. Built in 1730, it is believed to have belonged to the Miranda family, who later emigrated to Venezuela (see Plaza de los Reyes Católicos). It now houses a restaurant.

Casa de Miranda

Plaza Europa was given its present aspect in 1992. The style of architecture is modelled on that of the island's historic fortifications. The six cannon in the square date from the 18th and 19th c. Also in the square is the tourist information office.

Plaza de Europe

On the south-east side of the square is the Ayuntamiento (Town Hall), a trim modern building (1973) with typical Canarian timber balconies. Over the entrance is the town's coat of arms.

Ayuntamiento

Other sights

Some of the town's most comfortable hotels are in the La Paz (Peace) district, above the town centre to the east. It can be reached on foot on a stepped path that starts near the Centro Comercial Martiánez and runs into the Camino San Amaro, an attractively laid out pedestrian zone from which there are fine views of Puerto de la Cruz and the sea. There are a number of restaurants and cafés that may tempt you to linger. There are still better views from the nearby Mirador de la Paz. Facing this is the chapel of San Amaro, built by the Candia family in 1596 in honour of their patron saint.

La Paz

The flora of the Canaries is well represented in the Jardín de Orquídeas de Sitio Litre

From the Mirador de la Paz it is a 45 min. walk on the Camino de la Costa to the **Playa Bollullo**, a beautiful unspoiled beach. Beyond the Hotel Semiramis you leave behind the large hotels and apartment blocks. The path passes under the busy main road at the east end of Puerto de la Cruz and then follows a winding course through banana plantations, cuts across the Barranco de la Arena and continues straight ahead to the Bar Bollullo. To get down to the beach itself it is necessary to continue to the east end and take a flight of steps leading down to it. Sun beds and sun umbrellas can be hired, and there is a bar serving refreshments. Bathers should beware of the strong surf, which can make bathing hazardous.

Also in the La Paz district, on Avenida Marqués Villanueva del Prado, which leads to the motorway, is the ★★**Jardín Botánico** (Botanic Garden; officially the Jardín de Aclimatación de la Orotava). It was established by King Charles III of Spain (1716–88) in order to accustom tropical plants to a more temperate climate. The plants were successfully acclimatised to Tenerife, but the second part of the plan – to go on from there to accustom the plants to the climate of mainland Spain – was a failure. The Botanic Garden contains more than 200 species of plants and trees from all over the world, including breadfruit trees, cinnamon trees, pepper trees, coffee plants, mangoes and tulip trees; various species of orchids are grown in hothouses. There is a small water-lily pond in the upper part of the gardens, and also a fountain. Open daily 9am–7pm (winter 6pm).

Casa Abaco

In the district of El Durazno (to the south of the Jardín Botánico) is the Casa Abaco, a 17th c. Canarian mansion. Its luxuriant gardens are frequently the venue of various folk events, and on such occasions this beautifully furnished country house is also open to the public. For details contact the local tourist office (see Information).

High above Puerto de la Cruz, set in the beautiful Parque Taoro, is the **Casino Taoro**. It was originally opened in 1892 as a hotel, which was destroyed by fire in 1929. The Casino Taoro was opened in part of the building in 1975. The modern Congress Centre in the park was built in 1995.

Also in the Parque Taoro (entrance beside the Casino) is the little garden of **Risco Bello**, laid out in terraces with beautiful flowers, attractive ponds (waterfowl, water lilies) and an inviting café. Open daily 9.30am–6.30pm.

To the north-east, below the Casino, is another beautiful garden, the Jardín de Orquídeas de Sitio Litre. The history of the mansion (not open to the public) and gardens of Sitio Litre goes back to the 18th c. Among the many notable people who have stayed here have been Alexander von Humboldt, Sir William Wilde (father of Oscar Wilde) and Agatha Christie. Visitors can see a luxuriant display of the indigenous flora and a large collection of orchids. For those who want to enjoy the peace and quiet of Sitio Litre a little longer there is a pleasant café. Open daily 9.30am–6pm.

3 km (2 mi.) south-east of the town centre is the Bananera El Guanche, a banana plantation that gives visitors a general view of the cultivation and processing of bananas. A short video film and a series of displays explain the various stages of the banana plant, and In the rear part of the area there is a short circular route leading past other exotic plants of economic importance (including sugar cane, coffee, avocados and paw-paws). Included in the admission price is a free sampling of the banana liqueur produced on Tenerife. A brochure given to visitors with the admission ticket describes the methods of cultivation and the importance of the banana to the economy of the Canaries.

One of the great attractions in the Loro Parque is the Aquarium. Here, in an underwater glass tunnel, visitors come face to face with huge sharks

There is a free shuttle bus service to the Bananera El Guanche (at present buses depart from Avenida de Venezuela, otherwise the Playa Martiánez). Open daily 9am–6pm.

Oasis del Valle

Beside the Bananera El Guanche is the Oasis del Valle, where visitors can take a camel ride – small children may prefer the ponies. Open daily 10am–5pm; free shuttle bus service.

★★Loro Parque

You can enjoy at least a half day in the Loro Parque (Parrot Park) – going some way to justify the high admission charge. Even the journey to this park in the western district of Punta Brava is part of the fun: a brightly coloured train takes visitors there from Playa Martiánez free of charge. The park offers beautiful well-tended gardens and colourful parrots: amid tropical and subtropical plants, there are over 200 of the world's 335 known species of parrots. It is one of the objectives of the Loro Parque to breed species that are threatened with extinction, and the parrots are kept in pairs in spacious cages. The breeding station itself, however, is not open to the public. In the Loro Show more than 20 parrots of many colours perform their tricks. Other attractions are the beautifully orchestrated displays by sea lions and dolphins, which take place in a special amphitheatre against a beautiful scenic backdrop. The film show carries cinema to a wholly new level: with 60 images a second compared with the normal 24, the visual impact is extraordinarily powerful. The film shown here, "Natura Visión", was originally made by ICONA, the Spanish organisation concerned with the protection of nature, for the World's Fair in Seville. The crocodile enclosure, Tiger Island, the Bat Cave, the orchid house, and the penguins in Antarctic World are among the many other attractions in the park. Open daily 8.30am–5pm.

Surroundings

Mirador Humboldt

To reach the Mirador Humboldt, follow the signs to Cuesta de la Villa on the road leading east from the town, then turn right for La Orotava. A short distance along this road, to the right, is a viewpoint from which there is a panoramic view of the Orotava valley and Puerto de la Cruz. Inscribed on a commemorative stone is a remark by Alexander von Humboldt on the beauty of the Orotava valley.

Santa Úrsula

Places to the east of Puerto de la Cruz can be reached by road 820 parallel to the motorway. Santa Úrsula is a prosperous little town in which many visitors from northern and central Europe have a second home. At the near end of the town is a factory making leather goods, with a showroom selling its products at factory prices (free bus service from Playa Martiánez in Puerto de la Cruz).

La Victoria de Acentejo

Next to Santa Úrsula, and now joined with it, is La Victoria de Acentejo. There was bloody fighting in this area during the Spanish conquest, and the name of the town (The Victory of Acentejo) refers to a Spanish victory over the Guanches in December 1495.

La Matanza de Acentejo

The name of La Matanza de Acentejo (the Slaughter of Acentejo) commemorates a bloody battle in the spring of 1494 between the Guanches and the Spanish invaders led by Alonso Fernández de Lugo, after which the Spanish force was obliged to withdraw to Gran Canaria.

In the Old Town Hall is the **Museum of Canarian Art and Customs**. Open Tue.–Sun. 9.30am–1pm, 3.30–6pm.

Puerto de Santiago · Los Gigantes   A 3

Playa de las Américas

Altitude: sea level
Population: 800

Until the mid-1980s Puerto de Santiago was a small village enclosed by high rocky hills whose inhabitants lived mainly by fishing. Then tourism arrived, and Puerto de Santiago is now the centre of a holiday resort that extends along the coast for several kilometres, from the Los Gigantes development in the north to the attractive Playa de la Arena in the south. Compared with Playa de las Américas and Los Cristianos, Puerto de Santiago is a relatively quiet resort. Visitors looking for night life must go elsewhere: here there is not a wide choice of entertainment in the evening.

The street pattern of Puerto de Santiago and Los Gigantes reflects this desire to secure peace and quiet. Many of the streets lead only to apartment blocks and hotels and then come to a dead end. To drive through the resort from north to south is time-consuming, and many visitors prefer to take the bypass that gives the town a wide berth. The handsome hotels and apartment blocks indicate that Puerto de Santiago attracts a fairly prosperous clientele.

The life of the **resort** centres on the little fishing harbour of Puerto de Santiago and the promenade skirting the Playa de la Arena. Los

The tourist resort of Los Gigantes: beyond are the cliffs from which it takes its name

Gigantes has a modern yacht marina. From here excursion boats take visitors on trips along the cliff coastline and to the little beach at the mouth of the Barranco de Masca (see p. 104).

Puerto de Santiago is not well supplied with **beaches**. The most attractive is the Playa de la Arena, a small beach of dark sand with a promenade lined by palms and areas of grass. Between the elegant marina at Los Gigantes and the high wall of cliffs is another small but beautiful sandy beach, the Playa de los Guios. A new development is under way between the old fishing harbour of Puerto de Santiago and the Europa apartment complex, the Lago de Santiago. Like the Lido San Telmo designed by César Manrique in Puerto de la Cruz, it will have sea-water swimming pools and gardens that will greatly enhance the town.

Surroundings

★Acantilado de los Gigantes

A scenic backdrop to the holiday resort is provided by the sheer cliffs, the Acantilado de los Gigantes, just to the north of Los Gigantes.

Alcalá

5 km (3 mi.) south of Puerto de Santiago is the village of Alcalá, whose life still centres mainly on fishing. Every Monday there is a lively market in the square above the harbour.

San Juan

3 km (2 mi.) further south is San Juan, another fishing village. Visitors will be disappointed if they expect to find a picturesque harbour crowded with brightly painted fishing boats and lined by pretty whitewashed houses: a modern breakwater protects the harbour from the Atlantic breakers, and the village consists of rather plain houses several storeys high. San Juan mainly appeals to local people who have holiday apartments here.

San Andrés   E 1

Altitude: sea level
Population: 4000

San Andrés is a prosperous fishing village 8 km (5 mi.) north-east of
Santa Cruz, noted for its modest but good restaurants and for its beau-
tiful beach, Las Teresitas. It is a good centre from which to explore the
Anaga Hills (see Montañas de Anaga).

The **village** has managed to preserve much of its original character,
having so far remained unspoiled by any large hotel complexes or other
tourist facilities. Its Castillo was destroyed some 30 years ago by a storm
tide.

A short distance north-east of San Andrés on the road to Igueste is a   Viewpoint
viewpoint situated high above the coast. To the west there is a view of
Teresitas beach, to the east can be seen an number of small beaches of
dark sand.

Surroundings

The Playa de las Teresitas, at the north-east end of San Andrés, is an arti-   ★Playa de las
ficial beach. In the early 1970s the bay was closed off by a breakwater to   Teresitas
provide safe bathing and the beach was built up with sand brought by
boat from the Sahara. Large numbers of palms have been planted to
improve the amenity of the beach, which in spite of its nearness to a city
is remarkably clean and well maintained. A favourite resort of the population of Santa Cruz, it is very busy at weekends.

The Playa de las Gaviotas, reached by a made road 3 km (2 mi.) north-   Playa de las
east of San Andrés, is favoured by naturists.   Gaviotas

San Juan de la Rambla   C 2

Altitude: 63 m (207 ft)
Population (district): 4800

San Juan de la Rambla, chief place in the district of that name, lies on
the north coast of Tenerife, half way between Icod and Puerto de la Cruz.
As its name indicates (*rambla* , stream or torrent), it lies on a tongue of
land formed from deposits carried down by the Barranco Ruiz.

San Juan de la Rambla is a long straggling **village**, in the centre of which
is the simple village church, with a handsome tower. There are also a
number of houses that – in the island's traditional style – have artistically
carved balconies.

Santa Cruz de Tenerife   E 2

Altitude: 0–200 m (0–650 ft)
Population: 205,000

Santa Cruz de Tenerife, or Santa Cruz, capital of the Spanish province of
that name and of the island of Tenerife, lies in a sheltered bay at the foot
of the Anaga Hills in the north-east of the island.

The **city** owes its economic importance to the development of its harbour since the mid-18th c. Due to its situation at the intersection of important Atlantic seaways it is one of Spain's largest ports, handling some 13.6 million metric tons of freight annually. Major contributions are also made to the city's economy by an oil refinery, chemical plants and fish-processing and cigar-making factories. Visitors are attracted to Santa Cruz by its excellent shopping facilities – by far the best on the island.

The **history** of the town began in 1492, when Alonso Fernández de Lugo landed in the uninhabited bay that was later to become the site of Santa Cruz. From here he set out on the conquest of the island, and in 1494 he founded the town. In subsequent centuries Santa Cruz had repeatedly to defend itself against attack. In 1657 Admiral Blake tried unsuccessfully to take the town; in 1706, during the War of the Spanish Succession, an attack by Admiral Jennings was beaten off; and at the end of the same century Nelson himself had no better luck. In July 1797 he appeared off Santa Cruz with eight warships and bombarded the town's defences but was forced to retire under the return bombardment by the defenders, in the course of which he lost his right arm (see Baedeker Special p. 130). Another important date in the town's history was 1723, when Santa Cruz became the administrative centre of the archipelago in place of La Laguna, preserving this status until 1927, when the Canaries were divided into two provinces.

Although the tourist and holiday trade makes a major contribution to the economy of Tenerife, little of this is felt in the island's **capital**, which has preserved its own distinctive atmosphere.

In recent years numbers of handsome new buildings have been erected in the city centre, and modern office blocks and shops now dominate the Plaza de España and the Calle del Castillo pedestrian zone. Here and round the harbour there is perpetual hectic activity. A quieter part of the city is the area round the Parque Municipal García Sanabria, where upmarket citizens of Santa Cruz have their houses. The large numbers of inhabitants who are less well off, however, live in the continually expanding housing areas on the outskirts of the city, which is now gradually joining up with La Laguna (see entry).

Walk around Santa Cruz

From the Plaza de España a tourist train takes visitors on a tour (about 45 min.) of the main sights, with commentary in Spanish and English.

The floral Plaza de España, near the harbour, is the hub of the city's life. In the centre of the square is the Monumento de los Caídos, commemorating the dead of the Spanish Civil War (1936–9); in the base of the monument is a memorial chapel.

Plaza de España

On the south side of the Plaza de España is the **Palacio Insular**, a huge complex housing the Cabildo Insular (Island Council) and the National Tourist Office.

To see something of the bustling activity round the harbour it is worth taking a stroll along the Muelle Sur (South Mole), to the east of the Plaza de España, where cargo ships and tankers moor. Bananas and tomatoes are the main products shipped from Santa Cruz harbour, and crude oil is imported for the oil refinery near the town. Passenger ships, ferries and hydrofoils moor along the **Muelle de Ribera**.

Muelle Sur

The fishing harbour lies to the north-east of the town centre, on the

◀ *Playa de las Teresitas, formed of sand from the Sahara*

Santa Cruz: bustling with activity during the day, tranquil in the evening

road to San Andrés. The fishermen's catches are brought direct from the fishing boats to the large freezer plants here.

Plaza de la Candelaria

Adjoining the Plaza de España on the west is the Plaza de la Candelaria, an elongated pedestrian square surrounded by offices.

In the centre of the square is an early neoclassical sculpture in Carrara marble, the **"Triunfo de la Candelaria"** ("Triumph of the Virgin of Candelaria"; 1778), by the Italian sculptor Antonio Canova (1757–1822); the Madonna de la Candelaria, patroness of the Canaries, stands on a slender column with figures of four Guanche chieftains at her feet.

Casino de Tenerife

At the corner of the two squares is the mid-18th c. Casino de Tenerife, the premises of the island's oldest private club. The building is decorated with murals by leading Canarian painters (seen only with special permission).

Palacio de los Carta

The Palacio de los Carta, near the Casino, was built in the early 18th c. As the palace is now occupied by a bank it is possible to enter it during business hours and look into the inner courtyard with its elaborate wooden balconies.

Calle del Castillo

The city's principal shopping street, the busy Calle del Castillo, runs north-west from the Plaza de la Candelaria – crowded, particularly in the late afternoon and early evening, with an apparently endless stream of shoppers and promenaders.

Parlamento de Canarias

A little way along Calle Teobaldo Power, which opens off Calle del Castillo on the right, is the Parlamento de Canarias, a building in the style of a Greek temple erected in the 1880s.

Calle del Castillo runs into the busy Plaza de Weyler. In the centre of a small garden is a white marble fountain made in Genoa.

On the west side of the square is the Capitania General, a neoclassical building of 1880 that was the seat of the military governors of the island. General Franco resided here until the Spanish Civil War.

Plaza de Weyler

From Plaza de Weyler Calle Méndez Núñez runs north-east, lined by offices and government buildings. Here too is the Ayuntamiento (Town Hall), built in 1898 to the design of Antonio Pintor.

Ayuntamiento

Calle Viera y Clavijo runs north-west from Calle Méndez Núñez to Plaza Veinticinco de Julio, an oasis of quiet in the heart of the city. In the centre of this tree-shaded square is a fountain faced with tiles, and the attractive benches round the square are also faced with Seville tiles. Set into the backs of the benches are nostalgic old advertisements.

★Plaza Veinticinco de Julio

From the square Avenida 25 de Julio runs north to the Rambla del General Franco, a magnificent boulevard with a central strip lined by tall palms and bay trees that is the favourite promenade of the citizens of Santa Cruz in the evening, when the cafés and restaurants along the avenue are busy.

Rambla del General Franco

On the south side of the Rambla del General Franco is the Parque Municipal García Sanabria (named after a former mayor of Santa Cruz), one of the finest and largest (6 ha (15 acres)) municipal parks in the Canaries, with some fine mature trees and a profusion of tropical and subtropical plants. Shady avenues lead to an enormous fountain in the centre of the park. There are also animal enclosures, a children's playground and, at the south entrance, a flower clock. The numerous works of modern sculpture in the park and along Rambla del General Franco are the result of a competition held in the 1970s.

★Parque Municipal García Sanabria

From the park Calle del Pilar runs south to the quiet Plaza del Príncipe de Asturias, shaded by mature bay trees. Situated on rising ground, this was once the garden of a Franciscan friary.

Plaza del Príncipe de Asturias

The Municipal Museum of Fine Art, opened in 1900, is housed, together with the municipal library, in the former Franciscan friary. The collection, displayed on two floors, includes paintings and sculpture by contemporary Canarian artists as well as works by Dutch and Italian masters, among them Ribera, Brueghel, Madrazo, Van Loo, Jordaens and Guido Reni. There are also collections of coins, arms and armour, and a number of ship models. Open Mon.–Fri. 10am–8pm.

Museo Municipal de Bellas Artes

The Iglesia de San Francisco, adjoining the Museum of Fine Art, was founded in 1680 as the church of the monastery of San Pedro de Alcántara. Much restored in the 18th c., it has two retables of the 17th and 18th c. The church has a fine organ on which recitals are often given.

From here it is only a short walk back to the starting point of the tour, Plaza de España.

Iglesia de San Francisco

Other sights

There are a number of other features of interest in Santa Cruz, particularly in the southern part of the city centre.

The city's oldest and most important church, the Iglesia de Nuestra Señora de la Concepción, was built in 1502, and after being damaged by fire in 1652 was extensively restored in the 17th and 18th c. Its mid-18th c. bell tower was long regarded as the city's principal landmark and emblem.

Iglesia de Nuestra Señora de la Concepción

Santa Cruz de Tenerife

CONSULATE ABOVE BARCLAYS BANK

PLAZA DE WEYLER

Map labels:

LAS ACACIAS

Dr. Gonz. Coviella
Las Marañuelas
Pl. de Lavade
Doctor José
Wolfson
Henry Dunnat
Cam. Oliver
Dr. Zerolo
Dr. P. Camacho
Enrique
Rambla del Gen. Franco
Avenida 25 de Julio
Naveiras
Parque Municipal García Sanabria
Pl. E. de Virginia
Crist. Nelson
Plaza de Toros
Gen. Goded
Gen. Sanjurjo
Calvo Sotelo
Rambla del General Franco
Costa y Grijalba
Viera
Plaza Veinticinco de Julio
Numancia
Gen. Antequera
Ayuntamiento
Del Pilar
Pérez de Rozas
Robayna
Méndez Núñez
Robayna
Callao de Lima
Clavijo
San Clemente
Dieciocho de Julio
Rambla
Benavides
Álvarez de Lugo
Capitanía General de Pulido
Plaza de Weyler
San Lucas
San Martin
Suárez Guerra
Pl. Astu
General
Portier
Castillo
Imeldo Seris
Pérez Galdós
Parlamento
General Serrano
Ramón y Cajal
Pl. Pedro Schwartz
Angel
Carmen Monteverde
Miraflores
Patrono
Teobaldo Power
Teatro Güimer
Centro de Fotografía
Dugui
Parque Cultural Viera y Clavijo
Gral. Galcerán
de Santos
Alguera
Barranco
San Sebastián
Estadio H. R. López
Bern. Seman
López de Vega
San Sebastián
Observatorio Meteorológico
Pl. S. C. de la Sierra
Pte. Giral
Senador
Dc
La Huer
Jorge Manrique
LA SALLE
Parque de Don Quijote
Garcilaso de la Vega
Los Molinos
Fernández Navarro
Mercado N. S. de África
José Manuel Guim
Hu
La Laguna, Autopista
Avenida de la Salle
Avenida de
Leoncio
Buenos
Hernández Alfonso
Rodriguez
Aires
Calderón de la Barca
Tres de Mayo
Avenida del
Álvaro Rodríguez López
Estación de Autobuses
LOS LLANO

128

Parque Maríti
Autopista S

OS LAVADEROS

Playa de las Teresitas

Alejandro Cioranescu

Rambla del Gen. Franco

San Isidro

Museo Militar

Estación de Jetfoil

Muelle de Ribera

San Santiago

Miguel

ndez Núñez

La Rosa

San

San Martín

San Francisco

Avenida de Francisco La Roche

Ferrer

vier

La Rosa

Bautista

Muelle de Ribera

Puerto

La Marina

Dique Muelle Sur

Rosalía

San

Juan

Vicente

San Francisco

Pl. Isabel II

Em. Calzadilla

NATIONAL PARK OFFICE
CALLE EMILIA CALZADILLA 5
4TH FLOOR

de Padrón

Museo de Bellas Artes

San Francisco

Villalba

Hervás

Castillo

Casino

Pl. de España

Océano

tor Allart

Plaza de la Candelaria

Monumento de los Caídos

do Serís

ingo

Palacio Insular

so

Pl. de la Iglesia

Bravo Murillo

N. S. de la Concepción

seo de
cias
rales

Avenida de José Antonio Primo de Rivera

Atlántico

stián

Avda. de

Dársena Comercial

Dique Nuevo

Santa Cruz de Tenerife

200 m

© Baedeker

129

Nelson's Right Arm

He would return from the expedition either dead or crowned with laurels, said Nelson before his attack on the port of Santa Cruz de Tenerife in July 1797. He turned out to be wrong on both counts: he did not return with the laurels of a victor, for the attack ended in catastrophe for the British forces, nor did he lose his life – merely his right arm.

The idea of attacking Santa Cruz with a small naval force was Nelson's own. He did not set out to conquer Tenerife: what he sought was not territory, but fame and rich booty. He was not deterred by the port's strong fortifications, for he was convinced that his sailors and marines had only to be sufficiently motivated to make short work of the town's defences. His plan was supported by his commander-in-chief, Lord St Vincent; for the loss of the gold and silver held in Santa Cruz would weaken Spain – then allied with France against Britain – whose unstable economy depended on possession of these precious metals. The project was first discussed in April 1797 but was not carried out until July in that year. The operation might never have been attempted, for the army had refused to agree to Nelson's request for a contingent of land forces to take part in the attack, but for two incidents that encouraged the two admirals to carry on with the plan even without the army. At the end of May 1797 two British frigates had sailed into Santa Cruz harbour, taking the defenders by surprise, and had withdrawn unscathed after capturing a French frigate. This had been achieved in broad daylight: surely an attack by night would have an even greater element of surprise. It had

also become known that the "Príncipe de Asturias", richly laden with gold and silver treasure from Manila, lay at anchor in Santa Cruz harbour.

On July 15th 1797, therefore, Nelson put to sea with eight ships, under orders to capture Santa Cruz harbour, seize the treasure ship with the whole of its cargo and destroy all enemy warships in the harbour. On July 20th the little fleet reached Santa Cruz. The plan of attack had been carefully worked out. A force of sailors and marines was to make for the shore in assault boats, land and from there launch the attack on the town; they would then be supported by a bombardment of the town by the warships at first light. Fatally for the success of the enterprise, however, wind and weather turned against the attackers. While normally the wind blew towards the coast, on this occasion it turned against the assault boats, which also had to contend with strong currents. When Nelson's ships approached the town at dawn he saw that the boats had not yet reached land, and indeed were still a mile off the coast. The effect of surprise was thus lost, for all the Spanish lookouts had seen the enemy squadron. The attack was then called off, and for some days the British force remained at some distance from the coast.

The attack was renewed only on July 24th. The plan now was to land in a number of separate detachments, one of which was personally commanded by Nelson. The attackers waited until it was so dark that their movements could not be observed from the shore. Shortly before the British forces reached Spanish soil, however, they were seen by the

Spanish forces, which had been put on a state of high alert. Then all hell broke loose. But in spite of the heavy fire that poured down on them, killing and wounding many of the attackers, and in spite also of the heavy surf, many of them managed to reach land. Among the wounded was Nelson himself. As he left his boat, drawing his sword, to take part in the storming of the fortress his right arm was hit by a bullet from a musket. Feeling no pain under the influence of shock, he quickly transferred his sword to his left hand ; but his right arm was in such a bad way that he was compelled to withdraw from the attack. Members of his crew bandaged his arm and laid him in a boat that had arrived on the spot within seconds. On the way back to the flagship Nelson, though now half dazed, ordered the crew to pick up British sailors struggling in the sea. When a chair was let down from the ship to heave him on board he refused to use it, saying that he still had two legs and one arm, and made his own way up the ship's side, closely followed by an officer ready to catch him if he slipped. When he arrived on board his officers saluted him in the customary way by taking off their three-cornered hats, and Nelson returned their salute with his left hand, as if nothing had happened.

When asked by a surgeon whether an attempt should be made to save his arm, Nelson – who had already lost one eye in an attack on Corsica in 1794 – is said to have told him to lay the arm in a hammock alongside the brave fellows who had fallen at his sides. The surgeon's report recorded a "complicated fracture of the right arm caused by a bullet that broke the elbow or passed through a little above it, severing an artery; arm immediately amputated, then opium administered." There was no question of an anaesthetic in the modern sense: Nelson endured the operation fully conscious, with a drop of rum in his stomach and a small leather pad between his teeth. The arteries were then sewn up with silk thread; but in the process the median nerve was blocked, which caused Nelson to suffer pain in the stump for many months to come.

How did the battle end? One of Nelson's officers named Troubridge managed to make his way, with a handful of men, into the main square of Santa Cruz. From there he sent a message to the Spanish governor, saying that he would set fire to the town unless he was allowed to withdraw without hindrance – a bold threat, given that his force of a few hundred men faced something like eight thousand Spanish troops. But the governor, Don Juan Antonio Gutiérrez, was a chivalrous enemy: he guaranteed the British force an unhindered withdrawal, and even offered to lend them boats if they needed them – always provided that the British warships still lying off Tenerife refrained from any further bombardment of the town. He also offered to admit British wounded into hospitals in the town, and allowed the British force to take in supplies of food from the island. Nelson thanked the governor for his chivalrous attitude by sending him a cask of English beer and a round of English cheese. Three days later the British squadron put out to sea again, after burying the 150 soldiers, marines and officers – roughly a quarter of the attacking force – who had been killed.

Source: Ernle Bradford, "Nelson: the Essential Hero"

Sunday morning at the Mercado de Nuestra Señora de África: the flea market

The church contains some fine works of baroque art, including the high altar, with a figure of the Mater Dolorosa by Luján Pérez, and the pale marble pulpit (1736). Also notable are the finely carved choir stalls. After many years of restoration work the church was reopened in 1997.

★Museo de Ciencias Naturales

Facing the church of Nuestra Señora de la Concepción is the Museo de Ciencias Naturales, housed in a former hospital built in the 18th c. and much altered in the 19th c. It has two departments. The archaeological department has the largest collection of material on the history and culture of the ancient Canarians after that of the Museo Canario in Las Palmas (Gran Canaria). It includes skulls, mummies, tools and implements, sherds of pottery, simple pieces of jewellery and everyday objects. Display panels show the find-spots of the material and Canarian burial sites. There are also informative displays illustrating the process of mummification. Among the most important exhibits is the Zanata Stone, which threw fresh light on the origins of the ancient Canarians.

The natural history department presents a general survey of the flora and fauna of the archipelago. There is also a fine collection of minerals. Open Tue.–Sat. 10am–5pm, Sun. 10am–2pm.

Mercado de Nuestra Señora de África

From the Museum Calle de San Sebastián leads to the nearby Mercado de Nuestra Señora de África, the city's principal market (open in the morning), in the oldest part of Santa Cruz. In the arcaded central courtyard are innumerable stalls selling fruit, vegetables, flowers, meat and fish, as well as live animals. Even those who have no intention of buying will be fascinated by the Oriental atmosphere of the scene. Adjoining the market, in Calle J.M. Guimerá, are numbers of stalls selling souvenirs, leather goods, domestic items and clothing. On Sunday mornings there is a busy flea market here.

From the Mercado de Nuestra Señora de África the Puente del General Serrador leads north-east towards the city centre. In Plaza de Santo Domingo is the Teatro Gomerá, the hub of the island's cultural life. It hosts concerts (including the annual Festival of Classical Music) as well as opera and drama. The theatre is named after Ángel Guimerá (1849–1924), a poet and dramatist born in Santa Cruz.

Teatro Guimerá

The simple façade conceals a lavish interior, with crystal chandeliers and decorative stucco. The theatre was reopened in 1991 after extensive restoration.

In the adjoining Plaza Isla de la Madera is the Centro de Fotografía, housed in a market hall of 1851, which holds exhibitions of photography. Open Tue.–Sat. 10am–1pm, 5–8pm.

Centro de Fotografía

The people of Santa Cruz are particularly proud of the Parque Marítimo César Manrique, on the southern outskirts of the city, which was opened in 1995. It has two giant swimming pools, a children's paddling pool and a small beach. It was designed by the architect and artist César Manrique (see Famous People): not surprisingly, therefore, it shows similarities with the Costa de Martiánez in Puerto de la Cruz. Adjoining the park is a palm arboretum, with species from around the world.

Parque Marítimo César Manrique

Opposite the Parque Marítimo is the Recinto Ferial, a multi-purpose hall designed by Santiago Calatrava and opened in 1996. It seats up to 20,000 people.

Recinto Ferial

At the other end of the city is the Military Museum. It is housed in part of the Cuartel de Almeida, a fortified building dating from 1884 and now the military headquarters. The collection includes weapons used by the ancient Canarians as well as those of the Spanish conquerors and later periods. There are banners and standards of various regiments as well as uniforms and personal effects of famous military figures. Numerous exhibits recall the famous battle with Nelson's forces on July 25th 1797 (see Baedeker Special p. 000). As well as paintings of battle scenes there are the flags captured from Nelson following his ill-fated attempt to take the town. Perhaps the most famous exhibit is the cannon known as El Tigre (The Tiger), which shot off Nelson's right arm. Open Tue.–Sun. 10am–2pm.

Museo Militar

Immediately north of the Cuartel de Almeida, at the junction of Rambla del General Franco and Avenida de Anaga, is a huge monument to General Franco.

Franco Monument

At the north end of the town, just beyond the Club Náutico on the road to San Andrés, are the remains of the Castillo de Paso Alto. On a semicircular viewing platform are a number of old cannon.

Castillo de Paso Alto

Santiago del Teide   B 3

Altitude: 950 m (3117 ft)
Population (district): 7000

Santiago del Teide lies in a high valley between the Teno Hills to the west and the foothills of Mount Teide to the east. There is still some agriculture in the surrounding area, but the many uncultivated fields show that some of the inhabitants have sought employment elsewhere. For most visitors Santiago del Teide is merely a staging point on a tour of the island or a trip to Masca (see entry).

Santiago del Teide has no sights of tourist interest apart from its late

Church

17th c. church. The two white domes added in the 20th c. give it some-thing of the appearance of a mosque. It contains a 15th c. figure of Christ.

Surroundings

Arguayo

5 km (3 mi.) south of Santiago del Teide on the road to Chio is the village of Arguayo. At the north end of the village is the Centro Alfarero, where pottery is made in the traditional Guanche way, without the use of a wheel. Visitors can watch the process and can see an exhibition of tra-ditional pottery forms. Open Tue.–Sun. 10am–1pm, 4–7pm.

Tacoronte   D 2

Altitude: 447 m (1467 ft)
Population (district): 19,000

Tacoronte lies 20 km (12 mi.) east of Puerto de la Cruz in a fertile region near the north coast of Tenerife. The town is surrounded by large vine-yards, which yield an esteemed wine, and arable land. Here agriculture is possible without artificial irrigation. The many caves that have been found in the neighbourhood show that the area was inhabited before the coming of the Spaniards.

The best time to visit the town is at the weekend, when farmers come from the surrounding area to sell their produce in the Mercado del Agricultor (Sat. until 5pm, Sun. 2pm).

Tacoronte is a typical Canarian **town**, filled with bustling life in the little side streets. Its two churches are situated below the main street. On the road to Bajamar is a large dragon tree.

Iglesia de Santa Catalina

The Iglesia de Santa Catalina, built in 1664, has a number of late 17th c. altarpieces with sumptuous silver decoration. The square in front of the church is surrounded by tall Indian bay trees.
Iglesia El Cristo de los Dolores

A few hundred metres away is the town's other church, Iglesia El Cristo de los Dolores, which originally belonged to an Augustinian house. It has a much venerated 17th c. figure of Christ and a high altar of Mexican silver.

Bodegas Álvaro

The Bodegas Álvaro are the establishment of the largest wine merchant in Tacoronte. The cellars (with a tasting room) are on the road to La Laguna, some 2 km (1.2 mi.) from the town centre.

Surroundings

Mesa del Mar

A steep and narrow street flanked by flower beds runs down to the hol-iday development of Mesa del Mar, 3 km (2 mi.) north of Tacoronte. Some of the hotels look a little jaded, as do the sea-water swimming pools. Against this, however, almost all the holiday bungalows and apartment blocks have magnificent sea views. A tunnel gives access to a small beach of black sand.

El Pris

The neighbouring resort of El Pris is more attractive than Mesa del Mar. At heart it is still a quiet little fishing village.

Valle de Guerra

The name of the village of Valle de Guerra (Valley of War), in the valley

A fine view of the Valle de la Orotava from the Mirador Humboldt, on the road between Puerto de la Cruz and La Orotava

of that name, recalls the bitter fighting between the Guanches and the Spanish invaders.

The Casa de Carta, a handsome 17th c. Canarian country house about 1 km (0.6 mi.) outside the town, now houses a museum that illustrates the life of the islanders, and displays examples of Canarian handicrafts and a fine collection of traditional costumes. The house has beautiful gardens. Open Tue.–Sat. 10am–5pm, Sun. 10am–2pm.

★Casa de Carta

★Valle de la Orotava   C/D 2

The Valle de la Orotava (Orotava Valley) extends inland from Puerto de la Cruz in northern Tenerife. With its great width and length, measuring 10 km by 11 (6 mi. by 7), it is more like a large and gently rising plateau than a valley. The chief place in the valley is the town of La Orotava (see entry).

The Orotava valley became famous through Alexander von Humboldt's account of his travels. The landscape of the valley, however, is now very different from what it was in Humboldt's time. The lower parts of the valley have developed into a densely populated area, with older settlements and new developments jostling one another – a sea of houses interrupted here and there by luxuriant banana plantations. Above 400 m (1300 ft) the banana plantations give place to fields in which vines, vegetables, fruit and potatoes are grown, with flowering plants providing a colourful setting all the year round. In winter, when the deciduous trees have lost their leaves, the landscape is rather barer, though the tall bushy poinsettias help to make good the deficiency. This intensively cultivated agricultural region is bounded by a dense belt of forest, with Canary pines and tree heaths flourishing up to 2000 m (6500 ft). Above this begins the barren landscape of the Caldera de las Cañadas (see entry).

★Vilaflor C 4

Altitude: 1400 m (4600 ft)
Population: 1600

Vilaflor lies 7 km (4.4 mi.) north-west of Granadilla de Abona on the road that runs up to the Caldera de las Cañadas from southern Tenerife. The highest village in the Canaries, it is surrounded on the north by fragrant pine woods, on the south by plantations of fruit and vegetables. The terraced fields are covered with a layer of pumice, which stores the dew that falls overnight and prevents it from evaporating. Vilaflor is famed for its mineral spring, for its pillow lace, and for the excellent wine produced in the surrounding area.

With its little white houses and its many gardens, Vilaflor is an attractive village with an air of prosperity.

Corpus Christi procession

The Corpus Christi procession in the village takes an unusual form. While in most other places the procession passes over a carpet of flowers, in Vilaflor the carpet is made of volcanic earth. Religious subjects are marked out on the streets with chalk and filled in with volcanic earths of different colours brought from Las Cañadas for the purpose.

Iglesia de San Pedro

Narrow streets lead to a square in the upper part of the village, with the Iglesia de San Pedro, a simple church whose foundation stone was laid in 1550. It has a 16th c. alabaster statue of St Peter.

Vilaflor, in a charming hill landscape

The bizarre landscape of Paisaje Lunar

At the south end of the village, on the road from Los Cristianos, is a craft centre that shows a 20 min. video presentation on the Parque Nacional del Teide. Open daily 8am–6pm; shows every 30 min.

Multivisión Parque Nacional del Teide

At the north end of the village, above the main road near the Ermita de San Roque, is a viewpoint from which there is a fine view of the village and its surroundings.

Mirador de San Roque

At the Ermita de San Roque is a small theme park with a museum devoted to the origins and culture of the Guanches. There is also a restaurant. Open daily 10am–6pm; restaurant open until 10pm.

Parque San Roque

Surroundings

2 km (1.2 mi.) from Vilaflor on the road to the Caldera de las Cañadas is a mighty pine, 45 m (150 ft) high, with a girth of 8 m (26 ft).

Pino Gordo

The Paisaje Lunar (Lunar Landscape) is a series of tufa columns unique in the Canaries. It can be reached only on foot, starting from the Campamento Madre del Agua, a holiday camp. A rough track signposted to Lomo Blanco branches off the road above the Pino Gordo and comes in 9 km (5.6 mi.) to the camp. From the parking place follow the broad track round the camp and after about 1 km (0.6 mi.), after a sharp bend to the right, take a path on the left, which is marked, though not very clearly, by various signs, including white arrows. After 3.5 km (2.2 mi.) the tufa columns come into sight. The walk involves a climb of 200 m (650 ft).

★**Paisaje Lunar**

**Practical
Information
from A–Z**

Practical Information from A to Z

Air Travel

Airports

Tenerife has two airports. Almost all international flights use the Aeropuerto del Sur Reina Sofía (Reina Sofía Airport), 62 km (39 mi.) south-west of Santa Cruz, near El Médano. Spanish domestic and many inter-island flights mostly use the Aeropuerto del Norte Los Rodeos (Los Rodeos Airport), 13 km (8.1 mi.) north-west of Santa Cruz.

Gomera's airport is used only for inter-island and Spanish domestic services.

Island flights

The Spanish national airline Iberia and its subsidiary Binter Canarias, together with Air Europa, operate regular flights between the islands. From Los Rodeos Airport on Tenerife there are several flights daily to La Palma (about 7 flights daily), Hierro (2–3 daily), Gran Canaria (hourly), Lanzarote (3–4 daily) and Fuerteventura (2 flights daily).

Flying times between the islands range between 30 and 50 min. Since fares are relatively low, air travel is a popular means of transport with the islanders. Seats should, therefore, be booked in advance, particularly on public holidays and on flights to the smaller islands. Excess baggage is sometimes carried free or at a small extra charge.

Iberia

For all Spanish destinations tel. 902400500.

Arriving

Air

Most visitors to the Canaries arrive by air. There are several flights daily by Iberia from London to the Reina Sofía Airport in the south of Tenerife, usually with an intermediate stop at Madrid. It is also possible to fly from international airports to Madrid and get a connection from there to Tenerife. There are numerous charter flights to Tenerife from London and other European cities. See Air Travel.

Sea

There is a weekly car ferry service run by the Spanish shipping line Compañía Trasmediterránea from Cádiz to Santa Cruz de Tenerife. The crossing takes just under two days.

Gomera can be reached via Tenerife. From the Reina Sofía Airport the ferry port of Los Cristianos, 15 km (9.3 mi.) west, can be reached by taxi or bus. From the port there are several ferries daily to San Sebastián, with connections to Valle Gran Rey.

Beaches

The only beaches of any length with light-coloured sand are in the south of Tenerife. In recent years, however, a number of beaches of dark sand

◄ *Even at night Mount Teide dominates Tenerife's tourist metropolis, Puerto de la Cruz, and its bathers' paradise, the Costa de Martiánez*

have been created in the north of the island. Gomera has only small coves with beaches of dark sand.

Beaches on Tenerife

The longest and finest sandy beach on Tenerife extends to the west of the little fishing port and tourist resort of El Médano, in the south of the island. Here, except at the height of the season, it is still possible to find a relatively secluded spot. The only disadvantage is the strong wind that – to the delight of windsurfers if not of bathers – frequently blows here, carrying blown sand with it.

El Médano

This former fishing village transformed into a tourist centre, 20 km (12 mi.) west of El Médano, has a beach of light-coloured sand 400 m long and up to 100 m wide that offers safe bathing even for children.

Los Cristianos

A new beach has recently been constructed to the west of the harbour, the Playa de las Vistas.

In order to provide sufficient areas of beach for Playa de las Américas, the largest tourist centre in the south of the island, several small sandy beaches have been laid out in the last few years. Long breakwaters have been constructed to prevent the beautiful light-coloured sand from being washed away again by the sea and to provide safe bathing. In spite of this increased capacity, however, the beaches of Playa de las Américas are still crowded in the main holiday season.

Playa de las Américas

Sun beds and sun umbrellas can be hired, and there are numerous bars and restaurants close to the beach. There is also a full range of water sports on offer.

In Puerto de la Cruz, too, considerable efforts have been made in recent

Puerto de la Cruz

A beach in Playa de las Américas

years to provide new sandy beaches. In the western district of Punta Brava is the Playa Jardín, laid out to the design of César Manrique. Numbers of palm trees and other plants give this 1 km (0.6 mi.) beach an exotic atmosphere. The Playa de Martiánez has been created on the east side of the town, with dark sand and breakwaters to ensure safe bathing. In the centre of Puerto de la Cruz is the Lido San Telmo, also designed by César Manrique, with large sea-water swimming pools. To the east of the town is the unspoiled natural beach of Playa Bollullo.

Puerto de Santiago

This little resort in the west of the island has two small bays of black sand, one immediately below the cliffs of Los Gigantes, the other (Playa de las Arenas) to the south of the town centre. The latter is extremely well maintained and has a small promenade.

In Puerto de Santiago also the beach situation is being improved. There are plans to build two breakwaters, thus producing several natural swimming pools. The neighbouring coastal zone will be similar in design to the Lido San Telmo in Santa Cruz.

San Andrés

The beach of Las Teresitas at San Andrés, 9 km (5.6 mi.) north-east of Santa Cruz, was built up with sand brought from the Sahara and is protected from the heavy surf by a breakwater. Since it is mainly frequented by local people, it is usually busy only at weekends. For a beach so near the city it is extraordinarily clean, with shade provided by its fringe of palms. The Playa de las Gaviotas, 3 km (1.9 mi.) further to the north-east, is favoured by naturists.

San Marcos

The fishing village of San Marcos, 3 km (1.9 mi.) north of Icod, has a beach of black sand fringed by rugged cliffs. Usually not overcrowded (except at weekends), it is frequented both by local people and by visitors. There are a number of pleasant little restaurants along the beach.

One of Tenerife's finest beaches: Playa de la Arena in Puerto de Santiago

Beaches on Gomera

Playa de Santiago, in the south of the island, has a beach of black sand. There are sometimes dangerous currents here.

Playa de Santiago

The Playa de la Cueva, reached from the harbour through a tunnel, is particularly well maintained. 6 km (3.7 mi.) north of the town is the Playa de Avalo, one of the finest beaches on the island (crowded at weekends).

San Sebastián

There are a number of beaches at Valle Gran Rey, in the west of Gomera. The best bathing is on the Playa del Inglés to the north, the Playa Calera to the south and the Playa de las Arenas (two sheltered coves).

Valle Gran Rey

Naturist beaches

On Tenerife the beach most favoured by nudists is El Médano. Topless sunbathing is permitted in most resorts.

On Gomera nude bathing is common on the Valle Gran Rey beaches; elsewhere it is frowned on by local people.

Camping

Camping Nauta
Carretera 6225; km 1.5
Cañada Blanca
Las Galletas
Arona
Tel. 922785118
Open all year; 700 places

Tenerife

There are no official campsites on Gomera.

Gomera

"Wild camping" is permitted in many places. Before camping in a nature park, however, permission must be obtained from ICONA, Avenida Francisco la Roche 35, Santa Cruz de Tenerife; tel. 922286400. You need to show your passport when applying.

Camping sauvage

In Spain you are normally permitted to spend one night in a motor caravan parked by a road, or in a car park or rest area, but not in open country.

Car Rental

There are car-rental firms (with the sign *Alquilar de coches*) in all holiday resorts. It is a good plan to hire a car through one of the main international rental firms before leaving home. Rental charges on Tenerife are lower than in northern and central Europe, with rates vary depending on the size of car and the length of hire. The rental contract usually covers unlimited mileage. Comprehensive insurance cover is essential; damage to tyres on unmade tracks is sometimes not covered. Smaller rental firms will frequently undercut the charges of the larger organisations.

Consulates

Plaza de Weyler 8
Santa Cruz de Tenerife

United Kingdom

Tel. 922286863

United States

Alvarez de Lugo 10
Santa Cruz de Tenerife
Tel. 922286950

Currency

Euro

On January 1st 1999 the euro became the official currency of Spain, and the Spanish peseta (pta) became a denomination of the euro. Spanish peseta notes and coins continue to be legal tender during a transitional period. Euro banknotes and coins are likely to start to be introduced by January 1st 2002.

There are currently banknotes for 1000, 2000, 5000 and 10,000 pesetas and coins for 1, 5, 10, 25, 50, 100, 200 and 500 pesetas. Prices may be marked also in euros.

Currency regulations

There are no restrictions on either the import of export of currency, but very large sums should be reported to customs on arrival on Tenerife to avoid any difficulty in taking the money out again.

Currency exchange

Outside normal banking hours (see Opening Hours) money can be changed at bureaux de change, travel agencies and reception in the larger hotels. It will be changed everywhere at the official rate, but the amount of commission can vary considerably.

ATMs

The simplest and cheapest way of getting pesetas is through automated teller machines (ATMs, cash dispensers). These usually have instructions for use in English as well as Spanish. They accept Eurocards and various credit cards, but you will of course have to enter your personal identification number (PIN).

Credit cards

Banks, larger hotels and restaurants, car rental firms, and many shops accept most of the international credit cards. The loss of a credit card should be reported at once to the organisation that issued it.

Customs Regulations

Since the Canary Islands, along with the rest of Spain, are within the European Union, visitors from EU countries are allowed to bring in relatively large quantities of alcohol and tobacco without payment of duty. Visitors from other countries are restricted to the smaller quantities allowed for exports (see below). Since the prices of these products are so low on the islands the limits in either case are of little consequence to visitors.

But since the Canaries have a special status within the European Union and are exempt from certain taxes and duties, the amounts that visitors may take home with them are restricted to the quantities allowed from non-EU countries: e.g. for persons over 17 1 litre of spirits over 22 per cent volume or 2 litres under 22 per cent or 2 litres of sparkling wine; 2 litres of still wine; and 200 cigarettes or 50 cigars or 250 grams of tobacco.

Dress

Light cotton clothing, trainers or walking shoes, a pullover or light jacket should be taken on holiday. In the higher altitudes it can become quite cold in winter. A raincoat is a sensible precaution. In the luxury hotels smarter clothes may be required for evening wear. Do not wear swimsuits or similar casual wear when travelling around the island; and entering churches in shorts or off-the-shoulder dresses is frowned upon.

Electricity

Normally 220 volts. In the larger hotels the power sockets take plugs of standard European type (different to the British type).

Appliances with plugs of non-European type will require adaptors, which can be bought locally.

Emergencies

Dial 112 for medical assistance, the fire service or the police. Calls are answered in four languages (English, French, German and Spanish).

Thefts are everyday events in the large tourist centres of Tenerife. It therefore wise to leave valuables and identity papers in safes that are available in many hotels (though these do not offer complete security). Care should be taken, too, not to leave any belongings in a hired car or taxi.

Theft

Events

There are many festivals and occasions for celebration on Tenerife and Gomera. Every town and village has its own fiesta, a patronal festival in honour of its patron saint; and, particularly during the summer months, there is always a fiesta somewhere on the islands. These fiestas generally follow the same pattern, beginning with the religious part, a service in the church followed by a pilgrimage (*romería*) through the streets, which have been decorated for the occasion, with the inhabitants of a village wearing traditional costumes. This is followed by various secular events and entertainments – folk groups singing and dancing, a fair and sporting events such as Canarian wrestling (*lucha canaria*). The high point is the *verbena,* a dance that begins in the evening and usually goes on into the small hours. Often the celebrations end with a fireworks display. If the saint's day falls on a weekday the fiesta is usually held on the preceding or the following weekend, so allowing at least two nights for the celebrations; sometimes they last for several days.

Fiestas

In this section we list only the most important events on Tenerife and Gomera.

Santa Cruz (Tenerife): Cabalgata de los Reyes Magos; the coming of the Three Kings is celebrated with a colourful procession by the harbour.

January 5th

Garachico (Tenerife) and Valle Gran Rey (Gomera): Los Reyes, the feast of the Three Kings (Epiphany).

January 6th

San Sebastián (Gomera): patronal festival of San Sebastián.

January 20th

Los Realejos and Garachico (Tenerife): patronal festival of San Sebastián.

January 22nd

Icod (Tenerife): patronal festival of San Antonio Abad.

January/February

Dancing on a Volcano

Carnival in the Canaries – the European equivalent of the Carnival of Rio de Janeiro! Here too Carnival is a lively and boisterous affair: two weeks of uninhibited, noisy and colourful activity, continuing day and night. The fantastic, brightly coloured costumes are prepared weeks and months in advance, to be worn in the elaborate Carnival parades or displayed in the streets crowded with revellers, singing and dancing to the vigorous rhythms of salsa, samba and *merengue*. The dancers continue untiringly into the early morning – linking arms and swaying together, singing, yelling, and of course drinking.

Carnival in Garachico: even the children take part

During these two weeks almost everything is permissible. It was not always so. Only too often in the past the activities of Carnival incurred the wrath of the authorities. The first attempts to ban the festival date from the late 18th c., when the civic authorities took exception, either on political or on religious grounds, to the unbridled licence of the Carnival. During the

Franco dictatorship, too, the Carnival was prohibited in the Canaries. For forty years the Carnival became an unexciting "winter festival". Then, immediately after Franco's death in 1975, it came to life again. It is now celebrated on Tenerife, La Palma, Gran Canaria, Lanzarote and Fuerteventura; but the unchallenged stronghold of the Carnival in the Canaries is Santa Cruz de Tenerife.

The Carnival begins with the Concurso de Murgas, a competition between street musicians. But beautiful, melodious tunes are not to be looked for in this contest: the essential feature is noise. The *murgas* are equipped with drums and various wind instruments, which must have one principal quality – they must be as loud as possible. Nor is the speech song to which they are the accompaniment a delight for the ears. The things that appeal to the public, and to the judges of the competition, are the songs and rhymes dealing disrespectfully with leading public figures, politicians and events of the year (only the Spanish royal family being immune to attack). Apart from the texts of the rhymes and the songs and their musical accompaniment the judges also take account of the quality of the dancing and the costumes. The members of a group, in which all generations are represented, all wear the same costumes, the same shoes, the same jewellery and the same make-up, with no distinction of age.

The elaborate costumes worn by candidates for the title of Carnival queen can be very heavy – sometimes weighing as much as 60 kg

One of the high spots of the Carnival is the election of the Carnival queen, an event recorded by television cameras, when the beauties of the island parade before the judges on the catwalk. The judges, of course, also take account of a candidate's costume, an elaborate confection of silk and satin, paper and paste jewels, with a headdress that can be anything up to three feet high. An outfit of this kind may well cost between three and four thousand pounds.

The celebrations continue on Ash Wednesday, with the solemn funeral procession of the Carnival, the Entierro de la Sardina or Burial of the Sardine. This ceremony originated in Madrid in the late 18th c. A number of nobles had ordered sardines from northern Spain for the Carnival, but when they arrived they had gone bad. One of the nobles thereupon suggested organising a funeral procession for the sardines, after which they would be buried outside the city. The people of Madrid were so taken with the idea that thereafter all Carnivals ended with the Entierro de la Sardina, with huge papier-mâché sardines taking the place of the original rotten sardines.

The Canaries adopted the ceremony with enthusiasm. The outsize sardine is accompanied to its grave by a swarm of black-clad female "mourners", weeping and lamenting, and by "priests" and lamenting, and by "priests" and "bishops" who preside over the ceremony, praying and blessing the company.

In Santa Cruz the funeral procession ends with the ceremonial burning of the sardine in the Plaza de España and a great fireworks display. But this is still not the end of the Carnival, as celebrations continue through the whole night. Even this may not be enough for some people: some revellers prefer to begin celebrating some days late, and naturally they then continue longer.

Events

	Santa Cruz (Tenerife): Festival of Classical Music; concerts in Teatro Guimerá.
February	Many places: Carnival; the Carnival is celebrated with the most lavish splendour in Santa Cruz (Tenerife; see Baedeker Special p. 000).
February 2nd	Candelaria (Tenerife): Feast of Nuestra Señora de la Candelaria.
February 7th	Güímar (Tenerife): village festival in Barrio del Socorro.
March 2nd	La Laguna (Tenerife): patronal festival of San Benito Abad.
March 19th	La Guancha, Tanque (Tenerife): patronal festival of San José.
March/April	Many places: Semana Santa (Holy Week), with many processions and other religious and secular celebrations. One of the finest processions is at La Laguna.
April	Santa Cruz (Tenerife): Spanish Festival; theatrical and ballet performances.
April 25th	Icod, Tegueste (Tenerife), Agulo (Gomera): patronal festival of San Marcos.
May	Santa Cruz (Tenerife): Fiestas de Primavera (Spring Festival); operatic and folk performances, fireworks.
May 1st–5th	Santa Cruz (Tenerife): celebrations commemorating the foundation of the city.
May 15th	Granadilla, Los Realejos (Tenerife): patronal festival of San Isidro.
June	Many places: Corpus Christi; processions passing over magnificent carpets of flowers and volcanic earth; particularly impressive on Tenerife at La Orotava (where the celebrations last a week), La Laguna and Vilaflor.
June 14th	Granadilla (Tenerife): patronal festival of San Antonio de Padua.
June 24th	Arico, Icod (Tenerife): patronal festival of San Juan.
June 29th	Güímar/Tenerife: Fiestas de San Pedro.
First Sunday in July	La Laguna (Tenerife): Fiesta and *romería* in honour of San Benito Abad; pilgrimage, with folk celebrations.
July 15th	Puerto de la Cruz (Tenerife): Fiestas del Gran Poder de Dios; fiesta, with fireworks, exhibitions and other events.
July 16th	Santa Cruz (Tenerife): Fiesta de Nuestra Señora del Carmen; popular fiesta.
July 25th	Santa Cruz (Tenerife): celebrations commemorating the defence of the town against Nelson in 1797.
August 14th–15th	Candelaria (Tenerife): Romería de la Virgen de la Candelaria. This is the greatest festival in the Canaries, honouring the patroness of the archipelago, which draws tens of thousands of people every year.
August 16th	Garachico (Tenerife): Romería de San Roque (pilgrimage).
Last Sunday in August	El Cedro, Hermigua (Gomera): Fiesta del Cedro, honouring Nuestra Señora de Lourdes.

Los Cristianos (Tenerife): patronal festival of Nuestra Señora del Carmen.	August 30th
San Sebastián (Gomera): fiesta commemorating Columbus's departure for the New World.	Early September
La Laguna (Tenerife): Fiestas del Santísimo Cristo.	September 7th–15th
Icod (Tenerife): Fiestas del Cristo del Calvario.	Sunday after Sep. 17th
Fasnia (Tenerife): patronal festival of Nuestra Señora del Rosario.	October 3rd
San Sebastián (Gomera): patronal festival of Nuestra Señora de Guadalupe.	October 21st
Adeje (Tenerife): patronal festival of Santa Úrsula.	November 16th
Guía de Isora (Tenerife): Fiestas del Volcán (popular fiesta).	December

Many places, particularly in Santa Cruz (Tenerife): Fiestas de Navidad; a varied programme of pre-Christmas and Christmas celebrations, with exhibitions and other events.

Excursions

Holidaymakers in the main tourist centres on Tenerife are offered an inexhaustible range of coach trips by local agencies. Among the most popular excursions are a tour of the island, shorter trips to Las Cañadas, the Anaga Hills and the Teno Hills, and shopping trips to Santa Cruz and Puerto de la Cruz.

Coach

An easy and convenient way of seeing the sights on Tenerife and Gomera is to hire a car and explore the islands on your own. See Suggested Routes; Car Rental.

Car

A wide variety of boat trips are on offer, ranging from short trips along the coast or day trips to cruises lasting several days. Particularly popular are pirate, adventure and shark-fishing trips. Even the underwater world can be experienced from a boat. The Yellow Submarine, an 18 m (59 ft) long submarine, goes out on diving trips several times a day (free buses bring visitors from Playa de las Américas and Los Cristianos to the landing stage at Las Galletas). Also very popular are whale safaris (see entry).

Boat

For a change of scenery a trip from Tenerife to Gomera, or vice versa, can be recommended. It takes only 35 min. by hydrofoil (see Ferries). You can make your own arrangements for the trip, but you will want to hire a car on the island you are visiting. Another rewarding day excursion is a trip on the hydrofoil that plies between Santa Cruz (Tenerife) and Las Palmas (Gran Canaria), taking only 1 hour 20 min. for the crossing. Day trips to the other islands are not worth while in view of the greater distances involved, but there are attractive cruises, lasting several days, for example to Gran Canaria, Lanzarote and Fuerteventura.

Since each of the Canary Islands has its own distinctive character and air fares are relatively low, a day trip by air to one of the other islands offers variety of scenery and interest at very reasonable cost. Combined air and coach tours can be booked through travel agencies. Also on offer are short trips by air to Dakar in Senegal and Marrakesh in Morocco. See Air Travel; Information.

Air

Ferries

All the islands are regularly served by the Spanish national shipping company, Compañía Trasmediterránea, and by ships of Líneas Fred Olsen (Fred Olsen Line).

Tenerife–Gomera

The "Benchijigua" car ferry (Fred Olsen line) sails four times a day between Los Cristianos (Tenerife) and San Sebastián (Gomera). The crossing takes about 1 hour 30 min.

The Trasmediterránea line runs a hydrofoil service four times a day between Los Cristianos and San Sebastián (about 35 min.; passengers only). From San Sebastián there are fast launches to Valle Gran Rey (30 min.).

Tenerife–La Palma

From Santa Cruz de Tenerife there are ferries (Trasmediterránea) several times a week to Santa Cruz de la Palma. The Fred Olsen Line runs a daily ferry service from Los Cristianos (Tenerife) to La Palma, calling in at Gomera; Trasmediterránea runs a similar service three times a week.

Tenerife–Hierro

There is a daily ferry service between Los Cristianos and Puerta de la Estaca (on the east coast of Hierro), calling in at Gomera.

Tenerife–Gran Canaria

There is a car ferry several times a week between Santa Cruz de Tenerife and Las Palmas de Gran Canaria; the crossing takes 4 hours. A hydrofoil (passengers only) sails five times a day (except on Sundays) between Santa Cruz and Las Palmas (1 hour 20 min.), continuing to Fuerteventura (Morro Jable).

The "Bañaderos" and "Bajamar" (Fred Olsen Line) sail four times daily between Agaete, on the north-west coast of Gran Canaria, and Santa Cruz de Tenerife; the crossing takes about 2 hours.

Information and reservations

Compañía Trasmediterránea
Calle la Marina 59, Santa Cruz de Tenerife
Tel. 922243011

Compañía Trasmediterránea
Muelle, Los Cristianos
Tel. 922796178

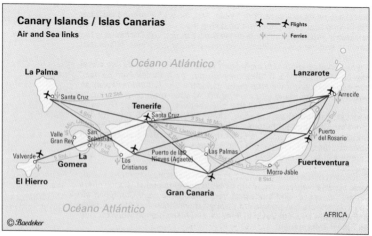

Compañía Trasmediterránea
Paseo de Fred Olsen, San Sebastián de la Gomera
Tel. 922871324

Líneas Fred Olsen
Muelle, Los Cristianos
Tel. 922790215

Líneas Fred Olsen
Paseo de Fred Olsen, San Sebastián de la Gomera
Tel. 922871007

Food and Drink

A light breakfast (*desayuno*) is followed by a substantial lunch (*almuerzo*) and dinner (*cena*). The two main meals are usually of three courses.
    The Canarians usually have lunch between 1 and 3.30pm, dinner between 8 and 10.30pm. The larger hotels and restaurants, however, now often serve meals at the earlier times to which most visitors are accustomed.

(Meals)

Elaborately prepared dishes are not to be looked for in the cuisine of the Canaries, but visitors will be surprised to discover how good the local seafood, freshly caught, and the substantial meat dishes can be. As in mainland Spain, much use is made of olive oil, garlic and a variety of herbs.
    Restaurants and hotels in the tourist centres tend to offer an international cuisine, usually of no more than average quality. In the smaller places and in country restaurants it is well worth trying some of the local dishes.

(Canarian cuisine)

For a snack between meals or as a preliminary to a meal there are the inevitable *tapas* (appetisers). Bars and *bodegas* as well as restaurants offer a selection of these tasty titbits, which may include goat's cheese (*queso blanco*), olives, smoked ham (*jamón*), small pieces of fried fish and other seafood.

(Tapas)

Gofio, made from roasted wheat, maize or barley flour, was the staple food of the original population of the Canaries and is still an essential element in the diet of the islanders, though it is unlikely to appear on a restaurant menu. It is eaten with various dishes in place of bread, and can be either sweet or salt.

(Gofio)

Visitors staying in coastal resorts should try the local fish soup (*sopa de pescado*), which at its best will include a variety of fish, mussels and other shellfish, together with vegetables. *Escaldón* is a thick soup made with gofio, *potaje de verduras* a substantial vegetable soup.

(Soups)

Fish (*pescado*) features prominently in the cuisine of the Canaries, usually grilled or fried. *Vieja* is a very tasty fish similar to a carp; it may be either fresh or dried. Also popular is *sancocho* (dried fish parboiled with potatoes, onions and garlic). Other fish dishes found almost everywhere are *calamares a la romana* (deep-fried cuttlefish rings) and *gambas a la plancha* (grilled prawns).

(Seafood)

Visitors who prefer meat (*carne*) will find a choice of pork (*cerdo*), mutton (*carnero*), lamb (*cordero*) and rabbit (*conejo*), either grilled or roasted. There are also typical meat dishes with unusual combinations of ingredients; among them is *puchero*, a stew of different kinds of meat and vegetables, varying according to season.

(Meat dishes)

You can sample all Tenerife's wines in the Casa del Vino La Baranda in El Sauzal

Mojo

Canarian fish and meat dishes are given their particular flavour by the piquant sauce called *mojo,* made from local herbs, garlic, vinegar and oil. *Mojo rojo* (red mojo) also includes saffron and red peppers, *mojo verde* (green mojo) parsley and coriander.

Papas arrugadas

An essential feature of the Canarian menu is *papas arrugadas* – jacket potatoes boiled in well-salted water. They are eaten in their jackets, which have a white deposit of salt.

Desserts

The people of the Canaries like sweet things, and desserts are always included in the meal. Very tempting, but with a high calorie content, are *bienmesabe* (whipped almond cream with egg and honey), *turrones* (almond cakes), *flan* (crème caramel), *frangollo* (a sweet made of maize flour and milk) and of course *helados* (ices) and fresh fruit. An attractive speciality in some restaurants is flambé bananas.

Drinks

The local mineral water (*agua mineral*) is excellent; it may be either still (*sin gas*) or carbonated (*con gas*). Beer (*cerveza*) and wine are commonly drunk with meals. The local country wine (*vino del país*), either red or white, is rarely to be had; it is normally mixed with wine from mainland Spain. The Canaries have long been celebrated for their Malvasía (Malmsey) and muscatel wines. The meal usually ends with coffee, either *café solo* (without milk), *café cortado* (with a little milk) or *café con leche* (white coffee). A further variant is *carajillo* (black coffee with a shot of brandy or rum).

Health

Medical services on Tenerife and Gomera are in line with European stan-

dards, and numerous well equipped medical centres provide emergency
services 24 hours a day. Visitors can also apply in a case of emergency
to one of the hospitals and casualty stations listed below.

British citizens, like nationals of other EU countries, are entitled to obtain **Insurance**
medical care under the Spanish health services (Instituto Nacional de la
Salud, INSALUD) on the same basis as Spanish people. This means that
they can get free treatment by a doctor in contract with INSALUD and
free hospital treatment but will be required to pay 40 per cent of the cost
of prescribed medicines (free if a pensioner) and the full cost of dental
treatment. A list of doctors in contract with INSALUD can be obtained
from offices of INSALUD or the Instituto Nacional de Seguridad Social.

Before leaving home British visitors should obtain from their local
health service or social security office, or from a post office, a booklet
called "Health Advice for Travellers" (T5), which contains an application
for form E 111. This is the document that they must present to the local
office of INSALUD when seeking treatment (except in case of emergency).

It is nevertheless advisable, even for EU nationals, to take out some
form of temporary health insurance providing complete cover and possibly avoiding bureaucratic delays, and nationals of non-EU countries
should certainly have insurance cover.

Calle Méndez Núñez 14   **INSALUD**
Santa Cruz de Tenerife, Tenerife
Tel. 922285001

Calle San Agustín 52   **Instituto Nacional**
La Laguna, Tenerife   **de La Salud**
Tel. 922250004

Calle Cologán 4
La Orotava, Tenerife
Tel. 922331834

Also in Icod and Güímar

Calle Ruiz de Padrón 2
San Sebastián, Gomera
Tel. 922872005

Centro Médico La Paz   **Medical centres**
Calle Aceviños
Puerto de la Cruz, Tenerife
Tel. 922384223

Centro Médico Salus
Calle República de Panamá 3
Playa de las Américas, Tenerife
Tel. 922796161

Centro Médico del Sur
Avenida Penetración
Los Cristianos, Tenerife
Tel. 922790486

Centro Médico Salus
Avenida Marítima 43
Los Gigantes, Tenerife
Tel. 922860432

Centro Médico
La Calera
Valle Gran Rey, Gomera
Tel. 922805804

Hospitals

Clínica General Urbanización Ofra
La Laguna (on La Laguna–Santa Cruz motorway)
Tel. 922646312

Hospital Insular
Barrio El Calvario
San Sebastián de la Gomera
Tel. 922140200

Chemists

Chemists are open Mon.–Fri. 9am–1pm, 5–8pm, Sat. 9am–1pm. At other times there is always a duty pharmacy open in places of any size. The address is given in a notice headed "Farmacía de Guardia" in every chemist's window. After 10pm only medicines on prescription are issued.

Hotels and Apartments

Tenerife and Gomera have an abundance of hotels, pensions (guest houses), club villages, apartment blocks and holiday bungalows – visitors can choose the particular type of accommodation that meets their needs.

Most visitors come to the Canaries on package holidays, with travel and accommodation arranged by a tour operator. Individual travellers who make their own way to the islands and then look for accommodation are likely to pay more and will not necessarily get a better room, since the large tour operators will have booked many of the best rooms for their customers. They will do well to apply to the local tourist office for a list of hotels and other accommodation, showing the amenities offered and the prices of rooms.

Paradors

Paradors (Paradores Nacionales de Turismo) are state-run hotels located at places of particular tourist interest. They are usually beautifully situated, offer every comfort and amenity, and have well trained staff. Tenerife has the Parador Nacional del Teide, Gomera the Parador Conde de la Gomera in San Sebastián.

Turismo rural

In recent years the Canaries have been concerned to throw off their image as centres of mass tourism and have developed the concept of *turismo rural* (country holidays), offering attractive holiday accommodation in restored cottages, farmhouses and country houses in rural surroundings. Holidays of this kind can be booked through tour operators. There are central reservation offices on Tenerife (Atrea, Carretera General Tacoronte Tejina, 38350 Tacoronte; tel. 922570015, fax 922572703) and on Gomera (tel. 922800000/75).

Hotels and
apartments

Hotels and apartment complexes are classed in various categories, hotels being awarded varying numbers of stars, apartments varying numbers of keys. The scale ranges from luxury hotels (5 stars) to modest hotels, *hostales* and pensions (1 star), and from comfortable apartments (3 keys) to more basically equipped apartments (1 key). The classification is based on the standard of amenity of the accommodation and not on the quality of service or food.

Tariffs

Hotel tariffs vary according to season. The rates given in the following table are a guide to the cost of a double room with breakfast; the rate for a single room ranges between 60 and 80 per cent of the tariff for a double room.

Category	Double room
★★★★★hotels	20,000–60,000 ptas
★★★★hotels	15,000–30,000 ptas
★★★hotels	10,000–15,000 ptas
★★hotels	5,000– 9,000 ptas
★hotels	3,000– 7,000 ptas

It is better value to book half board (dinner, bed and breakfast) in a hotel. In self-catering apartments the price is often not per person but for the apartment (with bathroom, kitchen and balcony or terrace).

On Tenerife most of the hotels and apartment complexes are concentrated on the north coast (Puerto de la Cruz and an extensive area around it), on the south coast (Los Cristianos/Playa de las Américas) and in Puerto de Santiago/Los Gigantes. On Gomera most of the accommodation is in Valle Gran Rey and Playa de Santiago.   Tourist centres

Hotels on Tenerife

★★Hotel Viña Vieja   Arico
Arico el Nuevo, E-38580 Villa de Arico (10 rooms)
Tel. 922161131, fax 922161205
Small hotel in the attractive town centre. Beautiful inner courtyard, library, drawing room. All rooms have bathroom, telephone, satellite television and safe.

★★★Médano   El Médano
Playa del Médano, E-38612 El Médano (90 r.)
Tel. 922177000, fax 922176048
Oldest hotel in the town, situated on the beach. Some rooms have sea views.

★★★★Hotel San Roque   Garachico
Calle Esteban de Ponte 32, E-38450 Garachico (20 r.)
Tel. 922133435, fax 922133406
An 18th c. mansion where modern design and avant-garde art combine happily with the historic setting. Beautiful patio, and a small freshwater swimming pool with sun beds on the roof terrace. Every room has a jacuzzi.

★★★Nivaria   La Laguna
Plaza del Adelantado 11, E-38240 La Laguna
Tel. 922264298, fax 922259634
A converted 18th c. mansion in a quiet quarter of the town centre. The hotel has two squash courts and a bar.

★Aguere
Obispo Rey Redondo 57, E-38240 La Laguna (20 r.)
Tel. 922259490, fax 922631633
A simple hotel in a former bishop's palace in the town centre.

★★★Hotel Victoria   La Orotava
Calle Hermano Apolinar 8, E-38300 La Orotava (14 r.)
Tel. 922331683, fax 922320519
An 18th c. mansion located in the historic centre of La Orotava. The rooms are comfortable and individually furnished. The restaurant serves regional specialities.

★★★★Hotel Paradise Park   Los Cristianos
Oasis del Sur, E-38650 Arona (280 r.)
Tel. 922794762, fax 922794859
Elegant modern hotel in Canarian style.

Hotels and Apartments

★★★Mar y Sol
Trasera Victoria Court, E-38650 Arona (150 r.)
Tel. 922750780, fax 922795473
Twelve two-storey apartment blocks surrounding a central block; the apartments are attractive and well equipped. Excellent facilities for visitors with disabilities (swimming pool with currents, exercise pool).

★★★Oasis Moreque
Avenida Penetración, E-38650 Arona (171 r.)
Tel. 922790366, fax 922792260
Located on the quieter south-east section of the seafront promenade, 500 m from the town centre (shops, restaurants and bars). Freshwater swimming pool in a beautiful palm garden.

★★Reverón
Calle General Franco 26, E-38650 Arona (40 r.)
Tel. 922790688
Established hotel in the town centre. Moderate prices.

Los Realejos

★★★★Maritim
El Burgado, E-38410 Los Realejos (306 r.)
Tel. 922379000, fax 922379037
High-rise hotel magnificently situated in a large subtropical park above the rocky coast. Sport and fitness facilities.

Parque Nacional del Teide

★★Parador de las Cañadas del Teide
Apartado de Correos 15, E-38000 La Orotava (34 r.)
Tel. 922383711, fax 922382352
Imposing hotel located at 2200 m (7200 ft). An ideal base for trips to Mount Teide and the Caldera de las Cañadas. Sauna and swimming pool. The restaurant serves traditional Canarian dishes.

Playa de las Américas

★★★★★Gran Hotel Bahía del Duque
Playa Fañabé, E-38670 Costa Adeje (362 r.)
Tel. 922713000, fax 922746925
Perhaps the best of Tenerife's luxury hotels. Located on the northern outskirts of Playa de las Américas, it consists of a group of buildings in a variety of styles and colours irresistibly reminiscent of Disneyland. With its quiet patios, elegant staircases, terraces and fountains, it has an atmosphere all its own. Five swimming pools (one heated). The restaurants offer Canarian, Spanish, Italian and international cuisine. The staff dress in traditional Canarian costume.

★★★★★Sir Anthony
Avenida Litoral, E-38660 Arona (72 r.)
Tel. 922797113, fax 922793622
One of the hotels in the Mare Nostrum Resort, a complex with five hotels, twelve restaurants and a congress and entertainment centre. Health and beauty salon, a swimming pool, and a sauna. Beautifully appointed rooms with satellite television, a balcony or terrace, and a magnificent sea view.

★★★★Hotel Jardín Tropical
E-38670 Costa Adeje (438 r.)
Tel. 922746000, fax 922752844
Attractive building in Moorish style set amid tropical vegetation (palms, flowers, exotic plants and waterfalls). There are a sea-water and two freshwater swimming pools, five restaurants and several bars, as well as a health and beauty centre.

★★★Parque Santiago 3
E-38660 Arona (748 apartments)
Tel. 922794302, fax 922797403

Complex of two- to four-storey buildings with various rooms, particularly favoured by families. Within the complex are shopping centres, restaurants, discos, a health and fitness centre, swimming pools and other sports facilities – a little holiday world on its own.

★★★Ponderosa
E-38660 Arona (150 r.)
Tel. 922790204, fax 922795472
Located in the centre of the resort, close to the beach. Tropical garden with two freshwater swimming pools. All rooms overlook the pool.

★★★★★Hotel Botánico
E-38400 Puerto de la Cruz (250 r.)
Tel. 922381400, fax 922381504
Located in a large and beautiful park near the Botanic Garden, the hotel has long offered great comfort and amenities. Distinguished visitors include King Juan Carlos of Spain and Queen Sirikit of Thailand. Shuttle bus service to the town centre. In addition to 200 comfortable standard rooms there are 40 magnificent "ambassadorial" rooms and ten penthouse suites. There are three restaurants: a grill room, an Italian restaurant and an Asian restaurant. There are also a health and beauty centre, and two swimming pools in the gardens.

Puerto de la Cruz

★★★★Atalaya Gran Hotel
Parque Taoro, E-38400 Puerto de la Cruz (183 r.)
Tel. 922384451, fax 922387046
Quiet location in the Parque Taoro above the town centre, with magnificent views of the town and the sea on one side, and the park, the Orotava valley and Mount Teide on the other. Comfortable, spacious rooms. There is a health and beauty centre, and the hotel offers a programme of entertainments.

★★★★Meliá
Avenida Marqués de Villanueva del Prado, E-38400 Puerto de la Cruz (300 r.)
Tel. 922384011, fax 922386559
Seven-storey hotel near the town centre, with magnificent views of the town, sea, the Orotava valley and (from the upper floors) Mount Teide. All rooms have a terrace or balcony. Tropical garden, terraces, freshwater swimming pools, and sports facilities including tennis and minigolf. Evening entertainments with live music.

★★★★Tigaiga
Parque Taoro 28, E-38400 Puerto de la Cruz (80 r.)
Tel. 9223835003, fax 922384055
Family owned for more than 30 years. Magnificent views of Mount Teide. All rooms have balconies with side views of the sea. The hotel offers an extensive entertainment programme (displays of Canarian folk dancing and Canarian wrestling, guided walking tours). Environment-conscious establishment (solar energy, own water supply, energy-saving lights).

★★★★El Tope
Calzada de Martiánez 2, E-38400 Puerto de la Cruz (216 r.)
Tel. 922385052, fax 922380003
Located above the town centre, a short walk from the beach, the Botanic Garden and a shopping centre. Most rooms have balconies, and all have views of Mount Teide and the sea. Swimming pool, sun terraces, a sauna and a beauty salon. Very friendly service.

★★★Marquesa
Calle de Quintana 11, E-38400 Puerto de la Cruz
Tel. 922383151, fax 922386950

An established hotel in the town's pedestrian area, occupying a mansion of 1712 that was converted into a hotel in 1887. There is a swimming pool on the roof terrace. The restaurant is popular with non-residents.

★★★**Monopol**
Calle de Quintana 15, E-38400 Puerto de la Cruz (92 r.)
Tel. 922384611, fax 922370310
The hotel occupies an 18th c. building in the pedestrian area. Attractive features are the glass-roofed patio and the traditional wooden balconies. There is a swimming pool on the roof.

Puerto de
Santiago

★★★★**Los Gigantes**
Flor de Pascua 12, E-38683 Santiago del Teide (225 r.)
Tel. 922861020, fax 922860475
Located beside the sea with magnificent views from most of the rooms. Sea-water swimming pool, sauna, tennis courts and a fitness centre.

Santa Cruz

★★★★★**Mencey**
Avenida Dr José Naveiras 38, E-38004 Santa Cruz de Tenerife (286 r.)
Tel. 922276700, fax 922280017
This luxury hotel is regularly host to the king and queen of Spain when they visit Tenerife. Stylish interior, with a spacious reception room, fine furniture and rooms in traditional Canarian style. The restaurant serves Canarian and international specialities. Guests can relax in the garden. The hotel also contains a casino.

★★★**Contemporáneo**
Rambla del General Franco 116, E-38001 Santa Cruz de Tenerife (126 r.)
Tel. 922271571, fax 922271223
A modest and reasonably priced alternative to the Hotel Mencey. Modern, well-equipped rooms.

Hotels on Gomera

Playa de Santiago

★★★★**Jardín Tecina**
E-38811 Playa de Santiago (434 r.)
Tel. 922145850, fax 922145851
This attractive modern hotel complex, set in a large park, is one of the finest hotels in the Canaries. Pleasant, simply equipped rooms. There is a varied programme of entertainments, plus sports and fitness facilities. The main restaurant offers an excellent buffet for lunch and dinner. A lift takes visitors down to the small beach at the foot of the cliffs.

San Sebastián

★★★★**Parador Conde de la Gomera**
Cerro de la Horca, E-38800 San Sebastián (42 r.)
Tel. 922871100, fax 922871116
Located high above San Sebastián, this parador is more like an 18th c. palace than a modern hotel. The rooms are tastefully appointed in traditional Canarian style. Beautiful garden, pool with a sun terrace, and a magnificent view of the sea.

Valle Gran Rey

★★★**Gran Rey**
La Puntilla, E-38870 Valle Gran Rey (120 r.)
Tel. 922805859, fax 922805944
Located next to a beach of dark sand, rock and shingle. From the hotel roof, with its swimming pool, there are fine views of the valley and the sea. Restaurants and shops close by.

★★**Los Tarajales**
La Playa, E-38870 Valle Gran Rey (40 apartments)
Tel. 922805301, fax 922805653

Quiet location beside the sea on the edge of the La Playa district. All apartments have a terrace or a balcony. Nearby are two unspoiled natural beaches.

Hotel de Triana   Vallehermoso
Calle Triana, E-38840 Vallehermoso (12 r.)
Tel. 922800528, fax 922800128
Located in the historic centre of Vallehermoso, in the north of the island. Comfortable, well-equipped rooms with bathroom, television, telephone and refrigerator.

Information

Internet

www.tourspain.es
Spanish National Tourist Office; includes information on Canary Islands.

www.canary-guide.com
Addresses and information about the Canary Islands, with useful links

www.eurosol.com
Tourist information about Tenerife.

www.cabtfe.es/inicio/index2.asp
Information from Cabildo Insular, Tenerife (in Spanish).

www.gomera-island.com
Information from Patronato de Turismo, Gomera (in Spanish and English).

Spanish National Tourist Office

22–23 Manchester Square   United Kingdom
London W1M 5AP
Tel. (020) 74868077, fax (020) 74868034

666 Fifth Avenue   United States
New York NY 10103
Tel. (212) 2658822

2 Bloor Street West (34th floor)   Canada
Toronto, Ontario M4W 3E2
Tel. (416) 9613131

Oficina de Turismo

Palacio Insular, Plaza de España, Santa Cruz   Tenerife
Tel. 922239897, fax 922239812

Plaza de Europa, Puerto de la Cruz
Tel. 922386000

Avenida Marítima 36–37, Puerto de Santiago
Tel. 922860348

City Centre, Playa de las Américas
Tel. 922797668

Urbanización Torviscas, Playa de las Américas
Tel. 922750633

Oficina Insular de Turismo

Gomera

Calle Real 5, San Sebastián
Tel. 922140147

Playa la Calera, Valle Gran Rey
Tel. 922805458

Language

English is widely understood in the larger hotels, restaurants and shops, but in small towns and villages on Tenerife and Gomera it will be a great help to have some idea of the pronunciation of Spanish, the basic rules of grammar, and a few everyday expressions.

Pronunciation

Vowels are pronounced in the "continental" fashion, without the diphthongisation normal in English. The consonants *f, k, 1, m, n, p, t* and *x* are normally pronounced much as in English; *b* has a softer pronunciation than in English, often approximating to *v* when it occurs between vowels; *c* before *e* or *i* is pronounced like *th* in "thin", otherwise like *k*; *ch* as in English; *d* at the end of a word or between vowels is softened into the sound of *th* in "that"; *g* before *e* or *i* is like the Scottish *ch* in "loch" otherwise hard as in "go"; *h* is silent; *j* is the Scottish *ch*; *ll* is pronounced like *l* followed by consonantal *y*, i.e. like *lli* in "million" (in many areas like *y* without the *l* sound); *ñ* like *n* followed by consonantal *y*, i.e. like *ni* in "onion".

Stress

The general rule is that words ending in a vowel or in *n* or *s* have the stress on the second-last syllable; words ending in any other consonant have the stress on the last syllable. Any departure from this rule is indicated by an acute accent on the stressed vowel. For this purpose the vowel combinations *ae, ao, eo, oa* and *oe* are regarded as constituting two syllables, all other combinations as monosyllabic: thus *paseo* has the stress on *e, patio* on *a*, without the need of an acute accent to indicate this. The accent is, however, required when the first vowel in the combinations *ia, ie, io, iu, ua, ue, ui, uo* and *uy* is to be stressed (e.g. *sillería, río*), and when the second vowel in the combinations *ai, au, ay, ei, eu, ey, oi, ou* and *oy* is to be stressed (e.g. *paraíso, baúl*).

Grammar

There are two definite articles in Spanish, the masculine *el* (plural *los*) and the feminine *la* (plural *las*). There is a neuter form *lo* that is used only in certain combinations such as *lo bueno,* the good. The indefinite articles are *un* and *una*.

Declensions: the genitive (meaning "of") is expressed by the preposition *de;* the dative (meaning "at" or "to") by *a*, which in the masculine singular are combined with the definite article to form *del* and *al*.

In the case of personal nouns the accusative case is preceded by the preposition *a:* e.g. *Veo a Juan,* "I see Juan".

Useful expressions

Yes/No	Sí/No
Perhaps	Quizás/Tal vez
Certainly!/Right!	¡De acuerdo!/¡Está bien!
Please/Thank you	Por favor/Gracias

Thank you very much	Muchas gracias	
Not at all	No hay de qué/De nada	
Excuse me	¡Perdón!	
Sorry?/What did you say?	¿Cómo dice/dices?	
I do not understand you	No le/la/te entiendo	
I speak only a little ...	Hablo sólo un poco de ...	
Can you help me, please?	¿Puede usted ayutarme, por favor?	
I should like ...	Quiero/Quisiera/Me gustaría ...	
I (do not) like ...	(No) me gusta ...	
Have you ...?	¿Tiene usted ...?	
What does it cost?	¿Cuánto cuesta?	
What time is it?	¿Qué hora es?	
Good morning!	¡Buenos días!	Meeting people
Good day!	¡Buenos días!/¡Buenas tardes!	
Good evening!	¡Buenas tardes!/¡Buenas noches!	
Hello!	¡Hola!/¿Qué tal?	
My name is ...	Me llamo ...	
What is your name?	¿Cómo se llama usted, por favor?	
How are you?	¿Qué tal (está usted)?	
Well, thank you. And how are you?	Bien, gracias. ¿Y usted/tú?	
Goodbye!	¡Adiós!/¡Hasta luego!	
See you soon!	¡Hasta pronto!	
See you tomorrow!	¡Hasta mañana!	
Left/right	A la izquierda/A la derecha	Travelling
Straight ahead	Todo sequido/derecho	
Near/far	Cerca/lejos	
How far is it?	¿A qué distancia está?	
I should like to hire ...	Quisiera alquilar ...	
a car	un coche	
a boat	una barca/un bote/un barco	
Please, where is ...	Por favor, ¿dónde está ...	
the (rail) station?	la estación (de trenes)?	
the bus station?	la estación de autobuses?	
the Metro	el Metro?	
the airport?	el aeropuerto?	
To the hotel, please	Al hotel, por favor	
I have broken down	Tengo una avaría	Breakdown
Would you please send a recovery vehicle?	¿Pueden ustedes enviarme un cochegrúa, por favor?	
Is there a repair garage near here?	¿Hay algun taller por aquí cerca?	
Where is the nearest filling station, please?	¿Dónde está la estación de servicio/la gasolinera más cercana, por favor?	Filling station
I should like ... litres of ...	Quisiera ... litros de ...	
standard grade petrol	gasolina normal	
diesel	diesel	
unleaded	sin plomo	
Fill up, please	Lleno, por favor	
Help!	¡Ayuda!/¡Socorro!	Accident
Watch out!	¡Atención!	
Caution!	¡Cuidado!	
Please call ...	Llame enseguida ...	
an ambulance	una ambulancia	
the police	a la policía	
the fire brigade	a los bomberos	
Have you a first aid kit?	¿Tiene usted un botiquín de urgencia?	

Language

	Can I have your name and address, please?	¿Puede usted darme su nombre y dirección?
Eating	Is there near here ...	¿Hay por aquí cerca ...
	a good restaurant?	un buen restaurante?
	a reasonably priced restaurant?	un restaurante no demasiado caro?
	Is there a restaurant here?	¿Hay por aquí una taberna acogedora?
	I should like to book a table for 4 people for this evening	¿Puede reservarnos para esta noche una mesa para cuatro personas?
	Your health!	¡Salud!
	The bill, please	¡La cuenta, por favor!
	Did you like the meal?	¿Le/Les ha gustado la comida?
	It was an excellent meal	La comida estaba excelente
Shopping	Where can I find ...	Por favor, ¿ dónde hay ...
	a market?	un mercado?
	a chemist's?	una farmacia?
	a baker's	una panadería?
	a photographic shop?	una tienda de artículos fotográficos?
	a shopping centre?	un centro comercial?
	a food shop?	una tienda de comestibles?
Hotel	Could you recommend ...	Perdón, señor/señora/señorita, ¿Podría usted recomendarme ...
	a hotel?	un hotel?
	a guesthouse?	una pensión?
	I have booked a room	He reservado una habitación
	Have you ...	¿Tienen ustedes ...
	a single room?	una habitación individual?
	a double room?	una habitación doble?
	with shower/bath?	con ducha/baño?
	for one night?	para una noche?
	for a week?	para una semana?
	with sea view?	con vista(s) al mar?
	What is the price of the room with ...	¿Cuánto cuesta la habitación con ...
	breakfast?	desayuno?
	half board?	media pensión?
Doctor	Can you recommend a doctor?	¿Puede usted indicarme un médico?
	I have ...	Tengo ...
	diarrhoea	diarrea
	a temperature	fiebre
	a headache	dolor de cabeza
	toothache	dolor de muelas
Bank	Where is there near here ...	Por favor, ¿dónde hay por aquí ...
	a bank?	un banco?
	an exchange office?	una oficina/casa de cambio?
	I should like to change ...	Quisiera cambiar ...
	pounds/dollars into pesetas	libras/dólares en pesetas
Post office	What is the cost of ...	¿Cuánto cuesta ...
	a letter	una carta
	a postcard	una postal
	to the UK/US?	para Gran Bretaña/los Estados Unidos?

Numbers	0 cero		13 trece		50 cincuenta
	1 un, uno, una		14 catorce		60 sesanta
	2 dos		15 quince		70 setenta

3 tres	16 dieciséis	80 ochenta
4 cuatro	17 diecisiete	90 noventa
5 cinco	18 dieciocho	100 cien, ciento
6 seis	19 diecinueve	200 doscientos/as
7 siete	20 veinte	1000 mil
8 ocho	21 veintiuno/a	2000 dos mil
9 nueve	veintiún	10,000 diez mil
10 diez	22 veintidós	
11 once	23 veintitres	½ medio
12 doce	24 Veinticuatro	¼ un cuarto

Menu

desayuno	breakfast
almuerzo, comida	lunch
cena	dinner
camarero	waiter
cubierto	place setting
cuchara	spoon
cucharita	teaspoon
cuchillo	knife
tenedor	fork
taza	cup
plato	plate
vaso	glass
sacacorchos	corkscrew

café solo	espresso	Breakfast
café con leche	coffe with milk	*Desayuno*
cortado	espresso with a dash of milk	
café descafeinado	decaffeinated coffee	
té con leche/limón	tea with milk/lemon	
infusión (de herbas)/tisana	herb tea	
chocolate	chocolate	
zumo de fruta	fruit juice	
huevo pasado por agua	soft-boiled egg	
huevos revueltos	scrambled eggs	
pan/panecillo/tostada	bread/roll/toast	
croissant	croissant	
churros	fritters	
mantequilla	butter	
queso	cheese	
embutido/fiambres	sausage/cold meat	
jamón	ham	
miel	honey	
mermelada	jam	

aceitunas	olives	Hors d'oeuvres, soups
alcachofas	artichokes	*Entremeses, sopas*
almejas	shellfish	
anchoas/boquerones	anchovies	
caracoles	snails	
chorizo	paprika sausage	
ensaladilla rusa	Russian salad	
gambas al ajillo	prawns in garlic sauce	
jamón serrano	air-dried ham	
mejillones	mussels	
morcilla	blood sausage	
panecillo	roll	
pinchos	appetisers	
pulpo	octopus	

Language

salchichón	type of salami
salpicón de marisco	seafood salad
tortilla (a la) española	omelette with potatoes (and onions)
tortilla a la francesa	plain omelette
caldo	meat bouillon
gazpacho	cold vegetable soup
sopa de ajo	garlic soup
sopa de pescado	fish soup
sopa de verduras	vegetable soup
(sopa juliana, sopa jardinera)	

Egg dishes
Platos de huevos

huevo	egg
huevo duro	hard-boiled egg
huevo pasado per agua	soft-boiled egg
huevos a la flamenca	eggs with beans
huevos fritos	fried eggs
huevos revueltos	scrambled eggs
tortilla	omelette

Seafood
Pescados y moriscos

frito	fried
asado	roast
ahumado	smoked
a la plancha	grilled on a hot iron plate
cocido	stew
almeja	river mussel
anguila	eel
atún	tunny
bacalao	cod
besugo	sea bream
bogavante	lobster
calamares a la romans	breaded rings of octopus
calamares en su tinta	octopus in its own sauce
camarón	shrimp
cangrejo	crab
dorada	dorada
gambas	prawns
langostinos	giant prawns
lenguado	sole
lubina	sea bass
merluza	hake
ostras	oysters
paella	a rice dish with seafood and/or meat
parrillada de pescado	dish of grilled fish
perca	perch
pez espada	swordfish
pulpo	octopus
rape	monkfish
rodaballo	turbot
salmón	salmon
trucha	trout

Meat and poultry
Carne y aves

asado	roast
buey	ox, bullock
cabrito	kid
callos	tripe
carnero	mutton
cerdo	pork
chuleta	cutlet
cocido	stew
cochinillo	sucking pig
conejo	rabbit
cordero	mutton, lamb

escalope	escalope
filete ruso	rissole
guisado	stew
higado	liver
lomo	loin
parrillada de carne	dish of grilled meat
pato	duck
pollo	chicken
riñones	kidneys
solomillo	sirloin
ternera	veal
vaca	beef

Vegetables
Verduras

aguacate	avocado
berenjenas	aubergines
calabacín	zucchini
cebollas	onions
col de Bruselas	Brussels sprouts
coliflor	cauliflower
escarola	endive
espárragos	asparagus
garbanzos	chick peas
guisantes	peas
hongos/setas	mushrooms
judías	kidney beans
lechuga	lettuce
lentejas	lentils
patatas	potatoes
patatas fritas	chips
pepino	cucumber
pimiento	pepper (red or green)
tomate	tomato
zanahorias	carrots

Desserts, cheese
and fruit
*Postres, queso y
fruta*

albaricoques	apricots
arroz con leche	rice pudding
cerezas	cherries
ciruelas	plums
flan	caramel custard
fresas	strawberries
higos	figs
macedonia de frutas	macédoine of fruit
melocotón	peach
melón	melon
naranja	orange
natillas	custard
pera	pear
piña	pineapple
plátano	banana
queso	cheese
queso de cabra	goat's cheese
queso de oveja	ewe's cheese
sandía	watermelon
tarta	cake, tart
toronja	grapefruit
uvas	grapes
bombón	sweet, candy
café helado	iced coffee
chocolate	chocolate
churros	fritters
copa de helado	sundae
dulces	sweets

galletas	biscuits
helado variado	mixed ice
nata	cream
tarta de frutas	fruit tart

Drinks
Bebidas

bebidas alcohólicas	alcoholic drinks
aguardiente	brandy
Jerez amontillado	a dry, slighty nutty sherry
botella	bottle
caña	a small glass of beer
cava	a sparkling wine produced by the *méthode champenoise*
cerveza	beer
copa	(small) glass
Jerez fino	a dry sherry
jarra	carafe, jug
litro	litre
Jerez oloroso	a strong dark sherry
(semi-) secco	(semi-) dry
vaso	glass
vino blanco	white wine
(vino de) Jerez	sherry
vino rosado	rosé wine
vino tinto	red wine
bebidas no alcohólicas	soft drinks
agua mineral	mineral water
batido	milk shake
gaseosa	aerated water
horchata	orgeat
jugo de tomate	tomato juice
leche	milk
zumo de naranja	orange juice

Language courses

Servicio de Idiomas
Universidad de La Laguna
Campus Central, Edificio de Becas
Tel./fax 922319199

The University of La Laguna runs Spanish courses for beginners and advanced students on the university campus. There are also Spanish courses in Los Cristianos.

Leisure Parks

Admission charges

The charges for admission to all leisure parks are fairly high, ranging between about £4 and £10 per head. The price often includes a bus service to the park. In Playa de las Américas and Los Cristianos visitors are picked up at certain hotels and taken to the parks. In Puerto de la Cruz the departure point for the buses is near the Playa de Martiánez. There is no charge for admission to the Parque Municipal in Santa Cruz, and only a small charge for admission to the Botanic Garden in Puerto de la Cruz.

Animal parks

Loro Parque
See Puerto de la Cruz

Parque Ecológico Las Águilas del Teide
See Los Cristianos

Birds of prey in the Parque Ecológico

Parques
Exóticos
See Los Cristianos

Tenerife Zoo
See Los Cristianos

Mariposario del
Drago
See Icod

Jardín Botánico
See Puerto de
la Cruz

Botanic gardens
and parks

Jardín de Orquídeas de Sitio

Litre
See Puerto de la Cruz

Parque Municipal García Sanabria
See Santa Cruz

Jardín Las Tosquillas
See El Sauzal

Parque Etnográfico Pirámides de Güímar
See Güímar

Open-air museum

Aguapark Octopus
See Playa de las Américas

Water park

Bananera El Guanche
See Puerto de la Cruz

Banana
plantations

Jardines del Atlántico
See Los Cristianos

International Go-kart Track
Carretera de Chio (between Guaza and Las Chafiras, on the Autopista del
Sur)
Open daily 10am–11pm

Go-karts

Karting Club Las Américas
On the road to Adeje
Open daily 10am–11pm
Also go-karts for children

Camel and donkey rides are popular with children and their parents.
They can be booked through travel agencies, or you can make your own
arrangements.

Safaris

Oasis del Valle
See Puerto de la Cruz

Guaza
East of Los Cristianos, on the Valle San Lorenzo–Las Galletas road
Open daily 10am–5pm

Camello Center

El Tanque (on the Santiago del Teide–Icod de los Vinos road)
Open daily 10am–6pm

Burro Safari
Arafo (exit 10 from the Autopista del Sur)
Donkey rides daily from 10am

Literature

Suggestions for further reading:
D.A. Brawn, "Tenerife South Walking Guide", 1995
D.A. & R.C. Brawn, "Tenerife West Walking Guide", 1998
R.C. Brawn, "Tenerife Plants and Flowers Guide", 1995
M.R. Eddy, "Crafts and Traditions of the Canary Islands", 1989
F. Fernandez-Armesto, "The Canary Islands after the Conquest", 1981
N. Rochford, "Landscapes of Tenerife", 1999
N. Rochford and A. Stieglitz, "Landscapes of Southern Tenerife and La
Gomera", 1993

Marinas

Tenerife

Real Club Náutico de Tenerife
Avenida Francisco la Roche, Santa Cruz

Tel. 922273700
No moorings; 60 anchorages

Puerto Deportivo Radazul
South of Santa Cruz
Tel. 922680933
100 moorings

Puerto Deportivo Los Gigantes
Acantilado de los Gigantes, Puerto
de Santiago
Tel. 922860630
370 moorings

Marina, Los Gigantes

Club Náutico Puerto Colón
Playa de las Américas
Tel. 922715651
Sailing boats, motor boats and
pedalos can be hired

Gomera

Yachts can put in at three harbours on Gomera – San Sebastián, Playa
de Santiago and Vueltas (Valle Gran Rey).

Media

Newspapers and
periodicals

Major British newspapers and periodicals are on sale on Tenerife and
Gomera on the day of publication or the following day at latest, as is the
"International Herald Tribune".

The English language "Holiday Gazette", published monthly and
available free from tourist offices, gives local news and information
about excursions, restaurants and events. Two other English language
publications, "Island Connections" and the "Island Sun" newspaper,
which cover all the islands, are available from newsagents.

Many hotels and bars have satellite television offering a wide range of British and American programmes. Listings are published in local and English language newspapers.

Television

The BBC World Service and the Voice of America can be heard on short-wave radio at night and in the early morning. Many local stations also have programmes in English.

Radio

Motoring

In the Canaries, as in mainland Spain and the rest of continental Europe, traffic goes on the right, with overtaking on the left.

In general, traffic coming from the right has priority. Exceptions to the rule are indicated by signs. On roundabouts, the vehicle already on the roundabout has priority.

An EU format (pink) driving licence is acceptable in Spain. With other national driving licences it is advisable to have an official translation (consult your motoring organisation about this). An international driving licence, obtainable from your motoring organisation, is also acceptable.

Car papers

The car's registration document must be carried, and the car must bear an oval nationality plate.

An international insurance certificate (green card) is required, and also a bail bond (issued along with the green card), since in the event of an accident the car may be impounded pending payment of bail.

120 k.p.h. (74 m.p.h.) on motorways.
100 k.p.h. (62 m.p.h.) on roads with two or more lanes in each direction.
90 k.p.h. (55 m.p.h.) on other roads.
50 k.p.h. (31 m.p.h.) in built-up areas.

Speed limits

On well-lit streets and roads (except expressways and motorways) driving with sidelights is permitted. A careful watch should be kept for vehicles driving without lights.

Lights

When overtaking the left-hand indicator light must be kept on during the whole process and the right-hand one operated when pulling in to the right again. Drivers about to overtake, or approaching a bend, must sound their horn during the day and flash their lights at night. Overtaking is prohibited within 100 m of a blind summit and when visibility is less than 200 m.

Overtaking

Seat belts must be worn at all times in both front and rear seats.

Seat belts

If you have a breakdown in a hired car (see Car Rental) contact the office of the firm from which you hired it.

Breakdown assistance

If you have a breakdown in your own car help can be obtained from the Policía Municipal in towns and from the Guardia Civil de Tráfico in the country.

Unleaded (*sin plomo*) normal and super petrol, and diesel (*gasoleo*) are obtainable in the Canaries. Prices are usually somewhat lower than those payable in northern and central Europe.

Fuel

On motorways and in large towns and tourist centres many filling stations are open all day. In rural areas most filling stations close at 8 or 10pm. On Sunday many filling stations, particularly on Gomera, are closed.

Filling stations

| Accidents | The towing of broken-down vehicles by private cars is prohibited. An accident can have very serious consequences for a foreign driver. Whether the accident is his fault or not, his car may be impounded (and may be released only after the completion of any judicial proceedings that follow); and in serious cases the driver may be arrested. After any accident the Spanish insurance company named on the driver's "green card" must be informed without delay, so that arrangements may be made for any payment required in the way of bail. In the event of an accident involving a hired car the instructions in the hire documents should be followed. |

| Automobile club | Real Automóvil Club de Tenerife
Avenida Francisco la Roche, Santa Cruz de Tenerife
Tel. 922659700 |

Museums

Art	Museo de Arte Contemporáneo See Garachico
	Museo Municipal de Bellas Artes See Santa Cruz
	Museo de Artesanía Iberoamericano See La Orotava
	Museo de Cerámica See La Orotava
	Centro Alfarero de Arguayo See Santiago del Teide
Natural history, science	Castillo de San Miguel See Garachico
	Museo de Ciencia y del Cosmos See La Laguna
	Museo de Ciencias Naturales See Santa Cruz
History	Museo de Historia de Tenerife See La Laguna
	Museo Arqueológico See Puerto de la Cruz
	El Pueblo Guanche See La Orotava
	Museo Militar See Santa Cruz
Ethnography	Casa de Carta See Tacoronte
Wine	Casa del Vino La Baranda See El Sauzal

Nightlife

Casino Taoro
Parque Taoro, Puerto de la Cruz
Tel. 922380550
French and American roulette, blackjack, gaming machines

Casino Playa de las Américas
Pirámide de Arona, Playa de las Américas
Tel. 922793758
Roulette, blackjack, gaming machines

Noches Mágicas
Pirámide de Arona, Playa de las Américas
Tel. 922796360
Spanish dancers; from 10pm

There are numbers of discos and night clubs, particularly in Playa de las Américas/Los Cristianos and Puerto de la Cruz. The Caballo Blanco (White Horse) on the promenade in Puerto de la Cruz, with a dance band, attracts an older clientele.

Casinos

Variety show

Discos

Opening Hours

Banks Mon.–Fri. 9am–2pm, Sat. 9am–1pm; most banks close Sat. Jun.–Sep.

Chemists See Health

Museums The opening times of museums vary: see entries in the Sights from A to Z section.

Filling stations See Motoring

Post offices See Post

Shops Mon.–Sat. 9am–1pm, 5–8pm, Sat. 9am–1pm. Supermarkets and other shops, particularly in the tourist centres, are often open outside these hours and sometimes Sunday too.

Post

All letters (*cartas*) and postcards (*postales*) from the Canaries go by air. Mail takes at least five days to reach northern and central Europe.
   Stamps (*sellos*) can be bought when buying postcards in souvenir shops as well as in post offices.

Post offices (*Correos*) are open Mon.–Fri. 9am–2pm, Sat. 9am–1pm. Faxes can be sent from post offices.

Public Holidays

Fixed holidays

January 1st	Año Nuevo (New Year's Day)
January 6th	Los Reyes (Epiphany)
February 2nd	La Candelaria (Candlemas)
March 19th	San José (St Joseph's Day)
May 1st	Día del Trabajo (Labour Day)
May 30th	Día de las Canarias (Canaries Day)
July 25th	Santiago Apóstol (St James's Day)
August 15th	Asunción (Assumption)
October 12th	Día de la Hispanidad (commemorating the discovery of America)
November 1st	Todos los Santos (All Saints' Day)
December 6th	Día de la Constitución (Constitution Day)
December 8th	Inmaculada Concepción (Immaculate Conception)
December 25th	Navidad (Christmas Day)

Movable holidays

Viernes Santo (Good Friday)
Día del Corpus (Corpus Christi)

The calendar of public holidays is laid down each year by the individual autonomous regions of Spain, and so there may be minor changes from these dates. If a public holiday falls on a Sunday the preceding Friday or the following Monday may be declared a holiday in lieu. In addition to these statutory public holidays each commune can add two further local holidays.

Public Transport

Buses

On Tenerife almost all towns and villages are served by buses running at relatively frequent intervals. The buses (*guaguas*) are usually punctual. Bus stops are indicated by a red/white/blue sign with the letter P (*parada*, bus stop). Timetables (*horarios*) can be obtained from tourist offices (see Information) and central bus stations. If you expect to do a lot of travelling by bus it is worth while getting a *bono* (voucher) for either 2000 or 5000 ptas. This gives you a discount of around 30 per cent of the normal fare, the appropriate amount for each journey being deducted from your "credit" on the voucher.

Free bus services

From Playa de Martiánez and Avenida de Venezuela in Puerto de la Cruz there is a free bus service, departing at regular intervals, to all the leisure parks (see entry) in the north of the island. In Playa de las Américas and Los Cristianos there are free services from various hotels to parks and other attractions; these are referred to in the descriptions of sights in the Sights from A to Z section of the guide.

Bus services on Gomera

Most places on Gomera can be reached by bus, but services can be infrequent. As a rule buses leave outlying towns and villages in the early morning and travel to San Sebastián, returning in the afternoon.

Religious Services

Churches are usually open in the morning and late afternoon as well as for services.

Puerto de la Cruz: every Sunday at 5pm in the Anglican church in the Parque Taoro.

Playa de las Américas: first and third Sundays in the month at 12 noon in the oecumenical church in the Pueblo Canario.

Puerto de la Cruz: Saturday at 6.30pm and Sunday at 11am in the chapel of San Telmo on the seafront promenade.

Restaurants

There are a large number of restaurants in the tourist centres on Tenerife. Most of them offer international cuisine, but there are also some that offer typical Canarian cooking; they are more likely to be found in country areas, in Puerto de la Cruz, a town of infinite variety, and in Santa Cruz, the island's capital, which is still relatively untouched by tourism.

Many restaurants on Tenerife and Gomera, particularly in country areas, serve what can be described as good family cooking. Restaurants in a higher category are mostly found in the leading hotels and the large tourist centres. Bars provide snack meals: they usually offer a wide range of *tapas,* appetising titbits of meat, fish, sausage, cheese, ham and so on, which are usually eaten at the bar counter. There are also "bar restaurants" that are a combination of both, serving drinks and tapas at the counter and regular meals at the tables.

Lunch is usually eaten about 2pm, dinner about 9pm; but in tourist centres the restaurants have adapted to the eating habits of their visitors, and many of them serve lunch from about noon and dinner from about 6pm.

In many restaurants the menu is in English as well as Spanish. In restaurants in the country, however, there may be no menu at all: instead the host or the waiter will recommend the restaurant's specialities personally; and if there are linguistic problems the guests will be taken into the kitchen to see for themselves what is on offer.

The bill will include a service charge as well as a cover charge and taxes. It is usual to reward good service with a tip of 5–10 per cent of the bill.

Like hotels and other establishments, restaurants and bars are required to keep a *libro de reclamaciones* (complaints book), which shows the prices approved by the Ministry of Tourism. They must also provide on request by a dissatisfied customer complaint forms (*hojas de reclamaciones*), and these are regularly inspected by the authorities. Complaints (preferably with name and home address) may be entered in English if required. If you have a complaint, however, you should first try to clear the matter up with the staff of the restaurant or bar.

Restaurants on Tenerife

Café Melita
Carretera General Punta del Hidalgo 171
Tel. 922540814
A German café with a tempting assortment of cakes.

El Rincón de Pepe
Carretera General del Norte

Restaurants

Tel. 922563806
Spanish cuisine. The restaurant is particularly popular with families and groups.

La Baranda

Casa del Vino
Autopista General del Norte, km 21
Tel. 922563388
An elegant restaurant in an old Canarian mansion, with a museum and a wine-tasting room attached. Exclusively Canarian cuisine.

Garachico

La Perla
Calle 18 de Junio 8
Tel. 922830286
A family-run restaurant whose specialities are seafood.

La Esperanza

Las Cañadas
Carretera La Esperanza, km 7.5
Tel. 922548030
A rustic-style restaurant, with a wood-burning oven, that provides Canarian and international cuisine and Canarian wines. Popular with local people.

La Laguna

Maquila
Calle Herradores
Tel. 922257020
An established restaurant that is a recognised institution in La Laguna. Superb cuisine and fine wines. Located in a narrow street near the cathedral, it is not easy to find.

El Rincón de Cereza
Calle Candilas
Tel. 922250240
A rustic-style restaurant serving Galician cuisine. Among its specialities are *empanadas* (pasties) and home-made bread. Attentive service.

La Matanza

Casa Juan Ahumadero
Calle de Acentejo
Tel. 922578543
A friendly restaurant with international and vegetarian cuisine. Specialities are various types of smoked fish and home-made sausages. Play area for children.

La Orotava

Los Sorales
Carretera de la Villa 60
Tel. 922310249
The restaurant has magnificent views of Puerto de la Cruz and the Orotava valley. Canarian and international specialities. Excellent wine list.

Los Cristianos

El Sol – Chez Jacques
Transversal General Franco
Tel. 922700569
Established restaurant in rustic Provençal style, with Provençal cuisine.

Los Realejos

La Finca
Calle El Monturrio 12
Tel. 922340143
Although *finca* means a farmhouse or country house, the interior design is more "nautical". The cuisine shows German influences – the owners are German – but the ingredients are exclusively Canarian.

Mesón El Monasterio
La Montaña 12
Tel. 922340707
As the name suggests, the restaurant is housed in a former monastery.
Generous portions of Canarian cuisine and grills. Open 9am–1am.

Chez Arlette
La Piedra
Tel. 922863459
Canarian home cooking, including cornflour cakes and roast lamb.
Beautiful garden.

Masca

El Duque
Gran Hotel Bahía del Duque; tel. 922713000
An elegant restaurant with Italian frescos and garden motif. Canarian
and French cuisine. Speciality: lasagne with seafood. Fine Canarian,
Spanish and French wines. Beautiful terrace.

Playa de las
Américas

El Patio
Hotel Jardín Tropical; tel. 922794111
The tables in this luxury restaurant are set round a beautiful patio.
International cuisine. The restaurant is one of the best on the island.

Mamma Rosa
Apartamentos Colón II; tel. 922794819
Italian restaurant with an elegant ambience; can be expensive.

Casablanca
Carretera General del Porís de Abona; tel. 922164296
Popular with local people and visitors. Specialities include goat's meat,
paella and home-made cheese. Canarian wines, some home produced.
Occasional live music in the evening.

Porís de Abona

Mi Vaca y Yo
Cruz Verde 3; tel. 922385247
Seafood restaurant in the old fishermen's quarter with typical Canarian
décor. Specialities: lobsters and crayfish; there are also meat dishes. The
patio has a profusion of plants. Pleasant service.

Puerto de la Cruz

Régulo
Calle Pérez Zamora 16; tel. 922384506
Old Canarian mansion with a beautiful patio. The cuisine is of the highest standard, the service friendly. Be sure to arrive early or book in
advance.

Carmencita
Calle San Felipe 9; tel. 922373075
Good establishment in the fishermen's quarter of Puerto. International
and Spanish specialities. Attentive service.

La Papaya
Calle del Lomo 10; tel. 922382811
Friendly restaurant in an 18th c. mansion beside the Archaeological
Museum in the pedestrian zone. Regional and international dishes.

Pancho
Playa de la Arena; tel. 922101323
Creative Canarian dishes can be eaten on the large terrace. Popular with
local families as well as visitors.

Puerto de
Santiago

Las Aguas
Calle La Destila 20; tel. 922360428

San Juan de la
Rambla

Friendly restaurant with rustic décor. Specialities include rice dishes and braised seafood.

Santa Cruz de Tenerife

Amós
Calle Poeta Tomás Morales 2; tel. 922285001
One of the most elegant restaurants in Santa Cruz, beautifully situated with views of the town and the sea. Canarian cuisine, particularly Hierro specialities. An extensive, changing menu.

Restaurante Cafeteria Olympo
Plaza de la Candelaria; tel. 922241738
Ideal for a quick snack or a coffee break. Not particularly cheap, but you can enjoy watching the bustling life in the square.

El Coto de Antonio
Calle General Goded 13; tel. 922272105
Attractive ambience in a side street off Rambla del General Franco. Exquisite Canarian and Basque specialities. Excellent Spanish wines. Attracts regular customers.

La Latería
Calle Benavides 28; tel. 922249778
Spacious restaurant housed in a former potter's workshop. Very good simple cooking. One of the pleasantest places in town for a meal.

La Frasca
Calle 18 de Julio 3; tel. 922243948
Bar with a magnificent range of tapas; the ham is particularly popular. Good wines too.

Santa Úrsula

Bodega Casa Antonio
Carretera General del Norte; tel. 922300606
Small restaurant on the main street with Spanish and Canarian cuisine. Speciality: tuna fish balls. Attracts regular customers.

Tacoronte

Los Arcos
Carretera General del Norte 254; tel. 922560965
Specialises in fondues; the sauces are particularly tasty.

Vilaflor

El Sombrerito – Casa Chico
Calle Santa Catalina 15; tel. 922709052
Rural décor. Canarian dishes, including hotpot, goat's meat, goat's cheese and rabbit.

Restaurants on Gomera

Arure

La Conchita
Carretera General; tel. 922804151
Authentic Gomeran cooking: cress soup, hotpot with good *mojo,* goat's cheese, Gomera wines.

Hermigua

El Silbo
Carretera General 102; tel. 922880304
Traditional Gomeran cuisine. One of the most attractive restaurants on the island, with historic photographs on the walls. Superb views of the sea, Tenerife and Mount Teide.

El Piloto
Playa Santa Catalina 16; tel. 922144120
Established restaurant serving regional dishes. Specialities: seafood. Magnificent views of Tenerife and Mount Teide.

Taller del Guano
Las Vueltas; tel. 922805192
One of the best restaurants in Valle Gran Rey. Speciality: fillet of beef
with a green pepper sauce or avocado puree. Fresh salads with a variety
of dressings.

La Islita
La Playa; tel. 922805500
Good Italian cuisine; the home-made pasta and vegetarian dishes are
recommended.

Telemaco
Avenida Marítima; tel. 922805755
Modest restaurant with a terrace and fine sea views. Freshly caught fish
and good salads.

Shopping

Since 1852 the Canaries have been a free trade (duty-free) zone. This
does not necessarily mean that all prices are low, for shops do not
always pass on the benefit of the tax exemption to the customer. Tobacco
goods will be found to be considerably cheaper than at home, and the
prices of spirits and perfumes are also relatively low. Cameras and other
technical equipment, and also jewellery and furs, can sometimes be
found at prices that appear very reasonable; but purchases should be
made only in specialised shops and after a careful check on quality.
Free trade zone

The widest range of goods is to be found in Santa Cruz; the main shopping street, with many small shops, is Calle del Castillo, a pedestrian
Shopping areas

A small shop in Afur: the customers don't just come to do their shopping

zone. Another good place to shop is Puerto de la Cruz. There are numbers of small shops and boutiques on the Lido San Telmo and in Calle de Quintana and the side streets opening off it. In bad weather you can do your shopping in the Centro Martiánez in Calle de Aguilar y Quesada, with many elegant shops. There are similar (if less elegant) shopping centres in other parts of Puerto de la Cruz and in the tourist resorts in the south of the island.

Bookshops

Newspaper kiosks and supermarkets offer a limited choice of light literature, much of it in English. The following is a selection of bookshops with a rather wider range of foreign literature.

La Isla Libros
Calle Robayna 2
Santa Cruz

Librería Bárbara
Calle Juan Pablos Abril 36
Los Cristianos

Librería Tenifer
Calle Delgado Barreto 36 (opposite the University)
La Laguna

Markets

Fruit and vegetables, flowers, and fresh meat and fish are offered for sale in quantity and variety in the Mercado de Nuestra Señora de África (see Santa Cruz, Sights from A to Z), the market in Avenida Blas Pérez González in Puerto de la Cruz, and the market in Plaza del Adelantado in La Laguna.

In the "Mercado del Agricultor" in Tacoronte, on Saturday afternoons and Sunday mornings, the local farmers offer their produce for sale. There is also an interesting farmers' market at El Médano (at the El Médano exit from the Autopista del Sur, beside a filling station).

In Playa de las Américas (Torviscas) there is a large market with more than 200 stalls on Thursday and Saturday mornings. On Sundays there is a market selling arts and crafts plus much else besides at the Gran Hotel Arona in Playa de las Américas.

The flea market held in the streets round the Mercado de Nuestra Señora de África in Santa Cruz attracts large numbers of customers and the merely curious on Sunday mornings.

Souvenirs

Tenerife is noted for its artistic hemstitch embroidery *(calados)*, in the form of tablecloths, place mats and articles of clothing. Another fine local product is Vilaflor lace, which resembles Venetian lace. Basketwork made from palm leaves, reeds and osiers is produced on Tenerife and Gomera. The finest pottery comes from Gomera (Chipude), where it is made in the traditional way without the use of a wheel and decorated with traditional designs. Seeds and seedlings of indigenous plants, or a bunch of strelitzias (sold in flower shops ready packed for the flight home) will provide an attractive reminder of the flora of the Canaries. For those who like to take back an alcoholic souvenir of their visit there are Canarian wines and the local banana liqueur.

Sport

Cycling

Bicycles and mountain bikes can be hired in tourist centres. Some agencies offer mountain bike tours, for example:

Creative Adventure Tours
Hotel Acapulco

Playa de las Américas, Tenerife
Tel. 922793584

Bike Station
Puntilla 7
Valle Gran Rey, Gomera
Tel./fax 922805082

The Canaries are a paradise for deep-sea anglers, with good fishing grounds only 3 km (1.9 mi.) off the coasts. Yachts sail daily from Los Cristianos harbour and Puerto de Colón in Playa de las Américas on fishing trips.

Deep-sea fishing

Tenerife's bizarre underwater world with its rocks, sea caves and gorges, and its abundance of fish offers tempting opportunities for divers. Visibility ranges between about 30 and 40 m (100 and 130 ft), and at temperatures of 24°C (75°F) in summer and 18°C (64°F) in winter diving is very pleasant all year round.

Diving

Gruber's Dive Center
Park Club Europe, Playa de las Américas
Tel. 922752708
Diving school, with daily diving trips by boat; special courses (wreck diving, underwater photography).

Atlantic Diving School
Hotel Maritim, Puerto de la Cruz
Tel. 922344501

Golf El Peñón
Tacoronte, near Los Rodeos Airport
Tel. 922636607
18 holes; non-members not admitted at weekends

Golf

Golf del Sur
near Reina Sofía Airport
San Miguel exit from Autopista del Sur
Tel. 922704555
27 holes

Los Palos Centro de Golf
Carretera Guaza–Las Galletas road, km 1.5
Exit 26 from Autopista del Sur
Tel. 922730080
9 holes; large practice area; coach; handicap not required.

La Rosaleda
Puerto de la Cruz (Los Orovales district)
Tel. 922373000
9 holes

There are facilities for parasailing, in suitable weather conditions, at Playa Troya in Playa de las Américas.

Parasailing

On some stretches of coast there are fairly strong winds, making these areas unsuitable for sailing novices (see Marinas).

Sailing and surfing

The Canaries are a rewarding destination for surfers. In winter the waves are higher, but in summer the trade winds blow more steadily. The great surfing resort on Tenerife, for both beginners and experts, is El Médano; but boards can also be hired at other resorts.

Squash Club Tenerife

Squash

Surfers on Tenerife's north coast: with its heavy surf and jagged rocks, this coastline is for experts only

Edificio Belitope
Urbanización El Tope, Puerto de la Cruz
Tel. 922384502
Open daily 10am–10pm

There are also squash courts in Hotels Europe, Conquistador, Gala and Palm Beach in Playa de las Américas and in Hotel Tenerife Sur in Los Cristianos.

Tennis

Most of the large hotels on Tenerife have excellent tennis courts, sometimes equipped with floodlighting. Coaching is available. Some hotels offer tennis holidays.

Walking

See entry

Canarian sports

Of particular interest to visitors are the traditional local sports, the best known of which is Canarian wrestling *(lucha canaria)*. In almost every place of any size there is a ring on which contests are held between twelve-man teams of wrestlers.

The *juego del palo,* a contest like singlesticks, with two sticks instead of one, is also fascinating to watch. Each contestant has to attack his opponent and ward off his blows, moving his body as little as possible.

Another Canarian diversion is cockfighting, which is the subject of heavy betting.

Taxis

Taxi drivers should switch on their meter for all journeys. In tourist areas in particular, however, they often fail to do so and charge as wish. To avoid any dispute it is advisable to agree on the fare before setting out.

The basic rate for any journey is 100 ptas per kilometre (0.6 mi.); if you book the taxi for the return journey it is considerably cheaper. There are extra charges for luggage, waiting and night journeys.

Telephone

International calls can be made from public payphones, using either coins or a telephone card. Telephone kiosks are usually open and therefore noisy. Payphones normally accept all peseta coins as well as telephone cards; cards *(tarjetas telefónicas)* can be bought for either 1000 or 2000 ptas.

For a call of some length it is preferable to go to a public telephone office *(teléfono público)* – found only in towns of some size – where it is quieter and payment is made on termination of the call. Telephone calls from hotels or holiday apartments can be as much more expensive than those from public telephones. Tariffs are considerably lower on Saturday afternoons and Sundays and in the evenings.

From Tenerife or Gomera:
　　to the United Kingdom: 0744
　　to the US or Canada: 071
To Tenerife or Gomera:
　　from the United Kingdom: 00 34
　　from the United States or Canada: 01134

Dialling codes

Spanish telephone numbers are nine figures. For calls within Spain no separate area code needs to be dialled, and for calls from abroad only the international code followed by the number.

National: dial 1003
International: dial 9198

Directory
enquiries

Theatre

The hub of Tenerife's cultural life is the Teatro Guimerá in Santa Cruz (see entry, Sights from A to Z), which is used for concerts (such as the annual Festival of Classical Music) as well as for operas and drama (usually in Spanish).

Time

The Canaries are on Greenwich Mean Time, one hour earlier than the time in mainland Spain and five hours later than Standard Time in New York. From late March to late September Summer Time (GMT+1) is in force, the same as British Summer Time and five hours later than Eastern Daylight Saving Time in New York.

Tipping

In general a service charge is included in bills, but hotel staff, waiters and taxi drivers expect an additional tip of 5–10 per cent of the bill.

Travel Documents

Personal papers

A valid passport is required by all visitors. No visa is required by nationals of the EU whatever the length or purpose of their visit. No visa is required by nationals of the US, Canada, Australia or New Zealand unless they intend to stay longer than 90 days.

It is advisable to make photocopies of your travel documents and take them with you. This makes it easier to get replacements if you lose the originals.

Walking

With their varied scenery, luxuriant vegetation and excellent climate, the western Canaries offer magnificent walking country throughout the year.

On Tenerife there are numerous waymarked routes, particularly in the Orotava valley, the Teide National Park and the Anaga Hills. The very useful green ICONA maps, issued free of charge by tourist offices (see Information), show walking routes in the different parts of Tenerife. On Gomera there is also splendid walking country, and there are many well waymarked routes in the Garajonay National Park. It is advisable to have a good walker's guide (see Literature).

Long walks should be undertaken only with proper equipment. The paths are sometimes rough and stony, requiring stout footwear, preferably boots. For protection against the strong sun a hat and sun cream are essential. In view of possible changes in the weather some protection against rain should be taken, and in winter warm clothing is necessary.

Guided walks

On Tenerife guided walks are organised by the large travel agencies and by a number of smaller firms. For example Gregorio offers a programme of walks in varying degrees of difficulty, with arrangements for picking up walkers from the Tigaiga and other hotels; tel. 639332761/629790156.

Walking holidays

Some travel firms offer regular walking holidays in the Canaries, covering accommodation and guided walks, sometimes confined to a single island but sometimes also taking in a number of islands.

Whaling Safaris

The waters round the Canary Islands, particularly between Tenerife and Gomera, are home to 24 out of the world's 68 species of whale, ranging in length between about 6 and 20 m (20 and 65 ft). The number of visitors who want to see these great marine mammals close up has been increasing year by year since 1995, and there are now some 70 boats in southern Tenerife offering trips to see the whales. The prices of these "whale safaris" range between 2000 and 6000 ptas. There is fierce competition between the owners of the boats, some of them seeking to attract customers by offering their money back if they see no whales. Regulations have been introduced for the protection of the whales – there must be no more than three boats within 200 m of the whales, and no boat may sail closer than 60 m – but these are rarely observed. As a result the whales are now showing symptoms of stress: the groups of whales are smaller, they are undernourished and shyer than a few years ago. Very similar observations were made about dolphins in 1998. There may be a case, therefore, for considering whether these whale safaris should be allowed to continue.

When to Go

The Canaries are sometimes called the "islands of eternal spring" – a reputation they owe to a climate that remains equable throughout the year (see Climate, Facts and Figures). The temperature variation between the coldest and the warmest month is only 6°C (11°F), and bathing is possible all year round. During the winter months, therefore, the islands attract large numbers of visitors from sun-starved central and northern Europe. It should, of course, be borne in mind that, particularly in winter, there can be a good deal of cloud and heavy rain on the north and east coasts of Tenerife and Gomera, while the south and west sides of the islands are much sunnier.

A good time to visit the Canaries is in March, when the flora of the islands is seen in all its splendour.

While in winter (particularly round Christmas and Easter) accommodation on the Canaries must be booked well in advance, during the summer many hotels are almost empty. Tenerife and Gomera are very agreeable at this time of year, when oppressively hot and sultry days are rare.

Climate Southern Tenerife Month	Temperature °C (°F)				Sunshine h/day	Rain	Rainfall mm (in.)
	Air			Sea water			
	Average maximum	Average minimum	Average mean				
January	22.5 (72.5)	15.0 (59.0)	19.5 (67.1)	19.0 (66.2)	6.1	9	36.65 (1.44)
February	23.0 (73.4)	15.0 (59.0)	19.5 (67.1)	19.3 (66.7)	8.9	2	8.25 (0.32)
March	26.0 (78.8)	14.7 (58.5)	18.6 (65.5)	18.7 (65.7)	7.7	2	1.8 (0.07)
April	22.3 (72.1)	16.2 (61.2)	19.6 (67.3)	19.0 (66.2)	7.7	6	11.55 (0.45)
May	24.7 (76.5)	17.5 (63.5)	20.6 (69.1)	19.7 (67.5)	8.7	2	1.85 (0.07)
June	25.8 (78.4)	18.2 (64.8)	21.2 (70.2)	20.9 (69.6)	10.3	0	–
July	25.8 (78.4)	20.0 (68.0)	23.5 (74.3)	22.2 (72.0)	9.8	0	–
August	28.5 (83.3)	20.5 (68.9)	24.2 (75.6)	22.3 (72.1)	8.3	0	–
September	26.0 (78.8)	19.5 (67.1)	24.0 (75.2)	23.3 (73.9)	6.0	3	6.2 (0.24)
October	25.7 (78.3)	20.2 (68.4)	23.0 (73.4)	22.3 (72.1)	5.9	2	3.7 (0.14)
November	23.8 (74.8)	18.1 (64.6)	20.9 (69.6)	23.1 (73.6)	5.6	9	58.2 (2.29)
December	22.7 (72.9)	15.5 (59.9)	19.0 (66.2)	20.2 (68.4)	5.0	4	9.6 (0.38)
Year	24.7 (76.5)	17.5 (63.5)	21.3 (70.3)	20.8 (69.4)	7.5	39	137.8 (5.43)

INDEX

Picture Credits

Imprint

85 photographs, 15 maps and plans, 1 large island map

German text: Birgit Borowski, Achim Bourmer (Baedeker Specials)
General direction: Rainer Eisenschmid, Baedeker Ostfildern (G)
Cartography: Franz Kaiser, Sindelfingen (G)

Editorial work English edition: g-and-w PUBLISHING
English translation: James Hogarth

Source of illustrations: see Picture Credits
Front cover: Images Colour Library

Back cover: AA Photo Library (Clive Sawyer)
3rd English edition 2000

© Baedeker Ostfildern
Original German edition 1999

© 2000 The Automobile Association
English language edition worldwide
Published by AA Publishing (a trading name of Automobile Association Developments
Limited, whose registered office is Norfolk House, Priestley Road, Basingstoke, Hampshire
RG24 9NY. Registered number 1878835).

Distributed in the United States and Canada by:
Fodor's Travel Publications, Inc.
201 East 50th Street
New York, NY 10022

Licensed user:
Mairs Geographischer Verlag GmbH & Co., Ostfildern

Typeset by Fakenham Photosetting Ltd, Fakenham, Norfolk, UK

Printed in Italy by G. Canale & C. S.p.A., Turin

ISBN 07495 2412 X

Principal Sights of Tourist Interest

The places listed above are merely a selection of the principal sights, of interest in themselves or for attractions in the surrounding area. There are many other sights on Tenerife and Gomera, to which attention is drawn by either one or two stars.

4,000 Pt   45 mins

Quad Bikes

Notes